LEGAL
HANDBOOK
FOR
Nonprofit
Organizations

LEGAL
HANDBOOK
FOR
Nonprofit
Organizations

Marc J. Lane

amacom

A DIVISION OF AMERICAN MANAGEMENT ASSOCIATIONS

346.73
L 266 L

Library of Congress Cataloging in Publication Data

Lane, Marc J
  Legal handbook for nonprofit organizations.

  Includes index.
  1. Corporations, Nonprofit—United States.
I. Title.
KF1388.L36   346.73'064   80-65702
ISBN 0-8144-5634-0

FIRST PRINTING

For Bee K. Schulman,
with great appreciation for her
friendship, talent, and dedication

Preface

THE NONPROFIT ORGANIZATION is under siege. For one thing, it is at war with the twin tyrants of inflation and recession. For another, the budget balancers and Proposition 13 advocates are attacking the voluntary organization. Their battle cry is: slice budget deficits by outlawing tax deductions for charitable gifts. So this book couldn't be timelier. Organization managers, hard pressed to comply with ever-expanding government obligations—and unable to obtain government money unless and until they do—now have a readable resource to guide them in their legal decisionmaking. And the liabilities they may incur and the responsibilities they have toward members, creditors, and all kinds of other would-be claimants are thoroughly explored as well.

One caveat. Although *Legal Handbook for Nonprofit Organizations* sets out the legal opportunities and pitfalls that may be encountered in organizing and operating a nonprofit organization, no book can replace your own lawyer. Only a lawyer knows all the nitty-gritty legal specifics that apply to your special situation. Only a lawyer can assess the impact of your state's laws (which, because of their diversity, have generally been excluded from consideration here). And only a lawyer will be aware of the very latest shifts in the direction of the wind coming out of Washington.

Marc J. Lane

Contents

1
An Overview

1 ▪ 1
THE WHYS AND THE HOWS

As anyone who ever ran one knows, never is it the object of a non-profit organization to operate unprofitably. Rather, the point is not to translate its profit into monetary gain for its members or managers, except as reasonable salaries paid for services actually rendered. Thus, the normal test for nonprofit status is whether or not dividends or other pecuniary benefits are distributed among members. But the law will look at motives, too. If moral, ethical, or social goals clearly dominate an enterprise, it will be considered nonprofit.

The profit motive must not be a basic purpose of a nonprofit organization, but profit need not be eliminated from all its activities for it to achieve nonprofit status. Practically speaking, its operation often requires its assets to be invested for profit. The profit, however, must be incidental. The motivation of the organization must be primarily that of public benefit, and its profits must be devoted to that altruistic purpose.

Nonprofit organizations can be classified by purpose into five major categories.

1. *Charitable.* These include educational, religious, civic, health, and similar organizations.
2. *Social.* Included in this group are fraternal orders and mutual benefit societies, but not Christmas clubs or nightclubs.
3. *Trade associations.* These include chambers of commerce, labor unions, employers' associations, and the like.
4. *Government.* All government and municipal organizations are included in this group, including administrative bodies such as the Civil Aeronautics Board and municipal corporations like road and water districts. Most government organizations are established and operated according to express legislative provisions.
5. *Political.* Included here are propaganda groups, political party organizations, and committees for legislative action.

Keep in mind that overlapping purposes are the rule of the day. Thus, achieving scientific goals may necessarily mean educational activities, too.

As incentives for, or in recognition of, services rendered, American communities offer, or reciprocate with, special advantages for nonprofit organizations:

- Full or partial exemption from federal income taxation, with the same exemption usually granted at the state level as well.
- Special postage rates.
- Eminent domain privileges granted to colleges in some states.
- Tort immunity in some states, but to an ever-decreasing degree.
- Exemption from labor union collective bargaining, particularly in the case of charitable hospitals.
- Exemption from certain customs duties for art objects used by charitable or educational organizations.
- Exemption from the statutory obligation to pay state or other unemployment compensation funds.
- The privilege of soliciting contributions, bequests, and gifts.

- Deductibility of charitable contributions made to certain non-profit organizations.
- An indefinable special preference the public and private sector alike accord charities.

In the conferring of these privileges, a complex set of laws and customs governing the creation and maintenance of nonprofit organizations has developed. And how does an organization gain nonprofit status? Self-designation is one way; in practice all states do require an organization to demonstrate in its articles that its purposes are nonprofit. But self-designation alone will not assure a nonprofit status. More important are an organization's methods and activities. The tests may be simple: Is income distributed as profits or dividends among the organizers or operators? Has dividend-paying capital stock been issued?

1 ▪ 2
WHO ARE THEY?

Nonprofit activities might most easily be studied by examining the organizations that encourage them and the evolving legal treatment that applies to those organizations.

Individual enterprise. Your encouragement of cancer research or my donation to the arts is likely to be supported by federal income-tax deductions. Within statutory limits, individual charitable contributions and public-charity work are allowed as tax deductions. But this is true only if the recipient is a formally organized entity, such as an association, trust, or corporation.

Regrettably, there is little legislative encouragement for individual charitable activity beyond tax relief. What legislation there is tends to be directed at unmasking swindlers who pose as philanthropists. The principal check on such abuses is licensing of both contributions solicitation and those who solicit contributions.

Association. Like a partnership, an association is a group of people joined in a common purpose, frequently without a formal charter. Ordinarily it is not incorporated, yet it usually employs the methods and forms used by corporations. In fact, the association is often treated by regulatory and tax authorities as a quasi-corporation. This is more likely, of course, if its organization and operation are governed by a written agreement among its members.

It is thought in legal circles that the unincorporated association has many disadvantages and only few advantages. The laws governing it are inadequate, vague, and still too few to define a reliable system of organization and operation. No wonder it is rarely viewed as a legal entity separate from the people who control it . . . except when it suits government purposes.

The number of important unincorporated associations has dwindled in recent years, while the number of incorporated associations, more logically called corporations, has increased considerably.

Corporation. Today this is by far the most popular form of organization for the majority of group enterprises. The corporation is an artificial person or legal entity with its own name, composed of individuals, yet regarded by the law as an aggregate body distinct from its members. Organized to meet lawful requirements and to exercise specifically authorized powers, it has a continuing existence even as its membership changes. Insulating its members from personal liability, the corporate form is most likely to dominate nonprofit structures in the foreseeable future.

Foundation. A foundation is a modern innovation to provide for the endowment of nonprofit enterprises and the establishment of a corporation or association to carry out its founder's plans. It is not a legal entity, but it is a philanthropic institution.

Most foundations are set up as charitable trusts. To use this form, the grantor of a foundation conveys money or property by a deed of trust to a named trustee or trustees, to be disbursed as the instrument directs.

The charitable trust, sometimes called an unincorporated foundation, is often managed by a board of trustees and operated by a small staff of officers. Although it may be incorporated, technically it remains a trust. Accordingly, when trust problems arise, they must first be considered in light of the law of trusts and only then in light of the law of corporations and associations.

The foundation has gained notoriety through its use by business corporations, which recognized opportunities in exchanging their stock for income-tax and gift-tax deductions, good public relations, low-cost research and product development, ready capital, a competitive advantage over fully taxed companies, and, to gild the lily, their perpetuation of control. The 1969 tax reforms, which have increased government regulation, were designed to curb these incredible abuses.

How does a charitable trust work? The grantor usually directs that a charitable corporation be formed to serve as a corporate trustee. The corporation itself is to be governed by a board of its own trustees, normally named by the grantor. Or the grantor may direct the named trustees to organize a charitable corporation that will become the corporate trustee. Occasionally, the grantor may even give the unincorporated group of trustees the option of incorporating or not, as it sees fit.

Technically, the *foundation* is the document of endowment or incorporation. In addition, the *founder* is the grantor (who can be an individual or an organization) and who normally specifies the purposes for which the assets are to be used. The *trustee* is actually the organization that is set up. In popular usage, though, the term *foundation* can mean the complete enterprise or, even more often, the organization that administers the fund.

1 ▪ 3
FOUNDING YOUR FOUNDATION

A foundation may be set up by an individual, a family, a corporation, or any combination of these. As a charitable trust, it is relatively easy to establish. Normally all that is required is the creation of a trust by will or deed, the transfer of property to the trust, and the acceptance by the trustees of the trust's terms. The foundation is then in a position to operate—unless it is to adopt the corporate form, in which case it will need to obtain a charter and comply with additional statutory provisions.

When the decision has been made to set up a foundation, certain choices must be made that will be reflected in the trust deed:

- Name selection. Do not pin your hopes on the selection of a name. It really will have no conclusive significance.
- Purpose clause or declaration of purpose. You will probably quote "the betterment of mankind" as your general intent, followed by more specifically detailed purposes.
- Transfer of property clause.
- Covenants by the trustees to fulfill their obligations.
- Successor trustee provision—just in case.
- Provisions for revocability (including alteration or amendment).
- Acceptance of the trust by the trustees.
- Compliance with state and federal laws and regulations.
- General provisions (filling of vacancies; retention of funds by trustees; authorization of perpetual existence; form of annual report, if one is required; investment in trustees of all the powers necessary to carry out the provisions of the trust, in addition to specific and general powers; and the provision that, if any of the other provisions is held invalid, those remaining "shall not be affected thereby").
- Schedule, or appendix, listing the original property transferred to the trust.
- Execution, by the settlor, accompanied by a statement that the trustees acknowledge "our promises, covenants, and agreements herein contained and in witness of our acceptance of the property herein described."

After the foundation is established, it is privileged to apply to the Internal Revenue Service (IRS) for tax-exempt status. Once obtained, the federal tax exemption ordinarily triggers state tax exemption, as well as state registration and regulation, usually by the attorney general.

We have said that the trustees are obligated to perform the duties imposed by the trust instrument. But those duties may be delimited or enlarged by state statute. For example, a statutory requirement may govern investments that trustees make, stating that it is improper for the trustees to invest speculatively. If the trust instrument calls for the trustees to invest "as they deem advisable," the effect of this clause will depend on the tradition of the state.

It is usually safe to apply the "prudent man" rule. Even so, if a power cannot be inferred expressly or implicitly from the trust instrument (for instance, to sell, mortgage, or make long-term leases on land), the trustees may be wise to obtain a court order and avoid potential problems.

More often than not, trustees of charitable foundations receive no payment other than reimbursement for their expenses. For smaller family foundations, nonpayment to trustees helps to avoid the suspicion that the foundation is a means for channeling tax-exempt income to family members or friends of the donor.

1 ▪ 4
PUBLIC VS. PRIVATE CHARITIES

To understand what a private foundation is, we must understand what it is not. The IRS, in its continuing attempt to police private foundations, has been most successful at defining them. Generally, they are exempt organizations organized exclusively for charitable, religious, and educational purposes, except those that are philanthropic, churches, schools, hospitals, and other broadly supported organizations. More simply put, a private foundation is a private charity, whereas the broadly supported charitable organizations are essentially public charities.

Every exempt U.S. and foreign charity that qualifies under Section 501(c)(3) of the Internal Revenue Code is a "private foundation" unless it sends the IRS a notice claiming that it falls into one of the categories specifically excluded from the definition of "private foundation." Broadly speaking, organizations that are not private foundations are public charities as described in Section 509(a) of the Internal Revenue Code. Public charities have wide public support or actively provide a supporting relationship to public charities.

Your organization is not a private foundation if it is a church or convention or association of churches, a school, a hospital, a government unit, a publicly or governmentally supported organization, a medical research organization operated in conjunction with a hospital, an organization operated for the benefit of certain state and municipal colleges and universities, or an organization organized and operated to test for public safety. These organizations are examples of charitable endeavors that can be loosely grouped as operating charities that often depend on public contributions for their support and fund-raising organizations that solicit public contributions and then make contributions to worthy causes.

An organization qualifies for "public charity" status if it meets the following criteria.

1. It receives more than one-third of its support by contributions, membership fees, and gross receipts from activities relating to its exempt function, as long as the contributions come from organizations qualifying for the 50 percent charitable deduction, government units, and organizations and persons not disqualified; and it normally receives no more than one-third of its support from gross investment income and income after tax from unrelated business taxable income.

2. It is operated, supervised, or controlled by or in connection with one or more public charities, but is in no way controlled by disqualified persons other than foundation managers. The organization itself is not publicly supported but is sufficiently related to one that is, so that the required degree of public control and involvement is present.

3. It normally receives at least one-third—or at least a "substantial amount"—of its support from government or public sources that qualify for the 50 percent charitable deduction. A substantial amount is measured by three yardsticks.

- The total amount of government and public support is at least 10 percent of its total.
- The charity has a bona fide and continuous program for the solicitation of funds from public charities, the general public, or government units.
- Other pertinent facts and circumstances suggest that the organization is one of a public nature. For example, the governing board is elected by a broadly based membership and composed of public officials.

4. It is operated solely for the benefit of one or more organizations that are exempt as social welfare organizations, civic leagues,

or labor, agricultural, or horticultural organizations. Keep in mind that the exempt organization benefited must meet the support test in Item 1 above. In addition, the organization operated for the benefit of a qualifying organization must not be controlled by disqualified persons other than foundation managers.

Remember, if your organization fits the description of a public charity, it will still be presumed to be a private foundation unless it gives timely notice to the IRS (Part VII, Form 1023) that it is not in fact a private foundation. Exceptions to these requirements are organizations not required to file Form 1023 and certain nonexempt charitable trusts. Timely notice for those required to file is within fifteen months from the end of the month in which the organization was organized.

What is a private foundation? It is a nonprofit, nongovernment organization having a principal fund of its own, managed by its own trustees or directors. It is established to aid or maintain charitable, educational, religious, social, or other activities serving the common welfare. It usually operates under state or federal charter and enjoys the privileges of tax exemption and a continuity of existence not accorded to noncharitable trust funds.

A private foundation is not a legal entity, but simply one kind of philanthropic institution. It commonly functions by disbursing its funds in the form of grants to operating charitable bodies, like hospitals, schools, and social service agencies. State law recognizes that the foundation can be organized as a trust (inter vivos or testamentary), as a corporation, or as an unincorporated association. It has been considered the principal vehicle by which an individual, family, or corporation can make substantial contributions dedicated to the public welfare and create all kinds of advantages for itself in the process.

Whereas the typical business organization uses private resources and means to pursue private ends, and government uses public resources to pursue public ends, the charitable foundation uses private resources to pursue basically public ends. To many, private foundations represent a desirable alternative to government's carrying on these same activities, since they take into account personal choices (as in religion, research, and social science) or private initiative and experimentation.

The foundation is generally created as a charitable trust and can be incorporated under state statute or special state or federal charter. The trend today is toward incorporation. Incorporation of a foundation is extremely attractive.

- It allows for greater freedom and less public control than a trust.
- Although it is permanent, it escapes the rule against perpetuities through the legal fiction that a corporation is a person in which the property has vested.
- It allows its founders to prevent the depletion of their principal.

But keep in mind that the administrative and operating expenses of an incorporated foundation will run higher than for one unincorporated. Incorporation is most practical for a fund with at least $100,000 a year.

1 ▪ 5
FOUNDATIONS BY THE NUMBERS

These categories are the most prevalent types of foundation:

General research foundations. These are large, endowed funds that make grants for education, research, welfare, health, and the like. One example is the Ford Foundation.

Family or personal foundations. These are smaller in scope, functioning primarily as instruments for channeling the annual contributions of their founders during their lifetimes and of their families thereafter. They can be a buffer between the giver and the many appeals directed at him, allowing time for investigation and planned giving; they can help level the rate of contributions between years of high and low income; and they can serve as a reservoir for the accumulation of the substantial funds that may be needed for a major project.

Company or corporation foundations. These are legal entities separate from their parent companies, although they derive most of their funds from the parent and have trustee boards consisting at least principally of the parent corporations' officers and directors.

Community foundations or trusts. These are formed to give central-ized administration to separate charitable funds in a single geo-graphical area, and are usually concerned with problems of social welfare. A particular variant of the community foundation is a common fund foundation, whereby contributions are pooled in a common fund, with the donor retaining the right to designate an-nually the income recipient organizations (so long as they qualify as 50 percent charities) and to direct by deed or will those who will eventually receive the corpus of the contributions. The common fund must pay out its adjusted net income to public charities by the fifteenth day of the third month after the close of the tax year in which the income is realized, and the corpus must be distributed within one year after the death of the donor.

Special-purpose foundations. Most are small funds formed for partic-ular purposes, like scholarship funds. Many are created by will or trust instrument rather than incorporation.

Government foundations. These are foundations set up and con-trolled by the U.S. government and financed by taxes. Favorite enterprises have been education, science, and the arts.

1 ▪ 6
A LOOK AT THE LAW

You can gain a healthy insight into the character of nonprofit or-ganizations merely by reviewing the manner in which they are regulated. On the federal level, nonprofit regulation generally translates into tax regulation, most notably exemption compli-ance. On the state level, however, all kinds of laws define the cate-gorization and operation of nonprofit organizations. Much of the state statutory classification that exists for nonprofit organizations is for the supervision of corporations.

Although the states have uniformly developed statutory schemes regarding the incorporation of business organizations, this is hardly true in their treatment of charitable and other nonprofit or-ganizations. Some states have enacted separate legislation, for ex-ample, for religious and educational corporations, different from that for other types of nonprofit activities. Others have included sections in their general business corporation statutes devoted to nonprofit corporations. Still others have made no reference at all in their statutes to nonprofit corporations.

A step toward consistency has been made in the Model Non-Profit Corporation Act, prepared in 1952 by the Committee on Corporate Laws and the Committee on Non-Profit Corporations of the American Bar Association, and revised in 1957 and 1964. This model act has been the basis for statutes in a number of states, helping to give some consistency to an area fraught with inconsistency. Even so, the committee that put together the model act was really concentrating on business and financial organizations.

In most states today nonprofit corporations do not use shares of stock. Instead, certificates of membership are issued to the members. Even if these certificates are referred to as shares or stock, dividends are not paid to the members. In this regard, some state statutes use the term "nonstock" as a synonym for nonprofit. The California general statute, for example, recognizes foreign and domestic corporations, and stock and nonstock corporations.

Once an organization has been classified, it falls under the specific statute or group of statutes that governs that class of organization. These classifications are significant in that they largely determine how an organization must be operated or dissolved, and, most important, what supervision it can expect from the public authorities.

Nonprofit organization statutes typically begin with a general procedural section addressed to all kinds of nonprofit organizations. Then they spell out the regulations governing special situations that particular groups are likely to encounter, generally through tailormade laws.

- In many states educational organizations must be established under the educational corporation statutes if they are to be nonprofit. These statutes generally require compliance with the education laws with regard to faculty, facilities, and academic standards.
- Churches must be formed under the church or religious corporation chapters of many state statutes.

- Social clubs, if incorporated, must be formed under the "general" nonprofit statutes in many states.
- Agricultural and horticultural corporations must be established under the general nonprofit statutes in some states and under specific agricultural corporations statutes in others.
- Fraternal benefit societies (and mutual indemnity organizations) are covered by state insurance statutes in most states.
- Nonprofit medical indemnity plan groups (such as Blue Cross) are subject to insurance statutes in many states and special hospital service or medical care statutes in others.
- Trade associations must be set up under special trade association statutes in some states, but under general nonprofit statutes in others.
- Foundations in most states must be organized under charitable corporations statutes if they intend to incorporate. If not, they must be set up under charitable trust law. And some states have charitable trust corporation statutes.
- Municipal corporations must be formed under city, town, or village corporation statutes, depending mainly on population. This group, although nonprofit in nature in many ways, forms a category of its own that is subject to unique municipal law statutes.
- Urban development corporations are governed by special law in many states.

1 ▪ 7
GETTING THE OK

Once organized, nonprofit corporations need special approvals for some special classifications. Yet most states do not have a single general approval agency. The attorney general or a judge sometimes gives a preliminary general approval, and additional approvals by particular agencies are often necessary for certain organizations and activities.

Here is a typical breakdown of special state approving agencies, the titles of which may vary from state to state.

- Asylums and homes for abandoned children: Department of social welfare.

- Cemetery associations: Cemetery board or commission, the clerk of the county in which the cemetery is to be situated, and the city, town, or village in which any part of the cemetery may lie. All three approvals are often required.
- Churches, synagogues, and parishes: Official consent of the bishop, synod, or diocese (or equivalent) is often required.
- Clinics or dispensaries: Department of hospitals or department of social welfare.
- Colleges or schools: Superintendent or commissioner of education and/or (in some states) state university and/or board of regents; also, for denominational institutions, denominational authorities. Other appropriate agencies, such as the Civil Aeronautics Board for flying schools and the state high court and/or the American Bar Association for accreditation of law schools, may have to give their approval.
- County professional societies: State (and, sometimes, national) professional societies.
- Cruelty prevention: State society for prevention of cruelty to children. The American Society for Prevention of Cruelty to Animals, despite its name, is a local New York organization. The nearest to a national organization in this field seems to be the National Catholic Society for Animal Welfare, Inc., which actually is a lay society supported by people of the Catholic, Protestant, and Jewish faiths.
- Hospital or medical expense groups: Both the superintendent of insurance and the department of social welfare.
- Labor organizations: Labor department or board of standards.
- Legal aid society: State appellate court and bar associations.
- Libraries: Department of education and local (town or city) school or other authorities.
- Military organization aid groups: Adjutant general.
- Monuments and memorials: Public authorities of the city, town, or village, if public property is to be used.
- Political party organizations: Chairman of county committee of the particular political party. (If he or she withholds approval unreasonably, a court may order it dispensed with.)

- Trade associations: Parent association's executive officers, pursuant to the parent constitution or bylaws. Such approval is not required for local or separate associations.
- Worker's organizations: Labor department or board of standards.

1 ▪ 8
CHECKING THE STATUTES BEFORE MAKING A CHOICE

If you are thinking about organizing a nonprofit entity for some special purpose, be sure to check your state statutes and administrative agencies to learn if such a group is likely to be accorded favorable treatment by legislative, judicial, and taxing bodies.

When your purpose is to dispense charitable funds, a study of your state statutes can help you and your attorney best determine whether the trust or corporate form will be more advantageous to your nonprofit organization. A state's requirements for establishing one form may be much more complex than for establishing the other. For instance, typical incorporation requirements follow.

- A specific number of incorporators—say seven—a majority of whom are residents of the state, may be mandated.
- Before a certificate of incorporation is issued by the secretary of state, the incorporators may be subject to examination (as are other matters related to the foundation), by officials of the municipal body in the city in which the foundation is to establish its premises.
- Before the articles of incorporation are approved, the commissioner of corporations or secretary of state may refer them to the department of public welfare or some comparable body. The latter may conduct its own investigation, holding a public hearing with publication of formal notice.
- If the commissioner of public welfare fails to give approval, an appeal may be made to a court of competent jurisdiction.

By contrast, the same state may have no statutory requirements for the creation of a charitable trust. Such a trust may be established and put in operation in the time it takes to draft the trust instrument and secure its execution. Furthermore, the trust provisions may be known only to the persons immediately concerned, the lawyer drafting the instruments, and the taxing authorities. Obviously, a check of a particular state's requirements is essential before selecting your organizational form.

Recently, there has been a marked preference for the use of corporations to manage charitable funds. These nonprofit corporations take different forms.

Membership corporation. In some states, a prescribed number of persons may form such an organization by preparing a certificate for judicial approval. It is then filed with the secretary of state. The membership corporation is exempt from state taxation and does not have to file a corporate tax return. The court may scrutinize its activities at any time on the motion of an interested party, who may be a member or the attorney general. This type of corporation functions through its directors, required to be at least three in number and elected by the members of the corporation. There are neither stockholders nor transferable interests.

Stock corporation. In states that allow the formation of a stock corporation to carry on the aims of a charitable foundation, the charter or certificate of incorporation should conform with the Internal Revenue Code in that no part of its earnings can inure to the benefit of any private stockholder or individual; this should be reiterated in the bylaws.

If you encounter difficulties forming such a corporation because stock companies are normally formed to make a profit, the certificate may be filed in Delaware, which will accept it. The corporation can then qualify in the home state, which may be less strict regarding out-of-state corporations. But why go to such trouble? The stock corporation has the advantage of limited liability for its stockholders, whereas the law regarding liability of the members of a corporation is less clear. Consequently, those who may be unwilling to be members of a membership corporation may become stockholders of a stock corporation.

The traditional form for management of charitable funds has been the lifetime—inter vivos—or testamentary charitable trust. It is generally a simpler form, created without reference to a court or a secretary of state. It is true, though, that in a number of states the trust must be registered with a government agency after its creation. And legislation may affect the trust instruments, although less often than legislation changes state statutes governing charitable corporations.

What other issues bear on your selection of the corporate or trust form?

Liability of trustees and corporate directors. In terms of care and skill, both must adhere to the standard of the ordinary prudent person in his or her conduct as measured in relationship to the trust's or corporation's charitable purposes. Neither is liable for reasonable errors of judgment nor for failure to foresee events not generally anticipated. And neither is liable for the wrongful acts of codirectors or cotrustees so long as they did not concur in the wrongful act.

The standard of care for trustees is no higher than that for corporate directors in terms of an organization's purposes. However, negligence and failure to exercise proper care and skill that would subject a trustee to liability is not considered as serious a deficiency in a director. The prohibitions of self-dealing and conflict of interest are not normally as strict for corporate directors. There must be proof of bad faith or gross or willful neglect before personal liability is imposed on the corporate director.

Tort liability. The traditional immunity doctrine for charitable organizations in tort actions has generally been abandoned by the courts. Tort liabilities are insignificant where an organization's purpose is to channel contributions rather than carry on charitable activities itself. And the problem of tort liability may be mitigated successfully through insurance. Nonetheless, where high-risk activities are carried on (for example, in a health or community center), the corporate form, with its limited liability, may be preferable.

Contractual liability. Although trustees are often bound to a contract, directors who negotiate contracts are agents of the corporation. They assume liability to a third party to a contract only if they fail to disclose that they were acting for the corporation.

International flexibility. Charitable contributions of a corporate donor to a trust are not eligible for the charitable deduction if the contributions are used outside the United States. For charitable contributions to a charitable corporation, the limitation does not apply.

State inheritance tax laws. The trust form is not advantageous in some states because of their inheritance tax laws. For instance, in Massachusetts, a bequest to a charitable trust will qualify for a deduction for inheritance tax purposes only if the purposes of the trust are to be carried out within either Massachusetts or states having reciprocal exemption laws. On the other hand, a deduction will be allowed for a bequest to a charitable corporation organized in Massachusetts, no matter where the corporation conducts its activities.

Federal tax considerations. If a trust is not tax exempt, it is taxed at individual and graduated rates. It has the benefit of the unlimited deduction for accumulations distributions and, in certain cases, amounts permanently set aside for charitable purposes. The exceptions are nonexempt charitable trusts and split-interest trusts treated as private foundations. The latter two take their charitable deductions under rules that apply to individuals. A corporation is subject to a flat-rate tax and a limited charitable contributions deduction.

In terms of tax savings, the best form to use depends on the type and amount of the organization's income and its actual devotion of funds for charitable purposes.

Control of trustees and directors. The biggest difference between a trust and a corporation may lie here. For a corporation,

- Directors are selected by the corporation's "members" or their fellow directors for a set term.
- They may vote to vary the administrative provisions of the corporation or to dissolve and terminate it, so long as they do not divert the funds from the general charitable purposes for which they were intended.
- They may resign with the simplest formalities, and their successors may be selected without any contact with the state.

- They can be removed by a court, or sometimes by vote of their fellow directors, or by failing to be reelected.

On the other hand, in a trust,

- The trustees are selected by the founder of the trust.
- They cannot amend the terms of the trust or terminate it unless expressly authorized by the trust's terms or by judicial action, following a judicial hearing.
- Absent a specific provision in the trust instrument, they may not resign without court permission, and their successors must be appointed by the court. They can be removed only by the court, after a showing of misbehavior or action adverse to the trust.

Powers. Trustees are under an obligation not to delegate acts they can reasonably be required to perform. They cannot transfer the management of the trust or delegate power to select investments, although they can solicit advice, particularly if it concerns professional skills or facilities not possessed by the trustees themselves.

Directors operate under modern statutes permitting the delegation of most board functions to executive committees. The board can delegate to subordinate officers and agents authority to act for and represent the corporation even in matters involving the exercise of judgment and discretion. However, the board remains obligated to supervise corporate affairs.

Both the trustee and corporate board have a fiduciary obligation, but the trustee must make the actual decision, whereas the board may delegate that responsibility and merely exercise general supervisory powers.

Some state statutes prescribe the decisional pattern outlined in the Model Non-Profit Corporation Act. The model places responsibility for management of the corporation on the board of directors. The board can delegate most of its duties to committees of two or more directors (but without relieving the board of its ulti-

mate responsibility) and can exercise power to elect or appoint officers and agents of the corporation and define their duties.

Generally speaking, the form to elect depends on considerations
of convenience of organization and operation. The IRS does not
seem to prefer one form over another. Indeed, the Internal Revenue Code defines organizations eligible for income-tax exemption
as corporations including associations, trusts, funds, foundations,
and the like. The choice, then, is a function of four considerations:
the grantor's wishes, the nature and purpose of the organization,
the amount of funds available, and applicable laws on the federal,
state, and local levels.

1 ▪ 9
SUMMARY

In selecting your organizational form, you and your lawyer must
consider the answers to these questions.

Exactly what does the creator want to do? Which form will best help
realize his or her intention, considering the statutory and case law
in that jurisdiction? Does the state's statute covering nonprofit
corporations allow the formation of a corporation to participate in
the type of activity the creator envisions? What would the situation be under trust statutes or common-law trust rules in that
jurisdiction?

Over what period of time is the organization to be operational? Will a
nonprofit corporation have perpetual life in the jurisdiction, or can
it exist for only a term of years? And is it difficult to renew the corporate charter? Although some states set fixed limits on the life of
nonprofit corporations that divest themselves of their property at
the end of such term, all states allow charitable trusts to exist in
perpetuity once the trust property has vested in the trustee.

What if new developments make a change of operation desirable? Does your state statute for charitable corporations permit
making amendments with ease or only by a complex process? Does
your state, through statutory or case law, allow for modification of
a charity created by a trust instrument?

Are there any operational problems that can be foreseen? If the organization holds stocks, bonds, or land, is it easier in your state to transfer

title when it is held by a trust or when it is held by a corporation? If the organization handles inherently dangerous assets, it may be very important to limit liability by use of the corporate form.

Is it easier or more difficult to provide for successor trustees or successors to the board and officers of the corporation under your state's laws?

What is the responsibility of corporate officers as opposed to that of trustees for handling the affairs of the organization? In some states an officer of a corporation may not be liable for exercising the same bad judgment as a trustee of a trust.

What are the tax consequences arising from the organization and operation of the charity? Trusts do not seem to be as exempt from local property taxes as corporations are.

Normally, no one answer will prompt the creator to select one form of organization over another, but a number of answers that cumulatively favor one form will determine the preferred one. Whatever your choice, make it a deliberate one. It will probably last the life of your organization and support the legal decisions it will make day in and day out.

2
Unincorporated Associations

2 ▪ 1
WHAT IS AN UNINCORPORATED ASSOCIATION?

An unincorporated association can best be described as a group of people joined together, often loosely, to meet common objectives. Labor unions, trade associations, fraternal benefit orders, sports clubs, civic societies, and political and propaganda committees are typical examples. Traditionally, an unincorporated association has not been treated as a separate legal entity. Instead, its rights and obligations are merely the cumulative rights and obligations of its members. All its members are jointly and severally liable for the obligations of the association—giving an adversary the right to sue one or more separately or all of them together at his or her option.

2 ▪ 2
LOOKING BACK AND LOOKING AHEAD

Historically, the unincorporated association's "nonentity" status has deprived it of the capacity to purchase, take, hold, or dispose of property; to sue or be sued; to contract in its own name; and to incur liability. Only recently have more realistic procedural rules displaced these common-law conclusions. Substantial rights and obligations are being created legislatively for the unincorporated association in these ways.

Capacity to deal in property. Under common law, conveyances to an association are held to be to its individual members, jointly or as tenants-in-common. Since each member in effect becomes a part owner, title can only be conveyed with each member's consent, subject to the rights of his family, heirs, and creditors. To avoid this problem of joint ownership, members can designate trustees to take, hold, and convey title in their behalf. The trustees can accept conveyances that would otherwise fall, such as property bequeathed to an association in its own name. As an alternative, members may prevent the loss of such a gift by incorporating the association within one year after the gift is made, but they should only consider incorporation if it is consistent with the association's objectives over the long term.

Under more enlightened statutes, an association is now allowed to hold property by virtue of the entity nature of associations in general, the nature of the use of the property, or the character of certain associations. In Indiana, for example, a statutory trust

- Limits property-holding rights to charitable-type associations.
- Sets a maximum on the number of acres that can be held.
- Specifies the purposes for which the land can be held.
- Requires the appointment of three to nine trustees to carry out the purposes of the association.

These regulations seem to eliminate the problem of several liability and help guarantee that the property will be used in a manner consistent with the association's purposes. Most states also allow entity recognition for the ownership of land by religious societies.

Capacity to sue or be sued. Under common law, the association has no standing in law or equity to sue or be sued. An action by or against it must be in the names of all its members with the right of notice and service of process required for all those named. Where there are too many members to join individually, the action can evolve into a "class" action by or against representatives of the members, complicating an already complex procedure. The best solution seems to be the designation and bonding of an officer— normally a director—for this purpose.

A majority of jurisdictions now allow an unincorporated association to sue or be sued in its own name or, less frequently, in the names of specified association officers. Does this mean, then, that individual members, even those who have not been joined as parties, are bound by a suit? Generally not. In most states, the individual member who has not been served incurs no liability. The Indiana statute, for example, provides:

> ... An unincorporated association may sue or be sued in its common name. A judgment by or against (it) shall bind the organization as if it were an entity. A money judgment against (it) shall not bind an individual. ... no judgment will be enforced against the individual property of any member unless he personally participated in the transaction surrounding the litigation.

Capacity to contract. Under common law, an association cannot contract in its own name, and all its members may be personally liable for its debts. Fortunately, simple membership does not necessarily trigger such liability. Therefore, when a plaintiff seeks to reach the member's assets he must establish association liability. Liability is established when the members expressly or implicitly assent to or ratify a contract and, as such, act collectively as "employers" or principals, thereby clearing the way to bind the association's assets. Each and every member need not assent to every group action; to incur liability, only enough members must have assented to satisfy constitution and bylaws requirements.

The courts have generally held associations' officers personally liable on any contract to which they are a party. Any officer would be well advised to secure a written ratification by vote of the association's membership according to its bylaws before executing a contract. This need for ratification and the threat of liability provide a good double-pronged argument for incorporation of many associations.

Also, if an association's assets are inadequate to satisfy a judgment, the plaintiff can then proceed against any member served for the unsatisfied balance. If any member pays more than his proportionate share, he can look to the other members for contribution.

The legislative trend is to exculpate individual members with respect to contracts made in the name of the association. This would parallel the insulation from liability that corporate managers have always enjoyed.

Capacity to incur tort and criminal liability. Under common law the association can be held liable for the wrongs it commits in the course and scope of its dealings outside the association. The association's liability depends on labeling its members as "principals." The actual wrongdoers will always be liable, whereas the association itself is not liable for the wrongs committed by one of its members.

But can a member sue the association in tort? Each member is both a principal and an agent with respect to all the other members. Consequently, a member as a principal has no cause of action against his coprincipal; the member would effectively be suing himself.

Courts have recently singled out labor unions as entities separate and apart from their memberships. This interpretation has done nothing to eliminate the joint and several liability of membership associations, but it has allowed a member to sue and name only the union as party defendant. Behind this exception lay the reality that individual members of a labor union are not principals of its officers or of its agents and employees. The same recognition of entity status is only beginning to be applied judicially to other unincorporated associations, and one criterion for selection seems to be size. Those given recognition as separate entities are the larger, well-organized associations that normally act through elected officers and in which individual members have little authority in day-to-day operations.

What of criminal liability? When an association has been granted entity status, only the association's assets are available to satisfy any fine imposed. But when an affirmative responsibility is placed on an officer by statute, he is personally liable for any penalty. Although members may occasionally be held accountable, officers are the most likely candidates to suffer criminal prosecution. Their visible positions of control render them more answerable for association activities and more open to a charge of affirmative responsibility. When practical, the association should bond its officers.

2 ▪ 3
TOWARD A DEFINITION

It is clear that the unvarying characteristics of an unincorporated association are few.

1. It is neither a partnership nor a corporation. Instead, it has a fluid, amorphous character.
2. It is viewed as a legal entity only in states with permissive, liberalized statutes. Without entity status, it has difficulties in acquiring, holding, and passing title to property; in making contracts; and in bringing or defending legal actions.
3. Its big advantage was once its lack of regulation. Government authorities are undertaking more and more regulatory administration, so for most purposes, the merits of that particular advantage are vanishing.

2 ▪ 4
LOOKING INSIDE THE ASSOCIATION

Each unincorporated association structures its own format and policies through three fundamental documents.

1. *Articles of association,* an agreement or contract among the original members, by which new members are also bound. Its purpose is to set up the general plan of organization, its goals, and the method of operation.
2. *Constitution,* the basic internal law of the association, analogous to a national or state constitution. It will sometimes be implicit in the articles of association.

3. *Bylaws,* the detailed set of internal laws covering internal procedures and regulations. It is equivalent to the specific statutes of
a state, rather than the general provisions of a constitution. The
bylaws sometimes are in the constitution or the articles.

These documents serve as evidence of consensual undertaking
among the members and as the private law of the association.
They prescribe the rights, duties, and liabilities of the members
and are fully enforceable in the courts unless they are legally unreasonable or contrary to public policy.

A document's validity is not diminished by its title, and termi-
nology may differ. "Articles of association" may be replaced by
"constitution" or "charter and bylaws." One set of articles may do
the whole job, yet be called "constitution and bylaws." Nonetheless, the rules of internal management are always the bylaws,
whether they are contained in the articles or are a separate document.

2 ▪ 5
GET A PERFECT FIT

Because of the far-reaching importance of these documents, they
should be carefully tailored to meet the needs and objectives of
your association, taking into consideration the association's purposes, funds, facilities, personnel, and agreed plan of operation.
This organizational form happens to be the least likely to follow a
standardized formula in drafting its governing instruments. Yet
the members' agreement should always be reduced to written articles. Only when they are duly adopted does the association formally come into existence.

In some states the articles must be filed with the secretary of
state and the clerk of the county in which the association's principal office is located. For a few states, a certificate that states the
name of the organization, its office location, and its officers is required. The use of an assumed (group) name may also require filing, in the nature of licensing, with penalties imposed for failure to
file.

2 ▪ 6
CHECKLIST OF INGREDIENTS

The essential ingredients of your articles include:

1. Name
2. Nonprofit purposes
3. Office location
4. Duration
5. Powers
6. Membership
7. Dues
8. Directors/trustees
9. Officers
10. Committees
11. Meetings
12. Resignation and expulsion
13. Amendments
14. Dissolution
15. Acceptance of articles
16. Signatures

If you are forming or reshaping an unincorporated association, Exhibit 1 (a typical form of governing instrument) should be helpful to you and your attorney in achieving good organization and operation. The form is generally suitable for any unincorporated association, but the specialized character of your organization may demand another approach. Exact wording does not appear in every section because certain sections must represent the agreement of the organizers.

2 ▪ 7
YOU CAN BE CHOOSY

Membership is generally open only to those whom the members choose to admit. They may be either natural persons or corporations. Evidence of membership may be certificates of membership or membership cards that are sometimes transferable.

Denial of membership or expulsion of existing members can

EXHIBIT 1

Articles of Association
of Unincorporated Association
(Schematic)

ARTICLE I
NAME AND PURPOSES

Section 1. We, the undersigned, desiring to form a nonprofit association for the purpose of . . . , do hereby constitute ourselves a voluntary nonprofit association under the name . . . Association.

Section 2. Our principal purpose(s) are all without pecuniary profit to any officer, director, or member.

ARTICLE II
OFFICE AND DURATION

Section 1. The principal office of this Association shall be located in the City of . . . , State of . . . .

Section 2. The duration of this Association shall be . . . years.

Section 3. The death, removal, or resignation of any member of this Association shall not result in the dissolution of this Association.

ARTICLE III
GENERAL POWERS

Section 1. This Association shall have the power to own, accept, acquire, mortgage, and dispose of real and personal property, and to obtain, invest, and retain funds, in advancing the purposes stated in Article I above.

Section 2. This Association shall have the power to do any lawful acts or things reasonably necessary or desirable for carrying out the Association's purposes, and for protecting the lawful rights and interests of its members in connection therewith.

ARTICLE IV
MEMBERSHIP AND DUES

Section 1. There shall be (only one) (two) class(es) of membership, namely (for example):
(a) Life Members (e.g., who contribute $100).
(b) Regular Members (e.g., who pay annual dues).
Section 2. Application for membership shall be: (specify; for example) submitted on Association forms, personally signed, and given to the Membership Committee.
Section 3. All membership applications shall contain a statement that the applicant agrees to abide by the Articles of Association (or Constitution), and the Bylaws (if any) as presently or hereafter duly adopted.
Section 4. (Specify method of acceptance or of election to membership.)
Section 5. (Specify any particular agreements or obligations that application for membership shall include.)
Section 6. (Specify the method and form of enrollment, initiation, or the like.)
Section 7. The annual dues of each member shall be . . . dollars, payable each year, on or before . . . .

ARTICLE V
DIRECTORS (OR TRUSTEES)

Section 1. The management and government of the affairs of this Association shall be vested in a Board of Directors (or Trustees) that shall consist of . . . members.
Section 2. (Specify their qualifications, terms of office, quorum, and other such general rules.)
Section 3. (Specify rules, notices, and procedures for their meetings.)
Section 4. (Specify the method of their election and of filling vacancies by directors.)
Section 5. (Specify what reports shall be made to the members,

when, and in what detail. At least one annual meeting of all members, and a report thereat, should be required.)

Section 6. Power to enter into contracts on behalf of the Association shall be vested in the President, who must be a member of the Board of Directors. But all such contracts shall be subject to ratification or disapproval by the said Board. (Or specify other rules for contracts.)

Section 7. All Directors shall serve without salary for their services as Directors, but they may receive reasonable compensation for special work or services rendered in other capacities at the request of the Board of Directors.

Section 8. (Specify methods of filling vacancies by members.)

Section 9. (Specify methods of removal, for what causes, and by what procedures.)

Section 10. (Specify other powers, such as procedure to hear complaints and to expel, suspend, or reinstate members; and special powers.)

ARTICLE VI
OFFICERS

Section 1. The Officers of this Association shall be: (specify titles, such as: President, Vice-President, Secretary, and Treasurer).

Section 2. The Officers of this Association shall be selected (or elected) by the Board of Directors, who also shall fix their salaries and who may remove them from office at the Directors' pleasure (or provide for removal by the members, and procedures).

Section 3. Legal counsel shall be selected by the Board of Directors (or by the President) on terms to be fixed by the Board.

Section 4. (Specify details for appointments, compensation, vacancies, removals, and chain of authority.)

Section 5. The President, who must be a member of the Board of Directors, shall (specify his powers and duties).

Section 6. The Vice-President (specify his powers and duties).

Section 7. The Secretary (specify his powers and duties).

Section 8. The Treasurer (specify his powers and duties).

Section 9. The Association's Counsel (specify his powers and duties).

ARTICLE VII
COMMITTEES

Section 1. (Specify committee selection, quorum, control, meetings, and reports. State which shall be standing committees. Specify a power to create special committees when necessary. Next, set forth for each committee, separately, its name, membership, powers, and duties, thus:)

Section 2. The Membership Committee. . . .

Section 3. The Executive Committee, exercising powers of the Board of Directors, under Board direction, when the Board is not in session. . . .

Section 4. The Budget Committee. . . .

Section 5. The Grievance Committee. . . .

Section 6. (Other committees). . . .

ARTICLE VIII
MEETINGS OF THE MEMBERSHIP

Section 1. An annual meeting of the members of the Association shall be held in the month of . . . , at a place in the City of . . . , State of . . . , to be designated by the Board of Directors (or in a place to be designated by the Board).

Section 2. At the annual meeting a report of the past year's activities and of projects for the future shall be made by the Board and by such others as the Board may invite to report. A financial report shall be made by the Treasurer.

Section 3. (Specify other regular matters on the agenda.)

Section 4. (Specify methods of sending notice.)

Section 5. (Specify procedures for election of directors.)

ARTICLE IX
EXPULSIONS AND RESIGNATIONS

Section 1. (Specify grounds and methods of expulsion, including notices, hearings, appeals.)

Section 2. (Specify procedures for resignations.)

ARTICLE X
AMENDMENTS

Section 1. (Specify methods and procedures for amending these Articles or the Bylaws.)

ARTICLE XI
DISSOLUTION

Section 1. (Specify procedures for dissolution.)
Section 2. (Specify methods of distribution of assets.)

ARTICLE XII
APPROVAL OF ARTICLES

Section 1. These Articles shall become binding and effective when they are duly accepted and signed by (specify the number of the organizers whose signatures shall constitute approval. At least two-thirds of the organizers should sign, if possible, in order to avoid later recriminations).

Signatures   Dates

_____   _____
_____   _____
_____   _____
_____   _____
_____   _____
_____   _____
_____   _____

(Note: Notarization of each signature may be attached below the group of signatures but is not required in most states.)

pose civil rights' problems. Usually a private association may limit its membership on, say, a racial or religious basis unless it is affected by a "strong public interest." The exceptions and limitations of such an interest are controlled by questions involving the Fourteenth and Fifteenth amendments to the U.S. Constitution regarding "state action," as opposed to private action.

2 ▪ 8
AGENTS—WHO'S TO BLAME?

An association, like a corporation, can act only through its agents or representatives. The amount of express authority an agent has must be determined by the executive board or the directors, pursuant to the powers granted by the members. And the members assume liability for the acts of their agents. Where the facts and circumstances give the agent the apparent authority to bind the members personally, the members may be bound to a third-person plaintiff showing reasonable cause to believe that the members actually did consent to the agent's actions. One exception: Agents of a union may bind the union only on the express authorization of its members. It has often been held that the employer acts at his peril if he relies on the implied or apparent authority of union representatives.

2 ▪ 9
PROTECTING THE FLOCK

An area of uncertainty involves how far an association may properly go in protecting the personal rights of its members by legal action. The boundaries are clear in the case of a professional society bringing suit to stop the unauthorized practice of a profession by unlicensed persons or organizations. On the other hand, if unlicensed persons commit criminal acts, public policy requires that public authorities, rather than private organizations, act to protect individuals' rights. At a minimum, though, an unincorporated association has the right to act on behalf of its members as a friend or adviser of the court. Whether or not the court chooses to listen is another matter.

Another labor union exception: The labor laws give the unions the specific right to act on behalf of their members to ameliorate working conditions and restore their rights as workers.

2 ▪ 10
CROSSING THE STATE LINE

A special duty arises when an association wants to operate in a state other than the one in which its home office is located. If under the laws of the other state it possesses the ordinary attributes of a corporation, it is required to register as a foreign organization in the other state and be licensed to do business there.

Registration includes the filing of a certificate with the secretary of state, who is designated as the agent for service of legal process against the association. The president, vice-president, or secretary usually must sign the certificate, and the signature must be notarized. The certificate should include the names and places of residence of its officers and directors, its principal place of operation, and its office address within the "foreign" state.

Punishment for failure to file is denial of the association's right to use the local courts to enforce its contracts within the state.

2 ▪ 11
WHERE DOES IT ALL END?

Since an association has no rights or obligations independent of those of its members, the association's existence depends on the continued existence of its members. What may trigger an association's demise?

- Involuntary judicial dissolution, such as action by state authorities for improper conduct.
- Expiration of a stated term, if one appears in the articles of association.
- Death or withdrawal of a substantial number of members without their replacement.
- Voluntary dissolution by consent of the members when the association's purposes have been achieved or abandoned.

The steps to an absolute dissolution are simple.

- All debts are paid.
- The remaining property is divided proportionately among the members.

However, dissolution is sometimes only partial. When a charitable association holds property in trust and the achievement of its purpose becomes impossible, a court will assign the property to some other trustee to devote the assets of the trust as nearly as possible to the original trust purpose. This is the doctrine of cy pres.

A recent trend in this vein is the idea of using the unincorporated association form for winding up a dissolved charitable corporation. Here is an example of the steps taken by a large corporation foundation that adopted such a solution.

1. After the foundation was dissolved, a trust agreement was drafted by the corporate officers to set up an unincorporated "final fund." The remaining unexpended assets were given to the final fund for completion of distribution.
2. A bank was made trustee for depository and distribution purposes.
3. Corporate directors were named to control the distribution of the final assets by the bank as trustee.
4. The agreement was filed with the secretary of state as part of the dissolution record of the incorporated and dissolved foundation.

2 ▪ 12
THE RESIDENT ASSOCIATION

Although the use of unincorporated associations has been on the decline generally, it has found some measure of popularity with owners of condominiums and cooperatives and with other resident associations. These "common-interest communities" are becoming more and more prevalent in our society as single-family dwellings are being replaced by multifamily unit developments. Their common characteristic is that each is an association of neighbors banded together for some common good. They are generally grouped into four types.

1. *Tenants' association.* Although this is not a "common-interest community" since its functions are not management and maintenance of realty, it does qualify as an association banded together for some common good. In this association of lessees, the common good is the abatement of tenant grievances through negotiation. Tenants' associations are usually formed and operated without detailed articles of association.

2. *Homeowners' association.* This is the means by which owners of freestanding dwellings join together for a common purpose or goal. Such an association may be formed as a joint venture to combat some problem facing the neighborhood (for example, rezoning that would lower property values). Title to any common property is granted to the association. When it has the responsibilities of managing and maintaining common property, it closely resembles a condominium association.

3. *Co-op association.* This is the managing body of a cooperative apartment building. In a cooperative the apartment units and common grounds are owned by a corporation, with each resident owning shares of stock in that corporation. A board of directors manages and maintains the complex as directed by its resident shareholders.

4. *Condominium association.* This is the governing association of a condominium development, one in which each unit owner has absolute title to his apartment unit with "common elements" collectively owned by all the unit owners. Each owner is a member of the condominium association by virtue of a membership covenant in his or her deed that runs with the land. Since the condominium is today's most prevalent resident association, it will serve as our frame of reference in the discussions to follow.

2 ▪ 13
THE DEVELOPER'S RULE

The time from which the developer of a complex initially organizes and sets the association in motion until the community and the association can become self-sufficient may be a period of concern and controversy between the developer and buyer. The responsibilities of the developer are to:

- Determine the legal form of the association (whether incorporated or not).
- Tailor the association to the project.
- Train the early residents in the administration and operation of the association.
- Guarantee that qualified managers are hired to run day-to-day operations.

Once the developer has met these responsibilities, he or she is obliged to transfer control to the unit owners. Failure of the developer to relinquish control has led to the enactment of statutes safeguarding the unit owners' rights of self-government without developer interference to the owners' detriment. Florida, for instance, has legislation that sets forth the following guidelines, designed to curb the developer's control:

- At such time as 15 percent of the units are sold, the unit owners may elect one-third of the association's board of directors.
- Within three months after 90 percent of the units are sold, or within three years after 75 percent of the units are sold, or when the developer stops his sales activity—whichever comes first—the unit owners have the right to elect a majority of the board of directors.

Developers, however, have been able to retain some control, as evidenced in the following situations.

Strings can be attached. In a case where the developer tried to retain control over the association's operation by reserving the right to "amend, alter, repeal, or modify" the association's declaration of restrictions, such a clause was held valid as long as it was carried on in a reasonable manner that would not destroy the general scheme or plan of the development. Another developer was allowed to keep an indirect interest in a project by reserving title to the common properties and leasing them to the association—as long as a standard of "good faith and reasonableness" was maintained.

2 ▪ 14
TO WHAT END?

The resident association is a minigovernment that alters or amends its rules once certain motives and voting requirements are met, taxes the members with monthly assessments, and can fine or expel a member for breach of its rules. This is especially true for associations with automatic and mandatory membership running with title.

The guidelines for the operation of a condominium association is provided by the declaration of condominium, its bylaws, and applicable state statutes. Your declaration and bylaws should be tailored to the project and the association's purposes. These documents should include:

1. A delineation of the various kinds of real-estate ownership—for example, a leasehold in the common areas, joint ownership of party walls, and fee simple ownership of each unit.
2. A designation of who is responsible for maintenance and repairs—whether it be the association, developer, or unit owner.
3. An explicit explanation in the bylaws of the house or "good behavior" rules.
4. A clear statement of the officers' and directors' powers and duties and the operational structure of the association.
5. A recitation of the rules for amendment of the bylaws and voter eligibility requirements. A particularly knotty area arises from clauses that grant the association the right to approve new members (new purchasers) or the "right of first refusal" to buy a unit from a member who is selling. As long as these clauses are reasonable and clearly drafted and have not been applied discriminatorily, they have been held valid. Any impermissible discrimination will expose both the association and its officers to civil liability.
6. An explanation of the areas of potential liability and a provision for insurance to protect against potential claims. Although members may be jointly and severally liable for the obligations of the association, there is a legislative trend to limit owner lia-

bility or to require an injured party to look to the association for satisfaction before he looks to the owners.

2 ▪ 15
WHO'S LIABLE?

You cannot overlook the officers' and directors' susceptibility to personal liability if they breach their fiduciary duty or get involved in a conflict of interest. Directors have often been held liable for injury to a third party that was caused by the negligent condition of the common property. Do not assume incorporation is the answer. The courts seem increasingly reluctant to allow a group of individuals to hide behind a thin corporate mask to the detriment of an injured party and sometimes conclude that the corporation is in truth an agent of its members. As a result, the members would be liable under the doctrine of respondeat superior—a principal is responsible for the negligence of his agent.

An adequate insurance provision for members would be one in which the risk of loss is deflected away from the personal assets of the association members. The cost of insurance is part of each unit's monthly assessment and contains cross-liability endorsements to cover liabilities the unit owners as a group may owe to an individual owner.

A special policy should also be provided for any volunteer officers and directors against risks like these:

- Misstatement of the association's financial condition.
- Overstepping authority under the association's charter or bylaws.
- Conflicts of interest of the director or officers with the association.
- Concealment of vital facts from association members.
- Unnecessarily incurred tax penalties against the association.
- Careless investments.
- Continual absence from directors' meetings.
- Permitting of improper acts by others.
- Failure to make or accept competitive bids.
- Failure to make proper reports to regulatory bodies.

- Failure to check auditing and accounting practices.
- Speculative investments on behalf of the association.
- Actions brought by regulatory bodies against directors or officers in their official capacity.
- Alleged mismanagement, negligence, or breach of fiduciary duties.
- Construction disputes.
- Indirect contract disputes from subcontractors, developers, or other third parties.
- Employment and/or labor disputes, including hiring, firing, terminating, and promoting.
- Disputes involving tax liens or assessment liens on property for nonpayment of property taxes or assessment fees.
- Interference with private (real-estate or insurance) business or competition with private business by the association directors or officers.

2 ▪ 16
THE ASSOCIATION AS PLAINTIFF . . . AND DEFENDANT

The courts have disagreed about a resident association's standing to sue, but are more receptive to suits filed on behalf of members rather than in its own capacity, unless it has an explicit procedural mandate to do otherwise. Furthermore, an association can institute a class action suit in a unit owner's name—usually an officer or director—on behalf of the total group of aggrieved unit owners.

A condominium declaration and bylaws are enforceable against an owner who purchased a unit with notice of the rules. Other remedies, including fines, injunctive relief, and even expulsion of the member, are available. For this reason, it becomes important that the house rules be incorporated into the bylaws, lest a court hold them unenforceable. Association rules must be followed by its members in much the same way a citizen is required to follow the rules of the municipality.

On the other hand, an association member does have recourse should he or she elect to challenge an association rule. The member will ordinarily be granted standing to attack a rule, but will not normally prevail if it is held to be reasonable and promulgated according to fair and stated procedures with adequate notice to the member.

An association member has a stake in the actions of the association. The officers and directors are personally liable for actions they take outside the scope of their authority and they must account for their negligent and fraudulent actions. Again, the importance of specifying the powers and duties of the officers and directors clearly in the association documents cannot be overstated.

2 ▪ 17
FINDING THE TAX BREAKS

Exemption from federal income tax is elective for resident associations. They are accorded much the traditional tax treatment afforded social clubs in that only "exempt function income" escapes taxation. "Exempt function income" includes amounts received as membership dues, fees, or assessments from association members. These are the requirements for exemption:

1. The association must be organized and operated to provide for the acquisition, construction, management, maintenance, and care of association property, and it must devote 90 percent of its annual expenditures to these purposes.

2. At least 60 percent of the association's yearly gross income must consist of exempt function income.

3. No part of its net earnings may inure to the benefit of any private shareholder or individual. Activities that do not constitute private inurement are acquiring, constructing, or providing management, maintenance, and care of association property and rebating excess membership dues, fees, or assessments.

4. A substantial number of all the dwelling units in the project must be used as residences.

Examples of taxable income are:

- Payments by nonmembers for use of the association's facilities.
- Payments subject to a specific $100 deduction.

- Deductions directly connected with the production of gross income (other than exempt function income).

Property taxes are paid by the association on the common property through assessment of its members. In turn, unit owners can personally deduct their pro rata share paid by the association. Since property taxes vary, counsel should consider local taxes in planning the development and projecting unit assessments.

Not all the tax laws favor the association. Consider, for example, the possibility of the U.S. Treasury's characterization of repairs and improvements to a unit owner's property furnished by the association as a constructive corporate dividend. If the IRS were to prevail in such a dispute, the unit owner would be obligated to include the value of the repair or improvement in his gross income, thereby increasing his personal tax liability.

2 ▪ 18
PROS AND CONS

The association is a relatively informal structure and its organizational vagaries, perhaps more than any other feature, tend to commend it. The form functions best for small, local organizations such as social, political, and sports clubs and local musical, literary, and religious societies.

At the same time, legislatures nationwide are imposing greater obligations on resident associations to their members through comprehensive disclosure requirements at sale and resale, expanded officers' and directors' liability, and stricter consumer protection standards. Not surprisingly, the unincorporated association continues to present a confused and inconsistent legal maze, one that should only be embarked upon with the guidance of competent counsel.

3
Charitable Trusts

3 ▪ 1
WHAT'S A TRUST?

An ordinary trust, simply put, is an arrangement whereby property legally owned by one person is administered for the benefit of another. Three parties are ordinarily needed for such an arrangement:

1. The settlor—who deeds or bequeaths his property for another's benefit.
2. The trustee—in whom the legal control of the property is vested.
3. The beneficiary—who benefits from the trust.

A charitable trust is one established for the benefit of the public or some class of it. The chief importance of a charitable trust is in the endowment of foundations and the support of public-benefit work. It is created by the appointment of a trustee to hold the trust property or fund and to manage or apply it for a charitable purpose. Its main characteristics may thus be summarized as the designation of a trustee to hold particular property and apply the property or its income to a specific charitable endeavor for unspecified beneficiaries who are of a specified class of the public.

3 ▪ 2
SAY IT LOUD AND CLEAR

A declaration of trust may be contained in a deed or will and, either way, must be crossed-t, dotted-i explicit. If created by will, the will must satisfy any local statute regarding the formality of wills. If created by deed, the instrument must be completely filled out, signed, and delivered.

If the subject matter is realty, the Statute of Frauds governing the enforceability of written documents must be satisfied. The declaration should state the donor's intention clearly and unequivocally to create a trust, the trust's purposes, and the rights, powers, and obligations of the trust parties. Of course, the settlor's objective must be legal.

How do we know if a trust has actually been established? At times, it may be difficult to distinguish between an absolute gift to a charitable organization to be used for its exempt purposes and a gift to the organization to hold as a trustee for charity. Words of trusteeship in the deed or will usually will be conclusive. But a statement that the property given is to be used as part of an endowment fund is not necessarily determinative. The need for expert draftmanship is underscored.

As you can see, the declaration is a complete package of all important information about the trust. Because the trust instrument defines the trust's purpose and the rights, powers, and obligations of the trust parties, and serves to convey title to the trust properties, it is indispensable. Courts will look to it to determine whether the properties are adequately defined or the purpose sufficiently charitable. Therefore, the importance of tailoring the trust instrument to the desired objectives cannot be overstressed. To get a clear picture of what this document may include, take a look at Exhibit 2, which is an IRS-sanctioned sample.

EXHIBIT 2

A Typical Declaration of Charitable Trust

The _____ Charitable Trust. Declaration of Trust made as of the _____ day of _____ , 19___ , by _____ of _____ , and _____ of _____ , who hereby declare and agree that they have received this day from _____ , as Donor, the sum of Ten Dollars ($10) and that they will hold and manage the same, and any additions to it, in trust, as follows:

First: This trust shall be called "The _____ Charitable Trust."

Second: The trustees may receive and accept property, whether real, personal, or mixed, by way of gift, bequest, or devise, from any person, firm, trust, or corporation, to be held, administered, and disposed of in accordance with and pursuant to the provisions of this Declaration of Trust; but no gift, bequest, or devise of any such property shall be received and accepted if it is conditioned or limited in such manner as to require the disposition of the income or its principal to any person or organization other than a "charitable organization" or for other than "charitable purposes" within the meaning of such terms as defined in Article Third of this Declaration of Trust, or as shall in the opinion of the trustees, jeopardize the federal income-tax exemption of this trust pursuant to Section 501(c)(3) of the Internal Revenue Code of 1954, as now in force or afterward amended.

Third: A. The principal and income of all property received and accepted by the trustees to be administered under this Declaration of Trust shall be held in trust by them, and the trustees may make payments or distributions from income or principal, or both, to or for the use of such charitable organizations, within the meaning of that term as defined in paragraph C, in such amounts and for such charitable purposes of the trust as the trustees shall from time to time select and determine; and the trustees may make payments or distributions from income or principal, or both, directly for such charitable purposes, within the meaning of that term as defined in paragraph D, in such amounts as the trustees shall from time to time select and determine without making use of any other charitable organization. The trustees may also make payments or distributions of all or any part of the income or principal to states, territories, or possessions of the United States, any political subdivision of any of the foregoing, or to the United States or the District of Columbia, but only for charitable purposes within the meaning of that term as defined in paragraph D. Income or principal derived from contributions by corporations shall be distributed by the trustees for use solely within the United States or its possessions. No part of the net earnings of this trust shall inure or be payable to or for the benefit of any private shareholder or individual, and no substantial part of the activities of this trust shall be the carrying of propaganda, or otherwise attempting to influence legislation. No part of the activities of this trust shall be the participation in or intervention in (including the publishing or distribution of statements) any political campaign on behalf of any candidate for public office.

B. The trust shall continue forever unless the trustees terminate it and distribute all the principal and income, which action may be taken by the trustees in their discretion at any time. On such termination, the trust fund as then constituted shall be distributed to or for the use of such charitable organizations, in such amounts and for such charitable purposes as the trustees shall then select and determine. The Donor authorizes and empowers the trustees to form and organize a nonprofit corporation limited to the uses and purposes provided for in this Declaration of Trust, such corporation to be organized under the laws of any state or under the laws of the United States as may be determined by the trustees; such corporation when organized to have power to administer and control the affairs and property and to carry out the uses, objects, and purposes of this trust. Upon the creation and organization of such corporation, the trustees are authorized and empowered to convey, transfer, and deliver to such corporation all the property and assets to which this trust may be or becomes entitled. The charter, bylaws, and other provisions for the organization and management of such corporation and its affairs and property shall be such as the trustees shall determine, consistent with the provisions of this paragraph.

C. In this Declaration of Trust and in any amendments to it, references to "charitable organizations" or "charitable organization" mean corporations, trusts, funds, foundations, or community chests created or organized in the United States or in any of its possessions, whether under the laws of the United States, any state or territory, the District of Columbia, or any possession of the United States, organized and operated exclusively for charitable purposes, no part of the net earnings of which inures or is payable to or for the benefit of any private shareholder or individual, and no substantial part of the activities of which is carrying on propaganda, or otherwise attempting to influence legislation, and that do not participate in or intervene in (including the publishing or distribution of statements) any political campaign on behalf of any candidate for public office. It is intended that the organization described in this paragraph C shall be entitled to exemption from federal income tax under Section 501(c)(3) of the Internal Revenue Code of 1954, as now in force or afterward amended.

D. In this Declaration of Trust and in any amendments to it, the term "charitable purposes" shall be limited to and shall include only religious, charitable, scientific, literary, or educational purposes within the meaning of those terms as used in Section 501(c)(3) of the Internal Revenue Code of 1954 but only such purposes under the law of trusts of the state of _____ .

Fourth: This Declaration of Trust may be amended at any time or times by written instrument or instruments signed and sealed by the trustees, and acknowledged by any of the trustees, provided that no amendment shall authorize the trustees to conduct the affairs of this trust in any manner or for any purpose contrary to the provisions of Section 501(c)(3) of the Internal Revenue Code of 1954 as now in force or afterward amended. An amendment of the provisions of this Article Fourth (or any amendment to it) shall be valid only if and to the extent that such amendment further restricts the trustees' amending power. All instruments amending this Declaration of Trust shall be noted upon or kept attached to the executed original of this Declaration of Trust held by the trustees.

Fifth: Any trustee under this Declaration of Trust may, by written instrument, signed and acknowledged, resign his office. The number of trustees shall be at all times not less than two, and whenever for any reason the number is reduced to one, there shall be, and at any other time there may be, appointed one or more additional trustees. Appointments shall be made by the trustee or trustees for the time in office by written instruments signed and acknowledged. Any succeeding or additional trustee shall, upon his acceptance of the office by written instrument signed and acknowledged, have the same powers, rights, and duties, and the same title to the trust estate jointly with the surviving or remaining trustee or trustees as if originally appointed.

None of the trustees shall be required to furnish any bond or surety. None of them shall be responsible or liable for the acts or omissions of any other of the trustees or of any predecessor or of a custodian, agent, depositary, or counsel selected with reasonable care.

The one or more trustees, whether original or successor, for the time being in office, shall have full authority to act even though one or more vacancies may exist. A trustee may, by appropriate written instrument, delegate all or any part of his powers to another or others of the trustees for such periods and subject to such conditions as such delegating trustee may determine.

The trustees serving under this Declaration of Trust are authorized to pay to themselves amounts for reasonable expenses incurred and reasonable compensation for services rendered in the administration of this trust, but in no event shall any trustee who has made a contribution to this trust ever receive any compensation thereafter.

Sixth: In extension and not in limitation of the common law and statutory powers of trustees and other powers granted in this Declaration of Trust, the trustees shall have the following discretionary powers:

(a) To invest and reinvest the principal and income of the trust in such property, real, personal, or mixed, and in such manner as they shall deem proper, and from time to time to change investments as they shall deem advisable; to invest in or retain any stocks, shares, bonds, notes, obligations, or personal or real property (including without limitation any interests in or obligations of any corporation, association, business trust, investment trust, common trust fund, or investment company) even though some or all of the property so acquired or retained is of a kind or size that but for this express authority would not be considered proper and even though all of the trust funds are invested in the securities of one company. No principal or income, however, shall be loaned, directly or indirectly, to any trustee or to anyone else, corporate or otherwise, who has at any time made a contribution to this trust, nor to anyone except on the basis of an adequate interest charge and with adequate security.

(b) To sell, lease, or exchange any personal, mixed, or real property, at public auction or by private contract, for such consideration and on such terms as to credit or otherwise, and to make such contracts and enter into such undertakings relating to the trust property, as they consider advisable, whether or not such leases or contracts may extend beyond the duration of the trust.

(c) To borrow money for such periods, at such rates of interest, and upon such terms as the trustees consider advisable, and as security for such loans to mortgage or pledge any real or personal property with or without power of sale; to acquire or hold any real or personal property, subject to any mortgage or pledge on or of property acquired or held by this trust.

(d) To execute and deliver deeds, assignments, transfers, mortgages, pledges, leases, covenants, contracts, promissory notes, releases, and other instruments, sealed or unsealed, incident to any transaction in which they engage.

(e) To vote, to give proxies, to participate in the reorganization, merger, or consolidation of any concern, or in the sale, lease, disposition, or distribution of its assets; to join with other security holders in acting through a committee, depositary, voting trustees, or otherwise, and in this connection to delegate authority to such committee, depositary, or trustees and to deposit securities with them or transfer securities to them; to pay assessments levied on securities or to exercise subscription rights with respect to securities.

(f) To employ a bank or trust company as custodian of any funds or securities and to delegate to it such powers as they deem appropriate; to hold trust property without indication of fiduciary capacity but only in the name of a registered nominee, provided the trust property is at all times identified as such on the books of the trust; to keep any or all of the trust property or funds in any place or places in the United States of America; to employ clerks, accountants, investment counsel, investment agents, and any special services, and to pay the reasonable compensation and expenses of all such services in addition to the compensation of the trustees.

Seventh: The trustees' powers are exercisable solely in the fiduciary capacity consistent with and in furtherance of the charitable purposes of this trust as specified in Article Third and not otherwise.

Eighth: In this Declaration of Trust and in any amendment to it, references to "trustees" mean the one or more trustees, whether original or successor, for the time being in office.

Ninth: Any person may rely on a copy, certified by a notary public, of the executed original of this Declaration of Trust held by the trustees, and of any of the notations on it and writings attached to it, as fully as he might rely on the original documents themselves. Any such person may rely fully on any statements of fact certified by anyone who appears from such original documents or from such certified copy to be a trustee under this Declaration of Trust. No one dealing with the trustees need inquire concerning the validity of anything the trustees purport to do. No one dealing with the trustees need see to the application of anything paid or transferred to or upon the order of the trustees of the trust.

Tenth: This Declaration of Trust is to be governed in all respects by the laws of the state of _____ .

Trustee _____

Trustee _____

3 ▪ 3
GIVE SOMETHING

It is clear that actual conveyance or transfer of ownership of the real, personal, or intangible property or estate must be made (which is accomplished simply by the trust instrument being contained in the deed or will). Thus, the grantor of the trust must be qualified to part with his interest. Most states impose all these requirements:

- The settlor must be competent when making the contribution.
- A contribution cannot violate statutory obligations to close relatives of the settlor.
- A testamentary contribution will be voidable unless made via a will executed at least a reasonable time before the death of the testator.
- A contribution will be ineffective if it is in excess of a certain proportion of the testator's estate if the testator left particular named classes of close relatives.

Only next of kin, heirs, and residuary beneficiaries can question the validity of the gift if the will was executed too close to the testator's date of the gift. As for the "excess" provision, only a member of one of the classes protected by the statute can object.

A legal title must be conveyed to a "capable" trustee and must give the trustee absolute ownership. Examples of capable trustees are the state, public officers, most individuals and corporations, unincorporated associations, if they have authority under the laws of their state to own property in their own name, and some nonresidents, aliens, and foreign corporations, again as provided by state law.

3 ▪ 4
WHAT'S CHARITABLE?

To be a charitable trust, the trust

- Must be held for the benefit of the public as a whole.
- Cannot be established to benefit a specific person or a few definite beneficiaries, as in an ordinary trust.
- Must have as its purpose to advance the public interest in a spiritual, mental, or physical manner.
- Must have an indefinite and general enough object or beneficiary to be deemed of common and public benefit. In other words, it must be a public charity.

Instead of identifying persons or corporations as beneficiaries, the settlor describes a purpose of substantial public benefit. Such charitable purposes include relief of poverty, advancement of education and religion, promotion of health, government or municipal purposes, and other purposes that benefit the community.

The courts determine whether the settlor intended to make the public the beneficiary by ruling on whether the settlor had a charitable purpose in mind when he or she set up the trust. If the object of a trust instrument falls within these charitable purposes, the courts will generally uphold the gift as charitable without much probing of its inner workings. However, where the trust's purpose fits into the "beneficial to the community" category, whether or not it will be considered charitable stands or falls on the court's subjective determination of what the end result may be. Remember, though, the settlor's personal motives are immaterial. The courts are looking to see if the trust will have charitable effects.

3 ▪ 5
OVERSEEING YOUR TRUST

How is a trust regulated? Most jurisdictions require trustees to make periodic accountings in court or to the appropriate state's attorney general, usually annually. And courts retain substantial control over trusts, which includes powers to do the following:

- To appoint a trustee if the original trustee refuses or is unable to carry out his duties.
- To construe the trust instrument.
- To remove or suspend an unfaithful trustee.
- To restrain a possible breach of trust, abuse, or power by the trustee.
- To correct any irregularities in administration.
- To protect the trust property from loss or diversion.
- To instruct the trustees when they are in doubt regarding their powers and duties.
- To direct the future administration of the trust.
- To order the sale of trust property.
- To rule on the validity of a provision for income accumulations in terms of reasonableness as to the length of time required.

How long does a trust last? Although charitable trusts are subject to the rule against perpetuities (providing that no property interest is good unless it vests—becomes a fixed right—no later than twenty-one years after some life in being at the creation of the interest), once a property has vested in a trustee, the trust may generally endure perpetually or for an indefinite period. The rule against perpetuities, in its proper legal sense, has relation only to the time of vesting of an estate, not the actual duration of the trust, and in no way affects its continuance once it vests. (The one exception to the rule involves trust property that, by the settlor's instructions, is to be transferred from one charity to another at some future date.)

The trust can be terminated by a specific provision in the trust instrument or by the accomplishment or failure of the trust's purpose. The latter may occur when there is no possibility of changing the trust to accomplish the stated purposes.

Because a charitable trust can be created for an indefinite duration or for any desired length of time, it may become necessary for the court to vary the precise terms of the trust. The court may exercise the equitable doctrine of approximation by varying the details of administration in order to preserve the trust and carry out the donor's purpose in light of changed conditions, or the doctrine of cy pres (limited to charitable trusts), in which the court finds that the donor's intended purpose has become impossible or impracticable owing to changed conditions and orders the trust corpus to be applied to a charity with an objective similar to that originally designated. The attorney general is a necessary party to such a court proceeding.

The doctrine of cy pres is part of the common law, and where there is no statutory regulation, the doctrine is applicable only after three conditions are met.

1. Either a valid charitable trust or a corporation that is considered a valid charity must exist.
2. The donor's intention must be impossible or impracticable to carry out.
3. The donor must have had a general charitable intention, as well as an intention to benefit the particular charitable group designated.

Where there is no court intervention, the activities of charitable trusts are seldom checked effectively. A private citizen interested in assuring that the settlor's intention is being carried out lacks judicial standing to initiate an action. Administrative supervision in most states is grossly inadequate. The state attorney general serves as the protector of the charitable trust, but all too often his office lacks the staff and facilities to provide the needed protection.

Ultimately, the attorney who drafts the trust instrument assumes the greatest responsibility. If he is careless in his drafting, the result may be the perversion of the settlor's intended charitable purpose. Worse yet, an unscrupulous trustee can take ambiguous phrasing and use it to frustrate the settlor's intended purpose.

3 ▪ 6
WHO'S THE BOSS?

Management of a charitable trust lies with its trustee, who may be subject to extensive regulations if it is a state bank or a trust company. In some states other types of corporations, usually of a charitable nature themselves, cannot receive title as trustees to property greater than a certain value or amount. Foreign corporations may be seriously handicapped to act as trustees or may be denied the right to conduct trust business.

What do trustees do?

1. They hold legal title to property for the benefit of another, who holds equitable title. Where property is given to a trustee for the benefit of a charitable corporation or unincorporated association, that corporation or association may in reality only be a conduit through which benefits are to flow to the public. As such, it may be said to be a subtrustee, rather than a beneficiary of the trust in the strict sense.

2. They are usually chosen by the settlor (who can decide how successor trustees will be appointed) or by judicial appointment. In certain cases they may be self-perpetuating if the trust instrument so provides.

3. They are usually granted all the powers necessary to administer the trust, either expressly or implicitly, by relevant statutes or by the trust instrument itself. Their powers include the power to delegate certain tasks requiring the exercise of minimal discretion.

4. The trustees are strictly accountable for exercising normal fiduciary standards in managing trust affairs and may be required to post bond. The standard of performance to which they are held is that of the ordinary skillful and prudent man in the management of his own affairs.

3 ▪ 7
THE TRUSTEE'S EXPOSURE

A trust is not treated as a legal person or entity. Instead, it is a "bundle of rights and duties" affecting the legal and equitable relationships among the trust properties, the trustee(s), the beneficiaries, and, sometimes, the settlor and his successors.

The trustee usually enjoys no independent legal status as a trustee; he or she acts as an individual. However, an increasing number of jurisdictions now provide by statute for actions taken against a trustee, in both contract and tort, solely in his or her representative capacity—although the right to proceed personally against the trustee remains alive. Here are examples of their fiduciary duties:

1. The duty of loyalty to administer the trust according to its provisions in good faith without seeking personal benefit.
2. The duty to protect and preserve the trust property by administering the trust in a businesslike manner in full compliance with the law.
3. The duty to make the trust property productive, including the duty to review and change investments continuously.
4. The duty to defend the trust against attack.

3 ▪ 8
TWO GOOD CHOICES

Two modern institutions are available to a settlor looking for a trustee for a charitable endeavor:

1. *The community trust.* Property is held and managed by corporate trustees subject to directives given by a distribution committee of civic leaders as to any limitations imposed by the donor. This is a good device for combining small funds, since separately each might not have the resources to attract personnel capable of wise and prudent management.

2. *The charitable foundation* (which can be in trust or corporate form). A large number of these have been established by wealthy

families to achieve public benefits, as well as to save themselves and their businesses from big tax bites.

3 ▪ 9
WHAT CAN A TRUST DO?

How much responsibility does a trust really have?

Capacity to own property. Legal title to the trust properties is vested in the trustee. If there is more than one trustee, they, as joint tenants, are ordinarily empowered by the trust instrument to sell the original trust properties and to invest in others. If this is not the case, they may have an implied power to do so in order to carry out the trust's purposes. Upon termination, the trustees distribute the net assets as directed by the trust instrument. In the absence thereof, there is a resulting trust for the settlor or his or her successors.

Capacity to sue and be sued. In contrast to some unincorporated associations, a trust may not litigate. Actions brought by or against the trust should be maintained in the names of the trustees.

Capacity to contract. The trustees usually have an express or implied authority to contract in administering the trust, express powers being conferred by statute or by the trust instrument. Contracts are made in the trustees' names and, barring relevant statutory provisions or a contractual stipulation to the contrary, will usually bind only the trustees. The trustees' ability to exclude personal liability by express contractual stipulation is literally recognized everywhere. The trustees may, within narrow limits, delegate the power to enter contracts to agents whose acts, under agency law, may bind the trustees personally as principals.

Capacity to incur liability. In third-person liability actions, a contract creditor may sue the trustees in their representative capacities and satisfy his or her claim only from the trust estate. Otherwise, the trust properties will remain beyond the creditor's reach. However, a number of states now recognize a creditor's right to go against the trust assets, whether or not personal liability of the trustee has been excluded.

If trustees suffer liability because of contracts properly executed on behalf of the trust, they normally have a right to be indemnified from the trust estate. And a creditor may reach trust assets by subrogating himself or herself to the trustees' right of indemnification. Trustees are personally liable both for the torts—noncontractual wrongs—they may commit and for those committed by their agents acting within the scope of their authority. Where the trustee's tort was committed as an inevitable consequence of administering the trust, recovery may be allowed directly against the trust estate, now that charitable immunity has been revoked in many states.

3 ▪ 10
CONCLUSION

Although the charitable trust differs structurally from the unincorporated association, the trust's trustees incur liability in much the same fashion as the association's managers. Both should be acutely sensitive to the risks they undertake as a representative of a regulated and legally restricted organization. And both should demand cautious guidance at every stage of legal decisionmaking.

4
Nonprofit Corporations

WHAT IS A NONPROFIT CORPORATION?

The most popular organizational form in use for nonprofit organizations is the nonprofit or not-for-profit corporation. A corporation is an entity separate and distinct from its members. It is a fictitious legal person and as such is usually given the same rights and is subject to the same obligations as natural persons. This makes its legal relationships easily definable and controllable.

Nonprofit corporations are governed by statutes that usually fall within three basic patterns:

1. General corporation statutes applying to both for-profit and not-for-profit corporations alike.
2. Not-for-profit statutes that closely follow business corporation statutes.
3. Not-for-profit corporation statutes that may have little resemblance to a more sophisticated business corporation statute or that may be supplemented by general provisions of the business corporation statute.

Here is a right-on-the-money definition of a nonprofit corporation, taken verbatim from such a not-for-profit statute:

A not-for-profit corporation is a corporation no part of the income of which is distributable to its members, directors, or officers; provided, however, that payment of reasonable compensation for services rendered and the making of distributions upon dissolution or final liquidation as permitted by statute, shall not be deemed a distribution of income.

4 ▪ 2
WHAT CAN THE NONPROFIT CORPORATION DO?

The nonprofit corporation's legal capacities and liabilities are as follows.

Capacity to deal in property. Nonprofit corporations usually have the power to take, hold, and transfer corporate property in the corporate name. Just how the net assets are distributed upon dissolution depends on the applicable statutes and provisions in the articles of incorporation.

Capacity to sue and be sued. By virtue of its entity status, a nonprofit corporation can sue and be sued in the corporate name. But unlike natural persons, it normally cannot appear in court without a duly licensed attorney.

Capacity to contract. Corporations are also empowered to make contracts in the corporate name. Such contracts should be executed in the corporation's behalf only by duly authorized officers or other agents, as specified in the bylaws or resolutions of the board of directors. The corporate seal should be affixed to minimize questions regarding the scope of the agent's authority and to ensure that the corporation—and not the agent—is bound by the contract.

Capacity to incur liability. Contract and tort claimants may sue the corporation in its own name and enforce any resulting judgment against corporate assets.

Members of the corporation have only limited liability, except when they are parties to a contract or take part in a tort. Their liability extends to any indebtedness to the corporation for unpaid dues, assessments, or fees.

Directors and officers are not personally liable unless they are parties to a contract or are themselves wrongdoers. If they are guilty of a wrong, but only through the exercise of their required duties to the corporation, they can be indemnified—secured against loss—by the corporation or through officers' and directors' liability insurance.

4 ▪ 3
YOUR MOST IMPORTANT DOCUMENT

When you incorporate your nonprofit organization, attend to the articles or certificate of incorporation or charter you adopt. This may be the first formal step in forming your corporation and will serve as its constitution.

The essentials of articles of incorporation are:

- The document's identity, whether it be articles or certificate of incorporation.
- The name of the statute under which incorporation is sought.
- The corporate name.
- The purpose clause.
- The statement regarding the corporation's nonprofit nature.
- The locality in which the corporation will conduct its activities.
- The location (city and county) of the corporate office.
- The minimum or maximum number of directors or trustees needed.
- The original directors' names and addresses.
- In some states, a statement that all those subscribing to the articles are legally qualified (of majority, U.S. citizens, and other such qualifications).
- The name and address of the designated agent for service of process.
- The signators' signatures, addresses, and acknowledgments.
- An approval statement from any government agency required to approve the document.

The articles are prepared for the organizers by an attorney. The language the attorney selects will vary with the provisions of the applicable state corporation statute, but should always be clear and understandable. Exhibits 3 and 4 are two contrasting formats for articles of incorporation. Reviewing them will enrich your appreciation of the thorough and thoughtful drafting process. (Note: The first is based on the charter of a local club, for which no approvals from any government agencies usually are required.)

EXHIBIT 3

Certificate of Incorporation of
The _____ Club, Inc.

We, the undersigned, desiring to form a Membership Corporation pursuant to the (Nonprofit) Corporation Law of the State of _____ , do hereby state:

One: The name of the proposed Corporation is The _____ Club, Inc.

Two: The purposes for which said Corporation is formed are as follows:

(a) To encourage interest in _____ .

(b) To provide economical _____ for its members, not for profit.

(c) To bring to more people the social benefits and pleasures of _____ activity.

Three: The powers of the Corporation shall be as follows:

(a) To own and hold and/or lease, purchase, mortgage, sell, or otherwise dispose of in its name personal property—namely, one or more _____ or _____ appurtenances—and to purchase in its name, lease, mortgage, sell, or otherwise divest itself of real property, or any interest therein for use in connection with its _____ activities, all property both real and personal to be used or disposed of only in the interest of the Corporation and in furtherance of its objects; and the Corporation shall operate as a nonprofitmaking enterprise; to perform or contract for the performance by others of any work or service deemed necessary or desirable in carrying on or furthering the purposes of the Corporation, and in the upkeep, improvement, or preservation of the Corporation's property interests;

(b) To promulgate rules and regulations governing the rights and activities of its members in their use of the Corporation's facilities; and

(c) To carry on all other business not specifically herein above mentioned and not inconsistent with law in furtherance of the above-stated purposes of this Corporation.

(Duration statement is required in some states.)

Four: The operations of this Corporation are to be conducted principally in the Counties of _____ and _____ , State of _____ .

Five: The office of the Corporation is to be located in the Village of _____ , County of _____ , State of _____ .

Six: The number of directors shall be not less than three nor more than seven.

Seven: The directors of this Corporation need not be members.

Eight: Any one or more of the directors may be removed either with or without cause at any time by a vote of two-thirds of the members of the Corporation at any special meeting called for that purpose.

Nine: The name and post-office addresses of the directors until the first annual meeting are as follows:

	Name	Address
1.	_____	_____
2.	_____	_____
3.	_____	_____
4.	_____	_____

Ten: The time for holding the annual meeting of the Corporation shall be the first Monday in the month of May or, if such day shall be a holiday, the next day thereafter.

Eleven: The majority in person or by written proxy of all the members of this Corporation entitled to vote shall be necessary to constitute a quorum at every regular or special meeting of the members, except as to a special election as provided for in the _____ Corporation Law.

Twelve: All the subscribers of the certificate are of full age, at least two-thirds of them are citizens of the United States, and at least one of them is a resident of the State of _____ ; at least one of the persons named as a director is a citizen of the United States and a resident of the State of _____ .

In witness whereof, we have made, subscribed, and acknowledged the certificate, this _____ day of _____ , 19___ .

(Acknowledgments)

EXHIBIT 4

Certificate, Charter of Incorporation, and Acknowledgment for Horticultural Society
(Tennessee)

CERTIFICATE
STATE OF TENNESSEE
DEPARTMENT OF STATE

I, _____, Secretary of State of the State of Tennessee, do hereby certify that the annexed Instrument with Certificate of Acknowledgment was filed in my office and recorded on the 15th day of September 198__ in Corporation Record Book Miscellaneous A-32, page 92.

IN TESTIMONY WHEREOF, I have hereunto subscribed my Official Signature and by order of the Governor affixed the Great Seal of the State of Tennessee at the Department in the City of Nashville, this 15th day of September A.D. 198__. /s/_____

Secretary of State

CHARTER APPLICATION

STATE OF TENNESSEE
CHARTER OF INCORPORATION

BE IT KNOWN that _____, _____, _____, _____, _____, and _____ are hereby constituted a body politic and corporate, by the name and style of _____ for the general purpose of operating a modified arboretum, promoting the conservation of resources by demonstrating to the public the need for conserving animal life, forests, water, soil, and a love of nature and its beauty, and acquainting the public with the history of the area in which _____ is located, including also the support and encouragement of agriculture, horticulture, and the mechanic arts, as, agricultural or horticultural societies, or societies for the promotion of the mechanic arts, or other objects of like nature.

The general powers of said corporation shall be:

1. To sue and be sued by the corporate name.

2. To have and use a common seal, which it may alter at pleasure; if no common seal, then the signature of the name of the corporation, by any duly authorized officer, shall be legal and binding.

3. To establish bylaws, and make all rules and regulations not inconsistent with the laws and Constitution deemed expedient for the management of corporate affairs.

4. To appoint such subordinate officers and agents, in addition to a president and secretary, or treasurer, as the business of the corporation may require.

5. To designate the name of the office and fix the compensation of the officer.

6. To issue income bonds, constituting an obligation to pay interest and liquidate principal by setting aside net operating income, to be used in payment of property bought by it, making improvements, and for other purposes germane to the objects of its creation, but no obligation may be executed that would be a general indebtedness on which a lien or judgment might be obtained, except one for purchase money on land bought.

7. To receive property, real, personal, or mixed, by purchase, gift, devise, or bequest, sell the same and apply the proceeds toward the promotion of the objects for which it is created, or hold any such property and apply the income and profits toward such objects; however, notwithstanding the powers herein given, it shall have no power to solicit gifts or money or property or to seek to raise funds from its members or the public.

8. Unless otherwise specifically directed in the trust instrument by which any real or personal property, money, or other funds are given, granted, conveyed, bequeathed, devised to, or otherwise vested in, the directors, the governing board, or the authorized finance committee thereof, when authorized by the corporation, shall have power to invest funds thus received or the proceeds of any property thus received, in such investments as in the honest exercise of their judgment they may, after investigation, determine to be safe and proper investments and to retain any investments heretofore so made.

9. The general welfare of society, not individual profit, is the object for which this charter is granted, and the members are not stockholders in the legal sense of the term, and no dividends or profits shall be divided among the members.

10. The said five (5) or more corporators shall, within a convenient time after the registration of this charter, elect from their number a president, secretary, and treasurer, or the last two (2) officers may be combined into one (1), said officers and the other corporators to constitute the first board of directors. They may also enlarge the board and the board may elect an advisory committee of such size and with such powers, privileges, and capacities as they may determine.

11. The term of officers may be fixed by the bylaws, the said term not, however, to exceed three (3) years. All officers hold office until their successors are duly elected and qualified.

12. At any time and for any period when the corporation does not have sufficient funds to carry on the objectives of the trust, it may (a) reduce the operation and employ a mere custodian who will be allowed to graze and farm the property, (b) rent to those who without hindering substantial development will be allowed to live on and utilize the property, (c) sell timber in sufficient amounts to maintain a custodian, or (d) adopt other expedients for mere preservation or conservation that will make the property available later for the general objectives.

13. To accept members, the incorporators or directors being such without the necessity of application, each incorporator or director to have the power of designating a successor and also naming two members, future members to be admitted upon such terms and conditions and with such privileges as may be fixed in the bylaws, etc., referred to in Section 3 above, but in any event to be by fee and classified as in like organizations, life membership to pass one time by will of the deceased member.

14. The members will meet periodically at such times as the directors fix, after five (5) years of operation have enabled them to form an opinion as to the need, and in all elections each member is to be entitled to one (1) vote either in person or by proxy, the result to be determined by a majority of the votes cast. Due notice of any election must be given by advertisement in a newspaper, personal notice to the members, or a day stated on the minutes of the board one (1) month preceding the election.

We, the undersigned, the incorporators above mentioned, hereby apply to the state of Tennessee for a charter of incorporation for the purposes declared in the foregoing instrument.

WITNESS our hands this, the 14th day of September 198___.

/s/ _____
/s/ _____
/s/ _____
/s/ _____
/s/ _____

Subscribing witness:
/s/_____

ACKNOWLEDGMENT

STATE OF TENNESSEE

COUNTY OF _____

Personally appeared before me _____ of said County, the within named _____, the subscribing witness and incorporator, with whom I am personally acquainted, and who acknowledged that she executed the within application for a Charter of Incorporation for the purposes therein contained and expressed; and the said _____, subscribing witness to the signatures subscribed to the within application, being first duly sworn, deposed and said that she is personally acquainted with the within-named incorporators, _____, _____, _____, _____, and _____ and they did in her presence acknowledge that they executed the within application for a Charter of Incorporation for the purposes therein contained and expressed.

WITNESS my hand and official seal at office in Chattanooga, Tennessee, this 14th day of September 198___.

/s/_____

                                        Notary Public

My Commission expires:

October 10, 198___.

State of Tennessee, Hamilton County

The above instrument and certificates were filed September 18, 198___ at 3:05 P.M. entered in Note Book No. 48, page 437 and recorded in Book 1239, page 557. Witness my hand at office in Chattanooga, Tennessee.

/s/_____, Register

/s/_____, Deputy Register

4 ▪ 4
PURPOSE GETS TOP BILLING

You will note the careful attention paid to the purpose clause. The purpose clause formally describes the aims of the corporation. It is preferably a one-paragraph summary of the stated reasons for the corporation's existence. The purpose clause serves several important functions. It gives public notice of the nature of the organization for the benefit of those who deal with it. It indicates to the corporation and its directors and officers the range and scope of their proper activities. It assures members that their membership will not involve them in any liability or activity they did not contemplate.

The following is a well-conceived purpose clause.

> The purpose of this organization shall be to unite the members of the profession of _____ in the area in and about the city of _____ ; to promote the ideals of _____ among them and in relation to the public; to aid and encourage cooperation and improvement in the practice of _____ ; to provide media for such cooperation and improvement; and to do all lawful things consistent with the purpose of the organization and helpful to it, its membership, and the profession, both as a separate organization and in cooperation with national, state, and other local organizations.

You and your attorney should consider these tips in drafting your organization's purpose clause:

1. The purpose clause should be stated briefly in simple words. The purposes themselves should be limited and practical, with alternatives provided only if it is essential.
2. Make certain that the purpose is neither contrary to the public policy of the state (for example, spreading racial and religious hatred) nor an evasion of other laws (for example, carrying on profitmaking activities to evade income taxes under the guise of the nonprofit form). Otherwise, the charter cannot lawfully be approved.
3. Say what you mean and mean what you say. Vagueness in the wording of the clause may lead to the rejection of the charter, and deceptiveness may result in the withdrawal of approval after it has been granted.
4. Be consistent. The charter will not be approved if the purposes stated are contradictory.

Along with a purpose clause, your certificate of incorporation should include a phrase or additional clause indicating its nonprofit intentions. This is often done with a disclaimer clause stating that it is not the purpose of the corporation to engage in an activity forbidden to it. The use of such a clause is especially important for obtaining tax exemption. A typical disclaimer clause may read as follows.

This corporation is not organized for the pecuniary profit of its directors, officers, or members; nor may it issue stock nor declare nor distribute dividends, and no part of its net income shall inure to the benefit of any of these persons; and any balance of money or assets remaining after the full payment of corporate obligations of all and any kinds shall be devoted solely to the charitable, educational, and benevolent purposes of the corporation.

4 ▪ 5
MORE POWER TO YOU

Another critical clause is the power clause. The power clause spells out the ability or capacity of the corporation to act as an entity. Every state allows a corporation to have and to use all the powers reasonably necessary to carry out its approved purposes.

These powers are:

- To use a corporate name or title and to have a corporate seal or symbol.
- To have continuous existence as a legal entity, even though the membership changes.
- To have perpetual existence, or to exist for any desired number of years.
- To acquire, own, deal with, and dispose of property, both real and personal.
- To appoint and compensate necessary officers and agents, and to act through them.
- To make bylaws consistent with the law for the internal regula-

tion of the corporation, and to establish procedures for carrying out its approved purposes.

- To sue and be sued in the corporate name.

Understand that the purpose clause, and not the power clause, is the real measure of your corporate authority. A general approval of its stated purposes amounts to implied approval of all reasonably necessary powers to attain the stated goals.

In addition to state corporation statutes and the corporation's charter and bylaws, we may discover its powers through a possible statute that governs the particular type of corporation in question (such as a religious corporations law); a special statute applicable to special activities (such as licensing for fairs); and/or case law applying to specific transactions or acts. Therefore, your power clause need concentrate only on emphasizing, classifying, or limiting particular powers.

An individual who challenges a corporation's powers has the burden of proving why they are illegal. Generally speaking, all the acts of a corporation are presumed to be within its proper powers unless they are conspicuously abusive.

Who can question the legality of a nonprofit corporation's powers? Under common-law rules, the doctrine of ultra vires is often invoked by persons who contracted with an organization and seek to avoid contractual compliance by arguing that the organization did not have the authority to contract. An ultra vires action is one that is outside the limits of powers stated in the organization's charter or bylaws, or beyond the implied powers reasonably necessary for carrying out its stated purpose. The same principle may give rise to a recession attempt by the organization or a state-initiated quo warranto proceeding to revoke the corporate charter.

To avoid the agony of analyzing whether or not a power should be listed in their charters, some nonprofit corporations rely on a so-called "all-powers" clause. Such a clause states that the corporation has all the implied powers reasonably necessary to reach its objectives. For example:

The foregoing statement of corporate purposes shall be construed as a statement of both purposes and powers, and not as restricting or limiting in any way the general powers of this corporation, or their exercise and enjoyment, as they are expressly or implicitly granted by the laws of the state of _____ .

More often, corporations elect to recite their most important powers. Your attorney will consult your state statutes to determine which powers must be stated to be preserved.

4 ▪ 6
THE LANGUAGE OF POWER

In drafting your organization's power clause your attorney will no doubt heed these pointers:

1. Where express powers are listed in the charter, exclusion is implied from those not listed, the exception being those reasonably needed to carry out those listed.

2. Any explanation and description following a general power is to be treated as a definition of that power. For example, a power to distribute charity to a specific church bars distributions to other religions.

3. If uncertainty exists as to the meaning of a certain statement of power, we must look for an explanation to public policy, legislative intent, judicial interpretation of customary powers of other corporations of the same type, and prior practices of other corporations in similar situations.

4 ▪ 7
MAKING IT OFFICIAL

After the articles of incorporation have been completed, they must be properly executed and legally recorded. Each incorporator must sign the certificate in its final form, and in some states the signing must be notarized. The certificate is then submitted for approval by the appropriate government approving agencies. The certificate is filed. The filing fee for the articles varies from state to state. The filing is carried out by sending the executed certificate, all the annexed affidavits and approvals, and the filing fee check to the secretary of state or some other designated officer. The secretary of state approves the certificate and the corporation is legally alive. Notice of approval is given in a receipt-acknowledgment-certificate mailed to the attorney, and normally serves as prima facie evidence of the incorporation.

4 ▪ 8
WHAT'S NEXT?

After the articles are filed, an organizational meeting should be held. It is best to hold your meeting as soon as conveniently possible, especially since some states grant only conditional existence until the organization begins the activities for which it was chartered. Failure to meet in a reasonable time can cause corporate existence to fail. This can mean that its members may become liable as partners, as in unincorporated associations.

One of the practical purposes of the organizational meeting is to examine the charter and make certain that all the required formalities have been satisfied. Should the corporation fail to complete its organization, defectively incorporate, violate a statute, or exceed its powers or fail to use them, the attorney general can bring about proceedings to revoke the corporation's charter. Your organizational meeting, therefore, is serious business. A nonprofit corporation's organizational meeting might proceed as follows.

After the opening amenities and the elections of both a temporary chairman and a secretary, the attorney is called upon to report on the organization's incorporation. After the attorney's brief review, he or she delivers to the secretary a copy of the articles, a receipt for its filing, the corporate seal, the minute book, and the book of membership certificates. (The articles and receipt will later be fastened into the minute book by the permanent secretary.) Following the elections of the directors and officers, the temporary chairman and secretary are relieved.

The bylaws are then read and adopted, with the names of the first-year directors and officers often filled in as they are elected. This practice can help to prolong control of the organization by the organizers. Waivers of notice of the organizational meeting can be signed if no written notice was sent. The treasurer, who is required to be bonded, collects the initiation fees and/or dues from all those present. The corporate seal is adopted, and the secretary is authorized to purchase and set up books and records.

Next, two officers (usually the president and treasurer) are authorized to open a bank account (by the bank's own form of resolution) in a named bank. The tax exemption application is directed to be filed, usually by the president and attorney. If state law requires, the agent for receiving legal process is designated. The treasurer is authorized to pay the expenses of organization, and a fiscal year may be adopted. The membership committee (when appointed) is given authorization to accept new members.

After the date of the next general meeting is set up, new business is discussed, followed by adjournment. The secretary prepares the minutes and signs them, for reading, correction, and approval at the next meeting.

4 ▪ 9
AFTER THE ORGANIZATIONAL MEETING

Meetings of the members, board of directors, various committees, and other special groups are the essence of nonprofit organization life. Immediately after the organizational meeting, the directors' first meeting is likely to be held. These kinds of decisions can then be made.

- Fixing the compensation of officers (if they are to be paid).
- Assigning certain tasks to the officers, according to the bylaws.
- Making committee appointments.
- Accepting contracts essential for the start-up of activities.
- Deciding on membership certificate forms and contents.

4 ▪ 10
ARE MEETINGS A MUST?

It is a basic rule that directors must meet and act as a board, not as individuals, in order to bind the organization by their acts. This is to protect creditors and any other interested third parties. But if no creditors' rights are affected, as is often the case with nonprofit organizations, and if public policy is not violated, directors' acts can be binding and effective without a formal meeting.

Many times directors hold meetings by telephone. When a decision has been reached, the impression is given in the record that a meeting actually took place. Or one board member might collect oral consents of the others in a series of luncheons, for instance. Although no protests are usually made about such "nonmeetings," there is always the risk of later trouble.

When the members go along with such slipshod procedures, the acts of the directors are binding and effective (as long as they are not otherwise beyond the scope of their powers). Moreover, when the directors or members acquiesce in a certain act, even though they know that a proper meeting was not held to authorize it, they are bound by it.

In some states, the informal authorization of acts that could be authorized at a meeting of directors or members is expressly sanctioned. But these statutes do require a written record of the action, signed by those who would have been entitled to notice of a meeting, and a filing with the corporate records.

Take special note that members normally will not be personally bound without their consent. The courts will not invoke estoppel against them as strictly as they will against members of business organizations.

4 ▪ 11
WHO CALLS THE DIRECTORS' MEETING?

The chairman of the board usually has the primary power to call a board meeting, while the sending of notices is the secretary's job. If the officer responsible for calling a meeting does not do so, the next in rank should (as long as no express alternative appears in the bylaws). In fact, if necessary, any other officer can do so. Unless the charter, bylaws, or a resolution of the directors sets a time or place for a regular meeting, notice should be given to all the directors. However, lack of notice does not invalidate a meeting if all the directors attend and participate without objection. Their presence at the meeting amounts to a waiver of the defect.

Notice is usually given by mail five to ten days in advance of the meeting. As for its contents, no particular form is prescribed. It should merely contain the necessary information, with only the time and place being essential. Oral notice is acceptable if it is your organization's custom, even if written notice is technically required. Directors' meetings only need to be called as is reasonably necessary, if the bylaws are silent on the issue.

A quorum is necessary for a board to act. Unless a specific rule is stated in the charter or bylaws, a quorum is a majority of the board members. A number of recent statutes allow the bylaws to require from one-third to four-fifths to constitute a quorum. If vacancies cause the board to constitute less than a quorum, the board must fill the vacancies before it can officially act.

4 ▪ 12
WHAT HAPPENS AT THE MEETING?

A well-organized board meeting should have an agenda to follow, which helps to keep order and prevent arguments about the priority of subjects.

The order of a typical board meeting follows:

- After assembly, a call to order.
- Roll call and announcement of a quorum.
- Reading of the previous meeting's minutes, any necessary corrections, and their approval as corrected.
- Reports of officers and committee chairmen.
- Old business.
- Elections, if any.
- New business, and appointment of officers or committees to deal with the new matters.
- Setting of time and place for next meeting.
- Adjournment.

At these meetings, as a director you will usually have the right to the presence and counsel of your own attorney.

A record of what went on at a meeting of members or directors is called the corporate minutes. The minutes are kept by the secretary and serve as the official memory, recollection, and record of the organization. For routine meetings the minutes should show the following:

1. The giving of due notice. (The dates of meetings are not scheduled if they are not prescribed in the bylaws.)
2. The presence of a quorum, so that the meeting is legally proper and effective.
3. A countersignature by another officer.
4. A clear and concise narrative of what went on at the meeting.

Unlike business corporations, nonprofit organizations often find it preferable to keep all their minutes in one book rather than two. Keeping informed of all the day-by-day activities helps the members maintain direct knowledge and control of their directors, viewed primarily as their agents rather than as managers. Such control by the members is the basic principle of nonprofit organization operation.

The minutes are considered prima facie evidence of what went on at a meeting. They are effective evidence of what was said and done. Refusal to produce them on court order cannot rest on the constitutional privilege against self-incrimination. The Fifth Amendment protects individuals, not artificial persons such as corporations.

Some state statutes specifically require nonprofit corporations to keep minutes of their meetings, along with complete books and records of account, but most have no such express requirement. If an organization's decisions and actions are otherwise valid, failure to keep minutes will not invalidate them. Nor will it provide a basis for denying the organization's responsibility for such decisions and actions.

In certain matters, state statutes do require records to be kept. Some require that a sale, lease, or mortgage of substantial assets may only be made with the consent of two-thirds of the members or directors, and the receipts of such contents must be recorded. For tax and regulatory purposes, the keeping of records is expressly required, and the minutes are often the primary record on which required tax and other reports must be based.

The members, at common law, have a general right to inspect the books and records. In many states, statutes expressly provide for the rights of members to examine the minutes and other books and records. But inspection rights in charitable organizations are limited for the protection of donors.

4 ▪ 13
LAWS TO LIVE BY

Your organization's bylaws are the rules of its internal management. For the members, they are second in force and binding effect only to the organization's charter. To be effective, they must always be consistent with the provisions of the charter.

Since well-drawn bylaws serve to resolve differences, their shortcomings can lead to friction and trouble in an organization. Although most state statutes allow, rather than require, nonprofit organizations to have bylaws, some states do require that they be adopted. The bylaws basically do the following.

- Regulate the organization's procedures and internal practices.
- Define the rights, duties, and relations of the members amongst themselves and in relation to the organization.
- Define the duties, powers, and limitations of the directors, officers, and other agents.

4 ▪ 14
DIFFERENCE BETWEEN CHARTER AND BYLAWS

What is the relationship between the charter and bylaws?

1. Since the charter is on file in a public office, it is constructive notice to the outside world of your organization's existence and structure. This is not the case with the bylaws, an internal document.
2. Although neither the charter nor the bylaws can override statutes or ordinances, either of these can override both the charter and bylaws. Today's charter does little more than state the purpose of the organization, whereas the bylaws define most management and operational policies.

3. Only members have an inherent right to see and make extracts from an organization's bylaws. As a public-record document, the charter is available at a public office for inspection by anyone desiring to see it.

4 ▪ 15
WHAT'S IN THE BYLAWS?

What is contained in the bylaws ultimately depends on the type of organization it regulates. They should be long enough to cover the subject but short enough to invite study. The differences in completeness are dictated by whether the organization is incorporated or unincorporated. If incorporated, many of the details in them are covered by the state's corporation laws. Consequently, a corporation's bylaws are not as exhaustive as those of an unincorporated association. Yet it is good policy to issue comprehensive bylaws. Customarily important provisions of the bylaws include:

- Restatement of purposes appearing in the charter.
- Membership qualifications, methods of admission, members' rights and privileges, initiation fees, dues, termination of membership by various means.
- Officers' titles, qualifications, powers, duties, terms of office, manner and times of election or appointment, and compensation for every office.
- Vacancies in offices or on the board of directors and how they are filled.
- Carefully detailed voting procedures and what number constitutes a quorum.
- Meetings for elections and other purposes (general and special), including notice, quorums and agendas, and voting qualifications.
- Directors' qualifications and their classification, the manner and times of election, terms of office, powers, duties, and meetings.
- Optional executive committee of the board of directors to exercise board powers between meetings.
- Bonding of particular officers and agents.
- Bank depository and which officers can handle funds.

- Property holding and transfer.
- Fiscal details regarding year and audits.
- Principal committees.
- Assembly and convention rules, if part of a larger entity.
- The seal—its adoption, custody, and method of use.
- Principal office and others.
- Books, reports, and records.
- Method and rules for amendment of charter and bylaws.
- Dissolution procedures and disposition of surplus assets upon dissolution.

4 ▪ 16
WHEN BYLAWS ARE DUE FOR A CHANGE

In most state statutes, the directors are permitted to amend or add to the bylaws only insofar as the general membership grants them the right in the charter or in the original bylaws.

Most bylaws provide fairly detailed procedures for their own amendment. The procedures include:

- That certain notice of a proposed change be sent.
- That the change be voted on at a formal meeting.
- That a certain majority or plurality vote be obtained to carry the proposal.

An amendment of bylaws will be valid if:

1. It is consistent with the charter as the supreme self-proclaimed law of the organization.
2. It does not violate vested contract rights. But keep in mind that it is invalid only for the member whose rights are violated.
3. It is consistent with the general law (as public law cannot validly be negated or altered by private law).
4. It is practical (and not impossible to obey).
5. It is reasonable.

The power to amend or repeal bylaws really rests in the members, not the directors. But the members may vest in the board of directors the power to adopt amendments, by resolution or approval of a bylaw providing for such. The granting of amendatory powers to the directors has proved to be safe and practical, so long as these powers apply only to routine matters. The granting of too-great powers may be a tempting means for directors to perpetuate power. Both charters and bylaws are subject to the reserved power of the state to amend or repeal the law. If the state so acts, there is no valid basis to complain unless contractual rights are destroyed. Therefore, a new statute that results in the voiding of an existing bylaw is a proper exercise of the state's reserved powers.

Be certain to follow amendment procedures carefully, whether they are set forth in the bylaws, the charter, or even in some state statutes. This, of course, is necessary for the amendment to be valid.

4 ▪ 17
MEET THE MANAGEMENT

The ultimate responsibility for management ideally vests in the members. Their basic means of control is their right to vote. It is their will alone that should be the standard in such extraordinary matters as:

1. Acceptance of the charter, adoption of bylaws, and election of officers.
2. Correction or amendment of the charter or bylaws.
3. Large donations or grants of organization property or funds.
4. Guaranteeing the obligations of others.
5. Real property sales, leases, or mortgages.
6. Extending a corporation's life if it is expiring.
7. Possibly insolvency or voluntary bankruptcy proceedings.
8. Voluntary dissolution.
9. Special matters for which the bylaws require meetings. For example, where conventions or assemblies are held to bring representatives of constituent organizations together by the parent body, the bylaws of the parent generally provide for the delegates' qualifications, selections, powers, and certain other functions. Furthermore, the delegates are usually given all the

rights, powers, and privileges of organization members in annual meetings.

The holder of legal power is the legal entity of the organization,
not the board of directors. Thus, the powers of the directors are inherent in the organization, not in themselves. Directors are obliged
to exercise the powers of the organization; they are not to own it.
Their powers are managerial in nature, not proprietary. For example, if members rather than directors were to bring or defend
suits in the organization name, mass confusion would most likely
result. Therefore, the directors need the power to act on behalf of
the organization, but this does not mean they are to have ownership powers within the organization.

Both statutes and case law vest the fundamental power to make
or change rules for the governing of corporations in the members.
The directors are only free to change policies and short-range purposes. However, in extraordinary matters, the will of the general
membership must rule, unless the charter or bylaws expressly allow
the directors to perform acts amounting to changes in fundamental purposes or policies of the organization.

In nonprofit organizations the normal rule is one vote per member, unless the articles or bylaws provide otherwise. Occasionally,
an organization will give each member more than one vote if that
member belongs to a particular class of members, such as those
who are donors.

The right to vote in most states is ordinarily considered an inherent part of membership in a nonprofit organization. The organization's membership rolls usually decide who is entitled to vote. To
base voting power on anything other than membership (for example, favoring holders of bonds or other creditors) is quite narrowly
restricted unless it is justified by statutory authority.

A proxy is a person appointed by another to act or vote for him.
It may also be the instrument containing the appointment of such
a person. This is the chief device for self-perpetuation of management and is widely used by nonprofit organizations. Although a
power to vote by proxy in nonprofit organizations did not exist in
common law, it has been affirmed in most state statutes, as well as

in charters or bylaws. Where it has not been so affirmed, the right expressed or implied in a statute prevails.

The charter and bylaws and occasionally statutes usually contain detailed regulations for elections in order to save time and prevent disputes. These are typical rules:

1. Directors not named in the articles of incorporation are elected by the members and other persons entitled to vote.
2. Majority vote is deciding unless otherwise provided by the charter, bylaws, or statute, which may make other requirements, such as higher than majority votes, as long as they are not unanimous or so close to unanimous that they defeat the basic control of the members, and a two-thirds vote for specific acts, like the making of a sale, lease, or mortgage of corporate assets.
3. Directors are elected annually by the members. This power of the members cannot be taken away from them.
4. Any reasonable method for balloting is normally allowed.
5. A member can change his or her vote or vote additional proxies until the formal results are announced (unless forbidden by the bylaws).
6. The actual closing of the polls occurs when the officer in charge of the election announces the result.
7. If there is a dispute as to the right of a member to vote, the organization's records are the true arbiters. Therefore, they should be at the voting place.
8. A disputed election is usually not void until such time as a court finds that an illegality occurred in the voting.
9. The appointment or election of inspectors of election is strongly encouraged in most states for overseeing the conduct of a vote, in an election or any other voting. The demand of a member for inspectors, even if not backed by bylaws, usually must be honored.

In most decisionmaking, the director of a corporation is a representative of the members. His charge is to carry on the affairs of the group that he represents. In many nonprofit organizations, the term "trustee" is preferred, since it conveys the functions of the office better than the "director" label. The trustee's status is akin to that of an elected legislator, with many of the characteristics of an agent's role and many of those of a trustee's position in a trust of property. The role of trustees in nonprofit organizations is similar to that of directors of other organizations, except for their somewhat limited power to deal with the organization's property. They often need the express consent of the general membership in dealings with property.

Do not compare trustee status in a nonprofit organization with the special status of a trustee of a private trust. Whereas a bequest to the trustee of a trust is a bequest to the individual, a bequest to the trustee of an institution is a bequest to the institution. We will use the term "director" in order to avoid any confusion between the director of a nonprofit corporation or association and the trustee of a trust.

In most states, all directors must be over twenty-one to qualify, with at least one a resident of the United States and at least one a resident of the state of incorporation. The number of original directors and their residences normally must be stated in the articles. Although five incorporators are often required, only three directors are mandatory.

The routine management of affairs lies in the hands of the board of directors. Their management includes three primary duties:

1. Directors are responsible for exercising reasonable care and good faith in organizational affairs. They can take advice and guidance from others, but they must use their own judgment in reaching final decisions.

2. Directors can also be described as fiduciaries, with a duty to act for the good of others rather than their own benefit. Their primary fiduciary duty is to exercise their powers for the benefit of all the members of the organization.

3. The directors must report the nature of their activities, along with the state of the organization's finances and affairs, to the members. In fact, a director's freedom from liability for the debts of the organization may well depend upon filing an annual report. This report must be available for the members' inspection, and a

bylaw that prohibits access to it is not valid. It should be no surprise that making false reports, failing to make reports, or keeping false financial records is a crime.

Some states hold directors personally liable only for a breach of fiduciary duty involving "gross negligence." But most states hold them personally liable for "ordinary negligence" in managing the organization's affairs. Personal liability attaches for failing to supervise subordinates or to choose them wisely; making decisions based on a propriety attitude (as if the trustees were the owners, not the servants, of the organization); and issuing false statements or reports.

Where directors are personally liable for fraud or bad faith, they are jointly and severally liable. A complaining party can sue any of them, all of them, or just one of them, as he or she chooses. Whomever is sued is liable for the total amount of the loss suffered by the plaintiff.

Many state statutes today suspend the Fifth Amendment privilege of refusal to incriminate oneself in testimony when it comes to directors. However, they are granted immunity from prosecution as a result of criminal conduct revealed by their forced testimony.

To protect themselves against unfair personal liability, directors should make certain that a written record is kept that indicates their good faith. If a director objects to a proposal that is carried out, that director should have that protest recorded in the minutes. He or she can also record objections in a letter, memorandum, or other writing. Such a paper is both desirable and valuable for self-defense.

4 ▪ 18
THE COMMITTEE'S FUNCTION

Directors do not work alone. Much of the important work of nonprofit organizations is done by committees of directors. Indeed, true cooperation in doing the work of the organization is much more common in nonprofit entities than in business organizations. Although the committee is essentially an administrative device, actual management or decisionmaking may be entrusted to it. In fact, many states permit the delegation of any authority of the directors to an executive committee. In practice, a committee is a group of members or directors, named by the organization's chief executive officer to study and make recommendations about some matter or to manage routine affairs.

Three general types of committees function in most organizations:

1. *Standing committees.* Their function is to carry on the regular administration of internal affairs. They include the executive committee and committees of finance, budget, membership, and grievance, a standardization committee in trade associations, and often an ethics committee in professional associations.
2. *Administrative committees.* They are like standing committees but only tend to administrative matters. In practice they often function as subcommittees to help the standing commmittees. They are most useful in larger organizations.
3. *Special committees.* They are temporary committees that are formed as problems arise. An example would be a nominating committee.

When a committee has done its work and is ready to report, that report should be brief and include the reason for the committee's appointment, the basic problems tackled, a summary of the study or action, and conclusions reached or recommendations made.

The executive committee is the most important committee in an organization, and its use is widespread. It generally is subject to the same rules that apply to the directors, and it may exercise all the power of the board of directors when the board is not in session. It can manage the routine affairs of the organization, but it cannot take extaordinary action, such as dissolving the organization, on its own discretion. In fact, its appointment is invalid if the charter, a bylaw, or a resolution fails to set reasonable limits on its authority. This means, of course, that the board cannot transfer all its power to the executive committee.

The executive committee functions as follows.

- It acts by a quorum and majority vote, unless otherwise expressly provided.
- It cannot delegate its powers. That even applies to one of its own members.
- Its power to act is suspended while the board of directors meets.
- In its dealings with third persons, the normal rules of express, implied, and apparent authority of agents apply.
- In general, its powers and functions depend on the charter and bylaws, on statutory limitations that require the directors themselves to act in certain matters, and on the purpose for which it was established.

Although important executive acts, such as the making of contracts and leases, may be delegated to a committee, how far the board of directors can delegate such executive (discretionary) powers is not that clear, except with regard to the executive committee. The answer seems to depend on the need for and reasonableness of such delegation and the nature of the duties involved.

It is clear, though, that not all powers can be delegated. For instance, statutes and the charter and bylaws often confer certain express or implied powers on particular officers or on the board itself. Moreover, the board cannot completely hand over to others the power to exercise the board's authority. The appointment of an executive committee cannot mean abandonment of board powers to that committee.

When the board or officers delegate authority to committees or to agents, they are not also delegating their responsibility. In other words, they must maintain a general supervision over the exercise of any powers they have delegated. If they do not, they may be liable for the consequences of any abuse of the delegated powers.

The board of directors has the power to delegate authority, but it is most often the president who exercises it. Any oral appointments of committees he may make are valid, but carefully drafted resolutions regarding the appointments are advisable. The clear record they provide can prevent later difficulties or disputes.

In making personnel selections for the various committees, knowledge of the characteristics and habits of the members is vital.

Which people will work well and efficiently together? A committee chairman, important enough to make or break his committee, should be selected for his qualifications and leadership ability.

Unless you are seeking trouble, it is best to avoid certain practices regarding committees.

1. Do not form committees just to bury an unpleasant issue. The likelihood is that it will just surface again.
2. Do not form them just for publicity purposes; the members may feel deceived.
3. Do not form them to flatter the members with titles. Flattery wears thin.
4. Finally, do not form them to button up an obstreperous member. It will only add fuel to his fire.

Once the committee is formed, keep its members enthusiastic. Always remember to extend the organization's thanks and appreciation to them.

4 ▪ 19
HOW MUCH LIABILITY?

As directors (and their committees) are permitted to rely on officers' and accountants' reports and on the advice of attorneys, they are generally not subject to the full degree of liability of a trustee. On the other hand, they cannot escape the personal liability that can result from ignoring organization affairs.

4 ▪ 20
OUSTING A DIRECTOR

Regardless of statutes, removal for valid cause is always possible. A director may be removed without cause if the charter, bylaws, or statute so provides. Some examples of removal for cause are:

▪ Failing to disclose information on business matters.
▪ Embezzling organization funds.
▪ Refusing to cooperate with the president or making unjustified attacks on the president.

- Gross or willful negligence, certainly; ordinary negligence only in some cases.

An accused director always has the right to a reasonable opportunity to defend himself or herself and must be given notice of the charges. Yet the director cannot vote on his or her own removal. Such removal is subject to court review.

4 ▪ 21
WHO ARE THE OFFICERS?

An officer of a nonprofit organization is any person elected or appointed for a fixed period of time to an office or position of authority, as the bylaws and sometimes the charter provides. He or she is usually elected by the directors or members and is compensated at a fixed rate. An officer has greater importance, independence, dignity, tenure, and authority than other employees. It is these differences in degree that primarily separate officers from rank-and-file employees. In addition, an officer must give bond, take an oath, and execute duties prescribed by internal or general law much more often than an employee.

By contrast, an employee or mere agent (other than an officer) of an organization does not hold any office. The employee is usually employed by the managing officer, and is subordinate to and controlled by the officers. Unlike the officers, he or she has no fiduciary relation to the members. The employee normally works a specified schedule of days or hours, and is paid a salary determined by the managing officer.

4 ▪ 22
WHAT DO OFFICERS DO?

One of the primary tests of an officer's status is the exercise of judgment and discretion. Unlike a director, the officer is primarily an agent of the organization (one who acts in the place of another by the latter's authority), subject to agency laws and the fiduciary duties of agents. Although also subject to the control of the directors and members, and carrying out the policies of either, the officer does hold a position of authority and trust in the organization.

However, as an agent, an officer cannot delegate the discretionary decisions necessary to his or her office. Rather, the officer may delegate only administrative powers.

4 ▪ 23
HOW MUCH POWER?

The powers and limitations of officers are whatever the bylaws declare them to be. Therefore, they should be drafted with exacting language. If an officer is given general management powers, in all probability that officer has the implied power to do anything reasonably necessary or proper to further the affairs of the corporation. Since a corporation cannot execute documents, the power to "sign" is often given to a particular officer and is considered an administrative power.

All this to the side, no officer can commit a corporation to something that its charter does not authorize. But the limitations of powers that are contained in the bylaws do not bind third persons unless they know of them. Such third persons must use reasonable caution, but not suspicious caution, in determining the extent of the authority of the officer with whom they are dealing.

4 ▪ 24
HOW MUCH LIABILITY?

A corporation is entitled to be protected from liability for any unauthorized acts of its officers. If the appearance of power and authority is created only by the officer's words or conduct, the corporation is not bound as to third persons misled by such appearance. On the other hand, if the corporation's conduct gives the officer the appearance of having power that he in reality does not have, the corporation will be so bound.

As for the officer, as an agent he or she is personally liable for any failure to reveal that he or she is acting for the corporation. The officer then is acting for an undisclosed principal, and as such, binds himself or herself. What's more, if the officer clearly exceeds his or her authority or acts without any authorization, that officer is personally liable. Note, though, that an act done without authorization can be ratified by the board of directors, if the board would have ratified it anyhow.

What if an officer exceeds his authority? All corporations have an inherent right to remove officers for cause, and some state statutes do permit removal with or without cause. Even when a bylaw allows removal, the contract status of an officer may bar such removal or suspension without cause. However, the corporation still has the power to remove in some states, but not the legal right. This means that if it does remove, it becomes liable for contractual damages.

In colleges and universities, rights to remain in office are governed by special rules. Until recently, the mere hiring of faculty members, for instance, practically amounted to a grant of tenure, meaning absolute job security. A more balanced interpretation of tenure is common today. This view has at times applied to officers and administrators in hospitals and some other organizations.

4 ▪ 25
THE PRESIDENT

The powers and duties of the president should be specified in the charter and bylaws of an organization. If they are not, the president could end up being a figurehead with no real powers to bind the corporation. Naturally, if the corporation ratifies or adopts the president's unauthorized acts, expressly or implicitly, it cannot deny his or her authority to act at some later date. Moreover, if it also allows the president to manage its affairs, it cannot suddenly do an about-face and deny his or her authority to someone who relied on it.

If the president has general management powers, he or she can do all that is reasonably necessary to accomplish his or her duties (which is usually less than allowed to the president of a business corporation). But the president is not authorized to borrow money or issue notes for the corporation.

Many state statutes give the president (along with the secretary) the duty of filing reports, such as financial reports, and signing other documents, such as a certificate of dissolution or of consolidation with another organization.

4 ▪ 26
THE VICE-PRESIDENT

The vice-president takes over the president's role, as next in rank, in the event of the president's absence, incapacity, or death. The vice-president has the power to bind the organization by his or her acts if the president has such powers. To avoid problems, the bylaws should address the issue directly.

4 ▪ 27
THE SECRETARY

The secretary's only inherent power is the care and keeping of the corporate records, the taking of minutes, and the custody of the corporate seal. Unless provided with authority, he or she ordinarily has no discretionary executive power to bind the corporation.

4 ▪ 28
THE TREASURER

The treasurer normally is the custodian and disbursing and accounting agent for the organization's funds, but may disburse them only as directed by the directors or other named authority. The treasurer normally has no other inherent powers. But if the corporation holds him or her out as having apparent authority, it may find itself bound by the treasurer's acts so far as third persons are concerned.

4 ▪ 29
THE EXECUTIVE MANAGERS OR SECRETARIES

Many nonprofit organizations employ an executive secretary, whose powers and duties should be specified in the charter and bylaws. The executive secretary is often a professional, full-time, paid employee who runs the daily routine operations. Since the executive secretary is normally hired on a contract basis, the bylaws should clearly spell out his or her functions and rights.

In the absence of charter or bylaw provisions, the executive secretary has the routine business powers of hiring administrative employees, entering into routine contracts, and getting legal advice on corporate problems. Third persons can rely on his or her apparent authority to do reasonably necessary acts in routine matters.

If it happens that an officer is given the powers of a general manager, that officer's broad managerial powers are not limited by his or her lesser powers as an officer.

4 ▪ 30
THE STATUTORY AGENTS

Many nonprofit corporation statutes require the organization to designate a statutory agent to represent it. This is the person upon whom any legal process, demand, or notice can be served. Often, the statutory agent must reside in the county in which the organization's principal office is located. Failure to meet this requirement could lead to cancellation of the corporate charter.

4 ▪ 31
INDEMNIFICATION

The personal risks one assumes when carrying out a corporate decisionmaking function are huge. Many corporations seeking to recruit and retain the best decisionmakers they can are committed to affording them the blanket protection of corporate indemnification.

Some state statutes do not deal with indemnification; others do, but only inconsistently. In some states, for instance, indemnification provisions are not self-executing; directors and officers have no indemnification right unless it is expressed in their organization's charter or bylaws or by resolution. Other state statutes make it mandatory to indemnify in certain circumstances, while some require judicial approval before indemnification becomes mandatory.

The majority of state statutes dealing with indemnification recognizes the rights of directors and officers to be reimbursed for the expenses of litigation resulting from acts performed in their official status. Within the limits of these statutes, the director or officer may usually obtain indemnification for reasonable expenses, including attorneys' fees, in an action alleging breach of duty, unless he or she has been found guilty of misconduct or bad faith. In the latter case, the director or officer is entitled to no reimbursement. He or she need not actually win the case, but must clear himself or herself.

In a minority of states a director or officer is entitled to the expenses of a lawsuit without statutory authority if his or her official acts are intended to preserve the corporation's property.

4 ▪ 32
INSURING THE OFFICERS AND DIRECTORS

To encourage talented and knowledgeable people to accept positions of responsibility in your organization, consider protecting them against the personal liability they may incur as an officer or director by insurance.

Good arguments are made for insurance coverage for directors and officers not only when the organization lacks the power or right to indemnify, but even when it has such power and does grant the right to indemnification to its directors and officers. These arguments center around the belief that an element of uncertainty is hidden in most indemnification arrangements.

1. Where states have enabling statutes empowering organizations to indemnify, but an organization has not provided for indemnification in its charter, bylaws, or agreement, its directors and officers are not protected.

2. Where a statute makes it mandatory to indemnify, the directors and officers still must depend on decisions by the board or legal advisers that they have met the appropriate standard of conduct. If a decision is unfavorable, they could be denied indemnification. Although a defendant-director could apply to the court to enforce his or her rights, such litigation involves additional expenses, a burden of proof on the part of the director, and a possible lengthy delay before the court decides the issue and orders indemnification.

3. To the extent that indemnification is allowed by statute, the organization decides as a policy question the form, extent, and scope of indemnification if its directors and officers are involved in litigation. Some provide indemnification on a par with that cited in the statute, but others would rather handle the question on a case by case basis, and a defendant-director may find himself or herself at the mercy of uncaring or hostile directors.

4. Without insurance the most a defendant can receive through indemnification are litigation costs and attorneys' fees. The defendant is not reimbursed for any amount paid in settlement where he or she has been adjudged liable for negligence, breach of duty, misstatement, omission, or other like wrongful acts. In this situation not only would the insurance benefit organization personnel by covering such wrongful acts; it could also best serve the public image of the organization by encouraging directors to settle quietly rather than litigate. Thus, directors' and officers' (D&O) insurance can be very important in diminishing financial damage both to an organization and to its directors and officers.

5. Should litigation proceed after a defendant-director leaves office, he or she may no longer be entitled to indemnification . . . but insurance would clearly still protect that person.

Directors' and officers' insurance is not new, but interest in it has risen sharply since the mid-1960s. This greater interest is attributable to:

1. The increased number of suits against directors and officers.
2. The higher standard of conduct required of directors and officers.
3. The tendency of the courts to place a greater responsibility on directors and officers.
4. The rising tide of consumerism, with its increasing recourse to the courts.

These policies essentially cover directors' and officers' errors and omissions that constitute breaches of professional duties. They are distinguished from umbrella policies, in that the latter cover bodily injury and property damage claims arising from accidents that take place entirely within the scope of employment. An example of an error and omissions policy is shown in Exhibit 5. (Text continued on p. 108.)

(Text continued on p. 108.)

EXHIBIT 5

Directors and Officers Liability and Company Reimbursement Liability

PART I: DIRECTORS AND OFFICERS LIABILITY

In consideration of the payment of the premium and subject to all the terms of this Policy, the Insurer agrees with the Directors and Officers of the Company (named in Item I of the Declarations) as follows:

1. Insuring Clause
If during the policy period any claim or claims are made against the Insureds (as hereinafter defined) or any of them for a Wrongful Act (as hereinafter defined) while acting in their individual or collective capacities as Directors or Officers, the Insurer will pay on behalf of the Insureds or any of them, their Executors, Administrators, Assigns 95% of all Loss (as hereinafter defined), which the Insureds or any of them shall become legally obligated to pay, in excess of the retentions stated in Item IV(a) and (b) of the Declarations, not exceeding the limit of liability stated in Item III of the Declarations.

2. This policy, subject otherwise to the terms hereof, shall cover loss arising from any claims made against the estates, heirs, legal representatives, or assigns of deceased Insureds who were Directors or Officers of the Company at the time of the Wrongful Act upon which such claims are based, and the legal representatives or assigns of Directors or Officers in the event of their incompetency, insolvency, or bankruptcy.

3. This policy shall automatically cover Directors and Officers of any subsidiaries acquired or created after the inception of this policy subject to written notice being given to the Insurer as soon as practicable and payment of any additional premium required.

4. Definitions

Definitions of terms used herein:

(a) The term ''Insureds'' shall mean all persons who were, now are, or shall be duly elected Directors or Officers of the Company named in Item I of the policy Declarations, except as noted in Item VI of the Declarations. Coverage will automatically apply to all persons who become Directors or Officers after the inception date of this policy, subject to (i) written advice of all such changes to the Insurer within 30 days after each anniversary date, or the termination date, and (ii) payment of any additional premium required.

(b) The term ''Wrongful Act'' shall mean any actual or alleged error or misstatement or misleading statement or act or omission or neglect or breach of duty by the Insureds while acting in their individual or collective capacities, or any matter not excluded by the terms and conditions of this policy claimed against them solely by reason of their being Directors or Officers of the Company.

(c) The term ''Loss'' shall mean any amount which the Insureds are legally obligated to pay for a claim or claims made against them for Wrongful Acts, and shall include but not be limited to damages, judgments, settlements, and costs, cost of investigation (excluding salaries of officers or employees of the Company), and defense of legal actions, claims, or proceedings and appeals therefrom, and cost of attachment or similar bonds; providing always, however, such subject of loss shall not include fines or penalties imposed by law, or matters that may be deemed uninsurable under the law pursuant to which this policy shall be construed.

(d) The term ''Policy Year'' shall mean the period of one year following the effective date and hour of this policy or any anniversary thereof, or if the time between the effective date or any anniversary and the termination of the policy is less than one year, such lesser period.

5. Exclusions

The Insurer shall not be liable to make any payment for loss in connection with any claim made against the Insureds:

(a) for libel or slander;

(b) based upon or attributable to their gaining in fact any personal profit or advantage to which they were not legally entitled;

(c) for the return by the Insureds of any remuneration paid to the Insureds without the previous approval of the stockholders of the Company, which payment without such previous approval shall be held by the courts to have been illegal;

(d) for an accounting of profits made from the purchase or sale by the Insureds of securities of the Company within the meaning of Section 16(b) of the Securities Exchange Act of 1934 and amendments thereto or similar provisions of any state statutory law or common law;

(e) brought about or contributed to by the dishonesty of the Insureds; however, notwithstanding the foregoing, the Insureds shall be protected under the terms of this policy as to any claims upon which suit may be brought against them, by reason of any alleged dishonesty on the part of the Insureds, unless a judgment or other final adjudication thereof adverse to the Insureds shall establish that acts of active and deliberate dishonesty committed by the Insureds with actual dishonest purpose and intent were material to the cause of action so adjudicated;

(f) which, at the time of happening of such loss, is insured by any other existing valid policy or policies under which payment of the loss is actually made, except with respect to any excess beyond the amount or amounts of payments under such other policy or policies;

(g) for which the Insureds are entitled to indemnity and/or payment by reason of having given notice of any circumstance that might give rise to a claim under any policy or policies the term of which has expired prior to the issuance of this policy;

(h) for which the Insureds shall be indemnified by the Company for damages, judgments, settlements, costs, charges, or expenses incurred in connection with the defense of any action, suit, or proceeding to which the Insured's may be a party or with which they may be threatened or in connection with any appeal therefrom, pursuant to the law, common or statutory, or the Charter or Bylaws of the Company duly effective under such law, which determines and defines such rights of indemnity;

(i) based on or attributable to bodily injury, sickness, disease, or death of any person, or to damages or destruction of any tangible property, including loss of use thereof.

It is agreed that any fact pertaining to any Insured shall not be imputed to any other Insured for the purpose of determining the application of the above exclusions.

6. It is warranted that the particulars and statements contained in the written proposal, a copy of which is attached hereto, and the Declarations are the basis of this policy and are to be considered as incorporated in and constituting part of this policy.

7. Limits and Retention

(a) The Insurer shall be liable to pay 95% of loss excess of the amount of the retentions stated in Item IV(a) and (b) of the Declarations, up to the limit of liability as stated in Item III of the Declarations, it being warranted that the remaining 5% of each and every loss shall be carried by the Insureds at their own risk and uninsured.

(b) Subject to the foregoing, the Insurer's liability for any claim or claims and/or costs, charges, and expenses shall be the amount as stated in Item III of the Declarations, which, regardless of the time of payment by the Insurer, shall be the maximum liability of the Insurer in (i) each policy year during the policy period or (ii) in the last policy year in which coverage is provided hereunder plus the period of ninety (90) days set out in Clause 13 if the right under such clause is exercised.

(c) This policy shall only pay the excess of amount stated in Item IV(a) of the Declarations for each of the Insureds against whom claim is made in respect of each and every loss hereunder but in no event exceeding the excess of the amount stated in Item IV(b) of the Declarations in the aggregate for all Insureds against whom claim is made with respect to each and every loss hereunder. The foregoing amounts include costs, charges, and expenses as described in Clause 8 and such amounts are to be borne by the Insureds as a retention and are not to be insured. Losses arising out of the same act or interrelated acts of one or more of the Insureds shall be considered a single loss and only one retention shall be deducted from each loss.

(d) It is understood and agreed that in the event a single loss as defined herein is covered in part under the Directors and Officers Liability Form, and in part under the Company Reimbursement Form, the retention stated in Item IV of the Declarations as applicable to each policy form shall apply to that part of the loss covered by each policy form and the sum of the retentions so applied shall constitute the retention for each single loss provided. However, the total retention as finally determined shall in no event exceed the amount of the Company Reimbursement stated in Item IV(c) of the Declarations.

It is further understood and agreed that, for the purposes of the application of the retention, loss applicable to the Company Reimbursement Form includes that for which indemnification by the Company is legally permissible, whether or not actual indemnification is granted.

(e) The foregoing provisions shall apply to this policy form and the Company Reimbursement Policy Form as though they constitute a single policy and the Insurer's maximum liability under both policy forms together shall not exceed the limit of liability as stated in Item III of the Declarations.

8. Costs, Charges, Expenses and Defense
No costs, settlements, charges, and expenses shall be incurred without the Insurer's consent, which consent shall not be unreasonably withheld. However, in the event of such consent being given, the Insurer will pay, subject to the provision of Clause 7, 95% of all such costs, settlements, charges, and expenses.

9. Loss Provisions
If during the policy period or extended discovery period:

(a) The Company or the Insureds shall receive written or oral notice from any party that it is the intention of such party to hold the Insureds responsible for the results of any specified Wrongful Act done or alleged to have been done by the Insureds while acting in the capacity aforementioned; or

(b) The Company or the Insureds shall become aware of any occurrence that may subsequently give rise to a claim being made against the Insureds with respect to any such alleged Wrongful Act; and shall in either case during such period give written notice as soon as practicable to the Insurer of the receipt of such written or oral notice under Clause 9(a) or of such occurrence under Clause 9(b), any claim that may subsequently be made against the Insureds arising out of such alleged Wrongful Act shall, for the purposes of this policy, be treated as a claim made during the policy year in which such notice was given or, if given during the extended discovery period, as a claim made during such extended discovery period.

The Company or the Insureds shall, as a condition precedent to the Insureds' right to be indemnified under this policy, give to the Insurer notice in writing as soon as practicable of any claim made and shall give the Insurer such information and cooperation as it may reasonably require and as shall be in the Insureds' power.

For the purpose of the above clauses notice to that individual named in Item VII of the Declarations shall constitute notice to the Company or the Insureds.

10. In the event of any claim occurring hereunder, the person or firm(s) as named in Item VIII of the Declarations shall be given notice on behalf of the Insurer.

11. Notice shall be deemed to be received, if sent by prepaid mail properly addressed.

12. Cancellation

This policy may be cancelled by the Company or the Insureds at any time by written notice or by surrender of this policy. This policy may also be cancelled by or on behalf of the Insurer by delivering to the Company or by mailing to the Company, by registered, certified, or other first-class mail, at the Company's address shown in this policy, written notice stating when, not less than thirty (30) days thereafter, the cancellation shall be effective. The mailing of such notice as aforesaid shall be sufficient proof of notice and this policy shall terminate at the date and hour specified in such notice.

If this policy shall be cancelled by the Company or the Insureds, the Insurer shall retain the customary short-rate proportion of the premium hereon.

Payment or tender of any unearned premium by the Insurer shall not be a condition precedent to the effectiveness of cancellation but such payment shall be made as soon as practicable.

If the period of limitation relating to the giving of notice is prohibited or made void by any law controlling the construction thereof, such period shall be deemed to be amended so as to be equal to the minimum period of limitation permitted by such law.

13. Discovery Clause

If the Insurer shall cancel or refuse to renew this policy, the Insureds shall have the right, upon payment of an additional premium calculated at 10% of the three-year premium hereunder, to an extension of the cover granted by this policy with respect to any claim or claims that may be made against the Insureds during the period of ninety (90) days after the effective date of such cancellation or, in the event of such refusal to renew, the date upon which the policy period ends, but only with respect to any Wrongful Act committed before such date. Such right hereunder must, however, be exercised by the Insureds by notice in writing to the Insurer not later than ten (10) days after the date referred to in the preceding sentence. If such notice is not given, the Insureds shall not at a later date be able to exercise such right.

14. In the event of any payment under this policy, the Insurer shall be subrogated to the extent of such payment to all the Insureds' rights of recovery therefor, and the Insureds shall execute all papers required and shall do everything that may be necessary to secure such rights, including the execution of such documents necessary to enable the Insurers effectively to bring suit in the name of the Insureds.

15. By acceptance of this policy the Company named in Item I of the Declarations agrees to act on behalf of all Insureds with respect to the giving and receiving of notice of claim or cancellation, the payment of premiums, and the receiving of any return premiums that may become due under this policy.

PART II: COMPANY REIMBURSEMENT LIABILITY

In consideration of the payment of the premium and subject to all the terms of this policy, the Insurer agrees with the Company (named in Item I of the Declarations) as follows:

1. Insuring Clause

If during the policy period any claim or claims are made against the Directors or Officers (as hereinafter defined) or any of them for a Wrongful Act (as hereinafter defined) while acting in their individual or collective capacities as Directors or Officers, the Insurer will pay on behalf of the Company 95% of all Loss (as hereinafter defined) that the

Company may be required or permitted to pay as indemnities due the Directors or Officers for a claim or claims made against them for Wrongful Acts, in excess of the retention stated in Item IV(c) of the Declarations, not exceeding the limit of liability stated in Item III of the Declarations.

2. This policy, subject otherwise to the terms hereof, shall cover loss arising from any claims made against the estates, heirs, legal representatives, or assigns of deceased Directors or Officers who were Directors or Officers at the time of the Wrongful Act upon which such claims are based, and the legal representatives or assigns of Directors or Officers in the event of their incompetency, insolvency, or bankruptcy.

3. This policy shall automatically cover Directors and Officers of any subsidiaries acquired or created after the inception of this policy subject to written notice being given to the Insurer as soon as practicable and payment of any additional premium required.

4. Definitions
Definitions of terms used herein:

(a) The term "Directors or Officers" shall mean all persons who were, now are, or shall be duly elected Directors or Officers of the Company named in Item I of the policy Declarations, except as noted in Item VI of the Declarations. Coverage will automatically apply to all persons who become directors or officers after the inception date of this policy, subject to (i) written advice of all such changes to the Insurer within thirty (30) days after each anniversary date, or the termination date, and (ii) payment of any additional premium required.

(b) The term "Wrongful Act" shall mean any actual or alleged error or misstatement or misleading statement or act or omission or neglect or breach of duty by the Directors or Officers while acting in their individual or collective capacities, or any matter, not excluded by the terms and conditions of this policy, claimed against them solely by reason of their being Directors or Officers of the Company.

(c) The term "Loss" shall mean any amount the Company may be required or permitted to pay as indemnities due the Directors or Officers for a claim or claims made against them for Wrongful Acts, and shall include but not be limited to damages, judgments, settlements, and costs, cost of investigation (excluding salaries of officers or employees of the Company), and defense of legal actions, claims, or proceedings and appeals therefrom, and cost of attachment or similar bonds; for which payment by the Company may be required or permitted according to applicable law, or under provisions of the Company's Charter or Bylaws; providing always, however, such subject of loss shall not include fines or penalties imposed by law, or matters that may be deemed uninsurable under the law pursuant to which this policy shall be construed.

(d) The term "Policy Year" shall mean the period of one year following the effective date and hour of this policy or any anniversary thereof, or if the time between the effective date or any anniversary and the termination of the policy is less than one year, such lesser period.

5. Exclusions

The Insurer shall not be liable to make any payment for loss in connection with any claim made against the Directors or Officers:

(a) that, at the time of happening of such loss, is insured by any other existing valid policy or policies under which payment of the loss is actually made, except with respect to any excess beyond the amount or amounts of payments under such other policy or policies;

(b) for which the Directors or Officers are entitled to indemnity and/or payment by reason of having given notice of any circumstance that might give rise to a claim under any policy or policies the term of which has expired prior to the issuance of this policy;

(c) based on or attributable to bodily injury, sickness, diseases, or death of any person, or to damage to or destruction of any tangible property, including loss of use thereof;

(d) based on or attributable to personal injury or bodily injury, sickness, disease, or death of any person, or damage to, destruction of, or loss of use of any property, directly or indirectly caused by seepage, pollution, or contamination, or the cost of removing, nullifying, or cleaning up seeping, polluting, or contaminating substances.

6. It is warranted that the particulars and statements contained in the written proposal, a copy of which is attached hereto, and the Declarations are the basis of this policy and are to be considered as incorporated in and constituting part of this policy.

7. Limits and Retention

(a) The Insurer shall be liable to pay 95% of loss excess of the amount of the retention as stated in Item IV(c) of the Declarations, up to the limit of liability as stated in Item III of the Declarations, it being warranted that the remaining 5% of each and every loss shall be carried by the Company at its own risk and uninsured.

(b) Subject to the foregoing, the Insurer's liability for any claim or claims and/or costs, charges, and expenses shall be the amount as stated in Item III of the Declarations, which, regardless of the time of payment by the Insurer, shall be the maximum liability of the Insurer in (i) each policy year during the policy period or (ii) in the last policy year in which coverage is provided hereunder plus the period of ninety (90) days set out in Clause 13 if the right under such clause is exercised.

(c) This policy shall only pay the excess of the amount stated in Item IV(c) of the Declarations in the aggregate with respect to each and every loss hereunder, including costs, charges, and expenses as described in Clause 8, and such amount is to be borne by the Company as a retention and is not to be insured. Losses arising out of the same act or interrelated acts of one or more of the Directors or Officers shall be considered a single loss and only one retention shall be deducted from each loss.

(d) It is understood and agreed that in the event a single loss as defined herein is covered in part under the Directors and Officers Liability Form, and in part under the Company Reimbursement Form, the retention stated in Item IV of the Declarations as applicable to each policy form shall apply to that part of the loss covered by each policy form and the sum of the retentions so applied shall constitute the retention for each single loss, provided, however, the total retention as finally determined shall in no event exceed the amount of the Company Reimbursement retention stated in Item IV(c) of the Declarations.

It is further understood and agreed that, for the purposes of the application of the retention, loss applicable to the Company Reimbursement Form includes that for which indemnification by the Company is legally permissible, whether or not actual indemnification is granted.

(e) The foregoing provisions shall apply to this policy form and the Directors and Officers Liability Policy Form as though they constitute a single policy, and the Insurer's maximum liability under both policy forms together shall not exceed the limit of liability as stated in Item III of the Declarations.

8. Costs, Charges, Expenses, and Defense

No costs, settlements, charges, and expenses shall be incurred without the Insurer's consent, which consent shall not be unreasonably withheld. However, in the event of such consent being given, the Insurer will pay, subject to the provisions of Clause 7, 95% of all such costs, settlements, charges, and expenses.

9. Loss Provisions

If during the policy period or extended discovery period:

(a) The Company or the Directors or Officers shall receive written or oral notice from any party that it is the intention of such party to hold the Directors or Officers or any of them responsible for the results of any specified Wrongful Act done or alleged to have been done by the Directors or Officers or any of them while acting in the capacity aforementioned; or

(b) The Company or the Directors or Officers shall become aware of any occurrence that may subsequently give rise to a claim being made against the Directors or Officers or any of them with respect to any such alleged Wrongful Act; and shall in either case during such period give written notice as soon as practicable to the Insurer of the receipt of such written or oral notice under Clause 9(a) or of such occurrence under Clause 9(b), any claim that may subsequently be made against the Directors or Officers or any of them arising out of such alleged Wrongful Act shall, for the purposes of this policy, be treated as a claim made during the policy year in which such notice was given or, if given during the extended discovery period, as a claim made during such extended discovery period.

The Company or Directors or Officers shall, as a condition precedent to the Company's right to be indemnified under this policy, give to the Insurer notice in writing as soon as practicable of any claim made and shall give the Insurers such information and cooperation as they may reasonably require and as shall be in their power.

For the purpose of the above clauses notice to that individual named in Item VII of the Declarations shall constitute notice to the Company or the Directors or Officers.

10. In the event of any claim occurring hereunder the person or firm(s) named in Item VIII of the Declarations shall be given notice on behalf of the Insurer.

11. Notice shall be deemed to be received, if sent by prepaid mail properly addressed.

12. Cancellation

This policy may be cancelled by the Company at any time by written notice or by surrender of this policy. This policy may also be cancelled by or on behalf of the Insurer by delivering to the Company or by mailing to the Company by registered, certified, or other first-class mail, at the Company's address shown in this policy, written notice stating when, not less than thirty (30) days thereafter, the cancellation shall be effective. The mailing of such notice as aforesaid shall be sufficient proof of notice and this policy shall terminate at the date and hour specified in such notice.

If this policy shall be cancelled by the Company the Insurer shall retain the customary short-rate proportion of the premium hereon.

If this policy shall be cancelled by or on behalf of the Insurer, the Insurer shall retain the pro rata proportion of the premium hereon.

Payment or tender of any unearned premium by the Insurer shall not be a condition precedent to the effectiveness of cancellation, but such payment shall be made as soon as practicable.

If the period of limitation relating to the giving of notice is prohibited or made void by any law controlling the construction thereof, such period shall be deemed to be amended so as to be equal to the minimum period of limitation permitted by such law.

13. Discovery Clause

If the Insurer shall cancel or refuse to renew this policy, the Company shall have the right, upon payment of an additional premium calculated at 10% of the three-year premium hereunder, to an extension of the cover granted by this policy with respect to any claim or claims that may be made against Directors or Officers during the period of ninety (90) days after the effective date of such cancellation or, in the event of such refusal to renew, the date upon which the policy period ends, but only with respect to any Wrongful Act committed before such date. Such right hereunder must, however, be exercised by the Company by notice in writing not later than ten (10) days after the date referred to in the preceding sentence. If such notice is not given, the Company shall not at a later date be able to exercise such right.

14. In the event of any payment under this policy, the Insurer shall be subrogated to the extent of such payment to all the Company's rights of recovery therefor, and the Company shall execute all papers required and shall do everything that may be necessary to secure such rights, including the execution of such documents as necessary to enable the Insurer effectively to bring suit in the name of the Company.

15. By acceptance of this policy, the Company named in Item I of the Declarations agrees to act on behalf of all Directors and Officers with respect to the giving and receiving of notice of claim or cancellation, the payment of premiums, and the receiving of any return premiums that may become due under this policy.

IN WITNESS WHEREOF, The Insurer has caused this policy to be signed by its President and Secretary, and countersigned on the Declaration Page by a duly authorized agent of the Insurer.

_____ , Secretary   _____ , President

Directors' and officers' liability insurance is issued with a deductible amount, the policy covering amounts that exceed this dollar figure. Such a self-insured retention is a negotiable amount; the lower the risk retained by the organization, the higher the premium. With the deductible amount protecting the insurance company from small claims, the insurer is better able to keep the cost of the policy at a more acceptable level. Furthermore, the deductible serves as an incentive for corporate personnel to be more careful and alert in carrying out their duties; after all, they become coin-surers of the policy. But do not assume that insurance can be had at budget prices. On the contrary, D&O coverage is very expensive. Why?

1. The difficulty of estimating the fair price of such a policy in light of the limited experience with it.
2. The absence of good statistical and actuarial data.
3. The uncertain trends and directions of state legislatures and the courts regarding stricter responsibilities and duties for directors and officers.

The cost of a corporate D&O policy seems to vary with the assets of the company, the number of directors' and officers' positions, the amount of coverage, and the deviations from standard policy terms (or endorsements).

But a D&O liability policy for nonprofit organizations is a specialized form of D&O policy. It does not have the normal minimum asset requirement. And the rate structure for nonprofit corporations is a good deal more favorable than for business corporations. This is because of a traditionally lower level of exposure on the part of nonprofit corporation officers and directors and, therefore, less risk for the insurance company. A nonprofit organization D&O policy will have two components: the first covering directors' and officers' liability and the second covering company reimbursement liability.

A typical directors' and officers' liability insuring clause may read:

> If during the policy period any claims are made against the Insureds or any of them for a Wrongful Act, while acting in their individual or collective capacities as Directors or Officers, the Insurer will pay on behalf of the Insureds or any of them, their Executors, Administrators, Assigns 95% of all Loss that the Insureds or any of them shall become legally obligated to pay, in excess of the retentions stated in the Declarations, not exceeding the limit of liability stated in the Declarations.

The insuring clause for company reimbursement liability may read:

> If during the policy period any claim or claims are made against the Directors or Officers or any of them for a Wrongful Act, while acting in their individual or collective capacities as Directors or Officers, the Insurer will pay on behalf of the Company 95% of all Loss that the Company may be required or permitted to pay as indemnities due the Directors or Officers for a claim or claims made against them for Wrongful Acts, in excess of the retention stated in the Declarations, not exceeding the limit of liability stated in the Declarations.

To understand the legal relationship between these two components, let us look first at the proposal form (application) completed by a potential insured and incorporated into the policy upon its issuance. Inevitably, the representations it contains will be certified by a corporate officer:

> No person proposed for insurance is cognizant of any act, omission, or error that he has reason to suppose might afford valid grounds for any future claims such as would fall within the scope of the proposed insurance except as follows. The undersigned authorized officer of the corporation declares that to the best of his knowledge and belief the statements set forth herein are true.

Such statements can be the source of a large problem for an organization and its directors and officers. If the officer-agent authorized to negotiate with the insurance company fails to disclose any facts and information that might otherwise provide grounds for a claim, the insurance policy can be declared void.

The authorized officer-agent who signs the application form acts as a "double agent." In terms of the directors' and officers' policy (the contract between the insurer and the individual directors and officers), he acts as an agent for the directors and officers. With regard to the reimbursement portion of the policy (a contract between the insurer and the corporation), he acts as an agent of the corporation. This means that the authorized agent's knowledge and representations are imputed to both the corporation and the individuals insured as his principals. The underwriter is as innocent a party as the directors and officers, but where one of two innocent persons must suffer by the fraud or negligence of a third, whichever of the two has accredited him ought to bear the loss. Consequently, the false representations of the agent can easily injure innocent directors and officers.

As long as an application form for D&O liability insurance does not include an additional statement binding only its signer (so that a forfeiture of his own rights due to his failure to reveal material information would not affect the rights of other insureds), directors and officers cannot be assured that they are protected under a valid insurance policy.

Another policy gap is its exclusion provisions. No coverage is provided, for example, in situations in which directors and officers are involved in illegal personal profit, trading on inside information, conflict of interests, self-dealing, fraud, dishonesty, libel, or slander.

4 ▪ 33
WHAT'S THE USE?

Surely insurance is not the whole answer. Does its utility warrant its high cost? Some doubts have been raised.

1. The lack of enough court decisions clarifying, approving, and interpreting some of the confusing provisions involved.
2. The probably mistaken belief by some organizations that the indemnification provision in their bylaws is broad enough to serve the same purpose as D&O insurance.
3. The difficulty in securing additional or specialized coverage for an organization believing its special needs warrant it.

4 ▪ 34
THE GOVERNMENT ANSWER

The insurance industry has long been under government control, more control perhaps than nonprofit organizations. Writing insurance is not a right, but a privilege granted by the state, which retains broad regulatory powers. A legislature can dictate a standard form that insurers are required to adopt or it can provide, and often does, that the policy include or exclude certain provisions. Directors' and officers' policies are not widely purchased, and legislatures have not yet exercised as much control over them as over other types of coverage. Insurance companies have been able to limit coverage and have been able to impose whatever conditions they want, subject to public policy considerations and competitive pressure.

But watch this trend: More and more enabling statutes are setting the risks a D&O policy ought to insure against. The Illinois Not-For-Profit Corporation Act, for example, has been amended to include the following text, where no comparable provisions had existed:

Each corporation shall have power:

(i) To indemnify any and all of its directors or officers or former directors or officers or any person who may have served at its request or by its election as a director or officer of another corporation against expenses actually and necessarily incurred by them in connection with the defense or settlement of any action, suit or proceeding in which they, or any of them, are made parties, or a party, by reason of being or having been directors or a director or officer of the corporation, or of such other corporation, except in relation to matters as to which any such director or officer or former director or officer or person shall be adjudged in such action, suit or proceeding to be liable for willful misconduct in the performance of duty and to such matters as shall be settled by agreement predicated on the existence of such liability.

(j) To purchase and maintain insurance on behalf of any and all of its directors or officers or former directors or officers or any person who has served at its request or by its election as a director or officer of another corporation against any liability, or settlement based on asserted liability, incurred by them by reason of being or having been directors or a director or officer of the corporation, or of such other corporation, whether or not the corporation would have the power to indemnify them against such liability or settlement under the provisions of this section.

The statute authorizes a nonprofit corporation to include in its articles of incorporation or bylaws a provision substantially in the language of the statute:

Sec. _____ Indemnification. The corporation shall indemnify any and all of its directors or officers or former directors or officers or any person who may have served at its request or by its election as a director or officer of another corporation, against expenses actually and necessarily incurred by them in connection with the defense of settlement of any action, suit or proceeding in which they, or any of them, are made parties, or a party, by reason of being or having been directors or a director or officer of the corporation or of such other corporation, except in relation to matters as to which any such director or officer or former director or officer or person shall be adjudged in such action, suit or proceeding to be liable for willful misconduct in performance of duty and to such matters as shall be settled by agreement predicated on existence of such liability.

The indemnification provided hereby shall not be deemed exclusive of any other rights to which anyone seeking indemnification may be entitled under any bylaw, agreement, vote of members or disinterested directors or otherwise, both as to action in his official capacity and as to action in another capacity while holding such office.

The statute, in allowing corporations to purchase and maintain insurance to insulate officers and directors from these risks, can be construed as a mandate to insurers about what ought to be included in and excluded from their Illinois D&O policies.

4 ▪ 35
TIME IS OF THE ESSENCE

Considerable time may elapse between the time a wrongful act is committed and when it is discovered to be the cause of current problems or losses. Does D&O insurance cover claims based on conduct that occurred prior to the effective date of the policy? Will your policy cover a claim made against the directors and officers after it has expired, based on a wrongful act committed during the policy period?

The standard loss provision makes it clear that D&O insurance focuses on the claim, rather than the wrongful act, and that the claim must be made during the policy period. Here is an example of such a provision.

> If during the policy period or during the discovery period, if any, claim is made against the Directors the Company shall as a condition precedent to its rights under this policy give to the Underwriters notice as soon as practicable in writing of any such claim.

It would appear that D&O insurance covers wrongful acts that occur prior to the inception date of the policy, so long as the claim is brought within the policy term and the insured was not cognizant of any wrongful act at the time the policy was issued. If a claim has not yet been sustained and the amount of loss is still unknown at the time the policy expires, the loss will be covered, so long as notice was given during the policy period.

A special "claim made" clause is usually included in the policy. If notice of the likelihood of a suit is given to the underwriters during the policy period, then any claim under this clause brought after the policy expires will be treated as a claim within the policy period.

In a situation in which the wrongful act occurs before or during the policy period, but is discovered only after the policy has expired or been canceled, a standard discovery clause generally provides an extension of the policy coverage with regard to a claim made against the directors for a period of 90 days after the effective date or expiration or cancellation. But this only applies to a wrongful act committed before such date. Since 90 days is a short time, the corporation and its directors and officers should try to obtain insurance coverage from another underwriter whenever the original policy is canceled or the insurer refuses to renew it.

4 ▪ 36
WHICH LAW TO FOLLOW

What law would govern a dispute involving the validity of an indemnification provision in a bylaw or the interpretation of an insurance policy clause? This question is not unique to indemnification and insurance, but it may become significant when a foreign corporation is involved in litigation and it is difficult to determine the principal place of its activities and the true location of its headquarters. The question is also important in light of the divergent public policies among the states.

An awareness of the conflict of laws problem will help a corporation and its directors and officers to avoid false expectations. Otherwise, a corporation may act in compliance with the corporate law and public policy of a state, anticipating that its laws will govern any controversy that arises, only to find that a court may be persuaded to apply a different law as the proper one to rule the matter in dispute.

The traditional view of the law calls for the corporation to be governed by the local law of the state of incorporation. This practice satisfies the need for predictability, certainty, and practicability.

As numerous cases indicate, the traditional view is beginning to give way to the view that the proper law to govern internal affairs is that of the place where the administrative headquarters is located and major activities are performed. Where the local law embodies a strong public policy, it may claim jurisdiction over a foreign corporation that has little or no contact with the state of its incorporation.

Without uniformity in corporate and insurance statutes and with the various public-policy approaches to the scope of D&O policy coverage, the insured organization may be wise to insist on stipulating which local law shall govern the policy. The best choice of law is that of a state with a substantial relationship to the parties and the insurance contract. The positive results of such a stipulation may be:

1. To protect the expectations of the insureds.
2. To reduce costly and unnecessary litigation.
3. To give the insureds some degree of certainty and predictability about the outcome of any potential litigation that might challenge the construction and validity of D&O liability policies.

If yours is a multistate organization, have your attorney determine which state's laws would be most beneficial to you and do your legal decisionmaking with that conclusion in mind.

4 ▪ 37
GETTING TOGETHER

Heightened awareness and sophistication may signal the need for the expansion of corporate resources or the acceleration of the corporation's timetable. Either way, corporation reorganization may prove a successful means.

The affiliation of two or more nonprofit corporations into one is a consolidation or merger. One corporation may absorb another, several may combine into one (a merger), or both may go out of existence with a new one appearing under either a new name or one of the old names (a consolidation). "Affiliation" refers to the consolidation of one organization as a branch of another organization.

Any two or more nonprofit corporations that were incorporated for related purposes may agree to affiliate or consolidate. This even applies to groups having different rules (such as different religious groups). However, if the agreement is contrary to any law that governs any of the constituent organizations, it takes only one dissenting member to set it aside.

Combinations may be put together on the charter level while the local-level organizations remain intact, with their bylaw rules remaining separate and distinct. For example, the affiliation of a local union with an international group may have no effect on the bylaws of the local, even though they differ from those of the parent, or even limit the parent's power over the local.

Affiliation or consolidation is a contractual agreement and, as such, may be anything the groups desire, subject only to the laws of contracts and general corporation laws.

4 ▪ 38
HOW CONSOLIDATIONS WORK

The procedure is compiled in separate nonprofit corporation acts in some states and in general business corporation statutes in others. Most state statutes call for the arrangement of the consolidation agreement by the directors of both corporations. The members of each then vote their approval, with a two-thirds vote often needed. The officers of the dominant (or either) corporation file a certificate of consolidation (in almost all the states) in the form required by statute to effectuate the agreement. Without state approval, consolidation is unlawful.

When nonprofit corporations consolidate, the old entity ceases to exist, except for the preservation of bequests or other specific reasons. The new corporation must assume all the obligations and liabilities of the constituent corporations. This means that creditors' rights with regard to either corporation cannot be ignored.

Combinations of nonprofit organizations and even conglomeration are on the rise, particularly in agricultural cooperative areas exempted from antitrust violation under the Capper–Volstead Act. Combinations effected by merger, affiliation, and consolidation have resulted in marketing associations and federations acounting for up to 70 percent and as much as 100 percent of certain commodities sold in a given year.

With concern for possible antitrust violations, we may see regulatory agencies devoting more attention to reviewing nonprofit corporation mergers, consolidations, and affiliations. Given the paucity of regulatory attention to nonprofit organizations, their reorganizations have gone largely unchecked. Since the scrutiny of nonprofit reorganizations can only increase, careful statutory compliance would be wise for any corporation contemplating expansion through corporate reorganization.

4 ▪ 39
WHERE DOES IT END?

Just as a corporation's purposes may best be achieved through consolidation, other times those purposes may be achieved or become
moot and dissolution becomes the logical step.

The duration of a nonprofit corporation is perpetual, unless the
articles of incorporation provide otherwise. In fact, even where
there is a limit provided, the corporation's existence usually can be
extended or even revived. On the other hand, the corporation's existence, no matter what its duration, can be terminated at any time
by forfeiture of its charter through an action by the attorney general or by dissolution, judicial or nonjudicial.

The dissolution process is made up of two principal phases. The
first is compliance with the procedural requirements for going out
of existence. Then, once dissolution has been implemented, the actual distribution of its assets is made. State statutes cover the dissolution process thoroughly.

The following are ways in which nonprofit corporations can be
dissolved:

▪ Withdrawal or death of most of the members without replacement by new ones.
▪ Repeal of the enabling statute under which the organization was
incorporated.
▪ Expiration of the corporation's stated period of existence without
extension or revival.
▪ Voluntary surrender of the charter, without court supervision,
by a predetermined vote of the members. State approval is required for such action by a corporation, and statutes in almost
every state specify how the dissolution is to take place and what
percentage of members must consent. Typical percentages range
from a majority to two-thirds vote of the members.

Members generally agree on a voluntary dissolution by adopting
a resolution at a duly called meeting. Certificates of dissolution
signed by the appropriate number of members must be prepared,
executed, acknowledged, and filed as the state statute directs. The

forms and filing procedures (including notice to creditors and clearance from state tax authorities) differ from state to state, and it is very important to follow the local statutory rules strictly.

In some states, dissolution may also be presented by 10 percent of the total number of members or by any director in the following cases:

- The votes needed for action by the board cannot be obtained because the directors are divided as to the management of the corporation's affairs.
- The members are too divided to get the votes required for election of the directors.
- Along with internal dissension, two or more factions of members are so divided that it would be beneficial to the members to dissolve.
- The controlling directors have looted or wasted the corporate assets, kept the corporation going for their personal benefit, or have otherwise acted in an illegal, oppressive, or fraudulent manner.
- The corporation can no longer carry out its purposes.

Voluntary surrender of a charter with court supervision may proceed on the petition of a member, a creditor, the attorney general, an interested person, or the members generally. In some states, voluntary dissolution must be carried on under court supervision, as a protection for interested parties who, upon the showing of good cause, can resist the dissolution or have it nullified.

Court-supervised dissolutions also serve to deal with a deadlock. If the directors are evenly divided into factions or the members cannot elect a board because they are evenly divided, a petition for voluntary dissolution can be filed with the state court.

A petition for this type of dissolution may be filed by the members or directors, and notice of the proceeding to dissolve must go to the state's attorney general. The court's decision on the petition rests on its determination as to whether dissolution will be beneficial to the interests of the members.

Involuntary dissolution may be ordered by reason of an organization's improper conduct. The attorney general may have the corporation terminated if it was formed through fraudulent misrepresentation or concealment of a material fact, or if it exceeded its lawful authority, violated a provision of law whereby it forfeited its charter, transacted business in a persistently fraudulent manner, or abused its powers contrary to the state's public policy.

If the corporation is insolvent, judicial dissolution may occur when it is necessary to protect the creditors. Judicial dissolution is also possible when the corporation can in no way accomplish its objectives. Moreover, no statutory authority is needed for courts of equity to order such dissolutions, although statutory affirmation of this general power is now found in many jurisdictions.

If an ordered dissolution results from a reorganization in a bankruptcy proceeding, a new corporation can be formed in its place. A certificate of dissolution or a new certificate of incorporation filed with an explanation will be enough to dissolve the old corporation.

In a few states, annulment of the charter for abuse or neglect of its powers, duties, or privileges (such as misuse of powers, fraud in incorporating, activities injurious to the public, or failure to pay taxes) is automatic without any further proceedings. However in most states, legal action by the state is required.

After a judgment in a formal court proceeding, only the state may act to forfeit a charter. State action to annul a charter or merely to oust a corporation from its improper activities is statutorily condoned. The attorney general is usually called on to bring such proceedings in equity courts for an order to annul the corporation.

Failure to pay taxes may result in suspension of a charter in some states. When payment is made (if it is done within the statutory time limits), a certificate to such effect may be filed (but with the imposition of a penalty), and the charter is revived. Before revival the suspended condition of a corporation cannot serve as a basis for denying the valid rights that come due during or after the suspension. If there is willful failure to pay taxes, the officers and agents of the corporation may be subjected to personal penalties.

A corporation can only be dissolved in the state of its incorporation. But a state does have the right to wind up a foreign (as well as a domestic) corporation's activities in that state.

4 ▪ 40
DISSOLUTION

The filing of a certificate of dissolution is, in reality, only the beginning of a dissolution. The organization's affairs must be wound up and its assets must be distributed or liquidated (or, if held in trust, arrangements must be made for their continued use). Therefore, for the winding up process to be practicable, the corporation must continue to exist under statutory provisions. In a voluntary dissolution, the trustees are charged with managing its affairs; but in an involuntary dissolution, the job goes to a court-designated receiver.

It is permissible for the organization to give the impression of its continued existence to outsiders during the winding up process. Still, it should be compiling a list of liabilities and creditors and doing everything necessary to fulfill its obligations. During this time it may continue to receive donations. These donations are put in a trust fund for creditors first, then for members.

In a number of states, directors and officers can stay in office during the winding up process, but they can only carry out activities having to do with the winding up. The directors in some cases have even been held to have the power to hold or convey real property, to contract in the name of the organization, or to sue and be sued during the windup.

How long the process takes depends on the kind of assets the organization holds and the complexity of the programs it supports. When there are few claimants or assets, the process is short. The mere filing of the certificate of dissolution can bring the corporation to an end. On the other hand, the process of winding up can be very lengthy, as in the case of a foundation or other charitable organization that is committed to a program requiring supervision through to completion.

An imaginative new technique to solve problems of winding up was developed for the Hanna Foundation of Cleveland. A three-man liquidating board of trustees was employed to supervise the completion of programs and grants to which all the remaining assets were committed. A bank-depository trustee was given charge of the detailed payment of disbursements and the keeping of financial records. Proper public notice and supervision was assured by the filing of the liquidation plan with the secretary of state after the filing of the certificate of dissolution. In less ingenious structures, the length of time usually considered reasonable for winding up is three years, and will be set by the statutes.

4 ▪ 41
DISTRIBUTING THE ASSETS

Assets of noncharitable nonprofit organizations may be distributed as the articles or bylaws provide. If there are no such provisions, the distribution takes place acording to a plan adopted by a vote of the members; if the members fail to act, then acording to a plan adopted by the trustees. Before assets can be distributed, all debts and liabilities must be discharged, followed by the return of any conditionally held assets, and, finally, any assets subject to a limitation, such as when a charity is dissolved.

In charitable organizations assets are held in trust for a charitable purpose. If the purpose cannot be achieved, the freedom with which the assets can be distributed is limited by the doctrine of cy pres, and is only applicable by the courts, being instituted by the attorney general. Before the court will employ this doctrine three tests must be met:

1. A valid charitable trust has to have been created so that the court can determine the valid charitable purpose of the gift. In practice the courts have implied such an existence when none was originally indicated.
2. It has become impractical or even impossible for the charitable trust to carry out its purpose. The standard of measure is the broad, underlying charitable purpose rather than the specific plan formulated by the donor. The determination of the donor's intent and the subsequent treatment of the property

are basic questions of trust law and, more specifically, of charitable trust law. They are only incidentally a matter of association or corporation law.

3. The donor must have had a general charitable intent, not a specific object or institution in mind.

The courts have great discretion in this area and make every possible effort to apply the assets of a dissolved charitable organization to a similar organization.

The cy pres doctrine is not always followed in decisions regarding corporations. A few state statutes provide that when any corporation dissolves, its excess assets are distributed among the members, no matter what the source of the assets.

It is the distinction between merely nonprofit and charitable organizations that forms the basis for modern statutory rule applicable to the distribution of assets.

In a charitable entity, the members are not considered to have a claim to the property. Usually the property goes to another, similar charity; but in some states, property bought by the organization may escheat to the state. Donated property may sometimes return to the donor.

In merely nonprofit entities, where assets may also come from various sources (for example, by gifts or by dues payments), a difficulty arises when the specific purposes of the gifts or their donors cannot be identified. If such assets are mixed with the assets of the members, the gift may well get distributed among them. If there are no members or creditors, the gift goes to the state.

In the case of an organization, such as a private club where no trust property (gifts for a public-benefit purpose) is involved, the rule is simple: distribution of the excess assets is made among the members.

Once the disposition of trust-purpose property is settled, the "free" assets of the organization will generally belong to the members. But if they have been given to the members before the creditors were paid, the creditors may not only recover them, but may also sue the directors personally.

4 ▪ 42
CONCLUSION

The historic resistance to the corporate form among nonprofit organizations is on the wane, and rightfully so. The uncertainties of
corporate existence are shrinking through statutory enlightenment
and the maturation of insurance and indemnification principles.
At the same time, the form offers the systematized and orderly
structure that has crystallized and improved business decisionmaking. Why not adopt the same sophistication in your endeavor?

5
Private Foundations: Their Funding and Granting

5 ▪ 1
DEFINITION

A private foundation is a tax-exempt religious, scientific, or charitable organization that isn't:

1. A church; a tax-exempt educational organization; a tax-exempt hospital or medical research organization; an organization holding property for state and local colleges and universities; the United States, a state, a U.S. possession or one of its subdivisions; an organization organized and operated exclusively for charitable, religious, educational, scientific, or literary purposes or for the prevention of cruelty to children or animals, if it normally receives a substantial part of its support from the government or general public; or a membership organization more than one-third of whose support comes from the public ... all these are characterized as "50 percent charities" because contributions to them are usually deductible up to 50 percent of the donor's "contribution base."

2. An organization that meets the Internal Revenue Code's "public support" tests.

3. An organization operated exclusively for the benefit of a 50 percent charity or a publicly supported organization and an organization not controlled by a disqualified person other than a foundation manager—that is, a substantial contributor.

4. An organization exclusively testing for public safety.

5 ▪ 2
TWO VARIETIES

There are two types of private foundations—the conduit type and the operating type.

The conduit foundation is a private "nonoperating" organization that must distribute all contributions it receives in any year, whether of cash or of property. This means that all income required to be used for charitable purposes received within a given year must indeed be used and distributed within that year. For most other purposes, however, the conduit runs much like the operating foundation.

The private operating foundation may hold over contributions to be distributed in following years. Also it must:

- Be nonpublicly supported.
- Devote most of its earnings and assets directly to the conduct of its exempt purposes, as opposed to making grants to other organizations.
- Spend at least 85 percent of its adjusted net income directly for the active conduct of its exempt activities—the so-called "income" test.

The awarding of grants, scholarships, or similar payments to individual beneficiaries to support active exempt programs will qualify the grantor as a private operating foundation only if it maintains some "significant involvement" in the programs. "Significant involvement" means that payments for the foundation's exempt purpose are made directly and without the help of an intervening organization or agency, and that the foundation maintains a staff that supervises and directs its exempt activities on a continuing basis.

5 ▪ 3
QUALIFYING

In addition to the income test, to qualify as an operating foundation, your organization must satisfy either the assets, endowment, or support test.

The assets test will be met if at least 65 percent of its assets (valued at fair market value) are stock of a corporation controlled by the foundation, at least 85 percent of the assets of which are devoted directly to the active conduct of its exempt activities, to functionally related businesses, or to a combination of the two.

To qualify under the assets test, the assets must actually be used by the foundation directly for the active conduct of its exempt purpose. Assets not qualifying are those held for the production of income, investment, or the like. If property is used for both exempt and other purposes, it will meet the assets test so long as the exempt use represents at least 95 percent of total use.

To meet the endowment test, an amount equal to two-thirds of its minimum investment return must be expended directly for the active conduct of its exempt activities (as under the income test). This test is appropriate for those groups actively conducting charitable activities, but whose services so far exceed its assets that the cost of such services cannot be met out of its endowment. The minimum investment return is 5 percent of the excess of the combined fair market value of all its assets (other than those used directly in the active conduct of its exempt purpose) over the amount of indebtedness incurred to acquire those assets.

Suppose your foundation has $400,000 of endowment funds and other assets not directly used for its exempt purpose, and it makes qualifying distributions of $20,000 during the year directly for the active conduct of its exempt function. Two-thirds of the foundation's minimum investment return is $13,333.33 (5 percent of

$400,000 equals $20,000; two-thirds of $20,000 is $13,333.33). Because the $20,000 distribution is greater than $13,333.33, your foundation meets the endowment test.

To satisfy the support test, 85 percent of your foundation's support (other than gross investment income) must normally be received from the general public and from at least five exempt organizations. It is further required that

- These exempt organizations are not disqualified persons with respect to each other or to the recipient foundation.
- No more than 25 percent of the foundation's support is normally received from any such organization.
- No more than half the foundation's support is normally received from gross investment income.

It is important to remember that support received from any one exempt organization can be counted toward satisfaction of the support test only if your foundation receives support from at least four other exempt organizations. Moreover, support from five exempt organizations is sufficient to meet the test even if there is no general public support.

Nonexempt organization support (except for that from a government unit) is included in general public support only to the extent that it does not exceed one percent of the foundation's total support. Many foundations today that meet the support test have developed expertise in a particular area and, as such, are targets for charitable contributions by other foundations for the purpose of helping to sustain particular programs in that area of specialization.

Note that for foundations created after 1969, the requirements for the income test and either the assets, endowment, or support test must be met for any three years during a four-year period made up of the three immediately preceding tax years to the tax year in question or on the basis of collection of all pertinent amounts of income or assets received, held, or distributed during the four-year period.

5 ▪ 4
CHANGE OF STATUS

Don't worry about the status of contributions or grants made to an operating foundation until notice of a change of its status is communicated to the general public. But be aware that if the contribution or grant is made after the contributor or grantor is aware of or is responsible for an action or nonaction that causes the organization to fail to meet the test requirements, the deductibility of the contribution or grant may be affected. This is true except where the contributor or grantor relied on a written statement by the grantee organization that the contribution or grant would not result in its inability to qualify as an operating foundation.

5 ▪ 5
PRIVATE OPERATING FOUNDATION VS. PRIVATE FOUNDATION

Both kinds of private foundation are subject to the 2 percent tax on net investment income (discussed later) and to the other requirements and restrictions generally applying to private foundation activity, but the operating foundation is treated in this way:

1. It is not subject to the tax on failure to distribute income.
2. Contributions to it qualify as 50 percent deductions, whereas contributions to other private foundations (except for the common fund and conduit types) are limited to 20 percent of the donor's adjusted gross income.
3. It may receive qualifying distributions from a private foundation if the private foundation does not control it.

On the other hand, the conduit foundation enjoys this treatment:

1. Its contributions also receive the benefits of the 50 percent contribution deduction. To qualify here, though, the contributor must obtain enough records or evidence from the foundation showing that it made the required qualifying distributions

within the time prescribed. This information must be attached to the return for the tax year for which the contributor is claiming the deduction.

2. The full value of appreciated property donated may be deducted if the conduit distributed an amount equal in value to all contributions received in a tax year to either public charities or to private operating foundations within two and a half months after the year of receipt.

3. The foundation or one or more disqualified persons may not control a recipient organization either directly or indirectly.

5 ▪ 6
GETTING IN THE OPERATING CLASS

To qualify as an operating foundation, your foundation must:

1. Submit a request to the district director of the IRS for a determination that it is not a private foundation.
2. Submit information that you are not a private foundation included in a properly completed and executed Form 1023.
3. Submit necessary supporting information to confirm that you are an operating foundation.
4. Submit a written declaration by an authorized official of the organization that there is a reasonable basis in law and in fact that you are an operating foundation, and to the best of the official's knowledge and belief, the information submitted is correct and complete.

5 ▪ 7
THE GOVERNING INSTRUMENT

Your private foundation can be neither tax exempt nor the recipient of tax deductible charitable contributions unless its governing instrument contains special provisions. For the most part, these provisions must require or prohibit the foundation to act or refrain from acting in order that it will not be liable for the taxes imposed by the Internal Revenue Code. Specific reference to these sections or language considered by the IRS to have the same full force and effect must be included in the governing instrument.

Keep in mind that a private foundation's governing instrument will be considered to have been amended to conform to this requirement if valid provisions of state law have been enacted that require it to act or refrain from acting so that the foundation will not be subject to the taxes imposed on certain prohibited transactions, or that treat the required provisions as though they were contained in the foundation's governing instrument. Your key district office will have a published list of states with these statutes, which the IRS periodically updates.

5 ▪ 8
EXAMPLES OF SPECIAL PROVISION

Most private foundations are set up in trust or corporate form. The following are examples of the specially required provisions as they appear in typical articles of incorporation:

1. The corporation will distribute its income for each tax year at such time and in such manner so that it will not become subject to the tax on undistributed income imposed by Section 4942 of the Internal Revenue Code of 1954 or corresponding provisions of any later federal tax laws. (This would not apply to an operating foundation.)

2. The corporation will not engage in any act of self-dealing as defined in Section 4941(d) of the Internal Revenue Code of 1954 or corresponding provisions of any later federal tax laws.

3. The corporation will not retain any excess business holdings as defined in Section 4943(c) of the Internal Revenue Code of 1954 or corresponding provisions of any later federal tax laws.

4. The corporation will not make any investments in a manner that would subject it to tax under Section 4944 of the Internal Revenue Code of 1954 or corresponding provisions of any later federal tax laws.

5. The corporation will not make any taxable expenditures as defined in Section 4945(d) of the Internal Revenue Code of 1954 or corresponding provisions of any later federal tax laws.

Examples of special provisions necessary for a trust indenture are:

Any other provisions of this instrument notwithstanding, the trustees will distribute its income for each tax year at such time and in such manner so that it will not become subject to the tax on undistributed income imposed by Section 4942 of the Internal Revenue Code of 1954 or corresponding provisions of any later federal tax laws.

Any other provisions of this instrument notwithstanding, the trustees will not engage in any act of self-dealing as defined in Section 4941(d) of the Internal Revenue Code of 1954 or corresponding provisions of any later federal tax laws, nor retain any excess business holdings as defined in Section 4943(c) of the Internal Revenue Code of 1954 or corresponding provisions of any later federal tax laws, nor make any investments in a manner that would incur tax liability under Section 4944 of the Internal Revenue Code of 1954 or corresponding provisions of any later federal tax laws, nor make any taxable expenditures as defined in Section 4945(d) of the Internal Revenue Code of 1954 or corresponding provisions of any later federal tax laws.

5 ▪ 9
FILING REQUIREMENTS

Close attention should be paid to the filing requirements. If your organization is exempt as a private foundation or has an application for recognition of income-tax exemption pending with the IRS and you acknowledge that your organization is a private foundation, you must file an annual return on Form 990-PF by the fifteenth day of the fifth month following the close of the organization's acounting period. If an extension of time to file is needed, this request can be made on Form 2758. If there is to be a complete liquidation, dissolution, or termination, the return must be filed by the fifteenth day of the fifth month following one of these actions. Form 990-PF should be filed as this list indicates:

1. If your organization fails to make a timely filing, it will be fined $10 for each day the return is late (not to exceed $5,000), unless it shows the failure to be due to reasonable cause.
2. As a private foundation, your organization is required to at-

tach to Form 990-PF a list of all states to which it reports in any manner regarding its assets or activities, or with which it has registered that it intends to be, or is, a charitble organization or a holder of property devoted to a charitable purpose.

3. Charitable or split-interest trusts that are not exempt but are treated as private foundations instead must file Form 5227.

4. In addition to, and not in lieu of, the annual return is an annual report that must be filed. The foundations managers of every private foundation (including nonexempt trusts) that has assets of at least $5,000 at any time during the tax year must file. They may use Form 990-AR as the report or make their own report, including the information shown in Form 990-AR.

5. Both the annual return and the annual report must be made available for public inspection, and newspaper publicity regarding where such inspection can take place is necessary.

6. In addition, a copy of the annual report must be furnished to the attorney general (at the same time it is filed with the IRS) of (a) each state listed on Form 990-PF; (b) the state in which the principal office of the foundation is located; (c) the state in which the foundation was created or incorporated; or (d) any state that requests it.

7. Attached to each copy of the annual report sent to state offices must be a copy of Form 990-PF and Form 4720, "Return of Initial Excise Taxes on Private Foundations, Foundation Managers, and Disqualified Persons" (if any) filed by your foundation for the year.

8. The penalty for failing to comply with the filing of the annual report is the same as that for failing to file the annual return within a reasonable amount of time. In addition, if the failure to file the report and to comply with the publicity requirements is willful, the person(s) responsible for the failure will be liable for $1,000 penalty for each report or publicity notice.

One variation: For special filing rules that may have to be followed for certain nonexempt trusts described in the Internal Revenue Code, your counsel will want to consult the regulations. Here's what the counsel will learn:

1. Form 1041 is required to be filed by all nonexempt trusts with gross income of $600 for the year, except those that are private foundations and owe no income tax.
2. Split-interest trusts with gross income of $600 must file Form 1041 (except for charitable remainder trusts described in Section 664).
3. Charitable remainder trusts must file Form 1041-B.
4. Split-interest or nonexempt charitable trusts that are not required under their governing instruments to distribute all their income annually must file Form 1041-A.

5 ▪ 10
A HAPPY ENDING?

Once your organization is determined to be a private foundation its status can be terminated voluntarily or involuntarily. Involuntary termination by the IRS is the result of willful, repeated acts knowingly committed in violation of the excise tax provisions. However, the IRS, in its increasingly stricter regulation of private foundations, imposes the same tax on both voluntary and involuntary termination, or, in essence, dissolution.

The termination tax and the other tax burdens imposed on private foundations can be avoided by voluntary termination in any of three ways:

1. The easiest solution is to distribute all the foundation's assets to a public charity that has been in existence for a minimum of sixty calendar months, so long as two requirements are met.
   - Proof of the preferred status of the transferee must be obtained by the foundation.
   - The foundation as the transferor may not put any material restrictions on the handling of the funds by the charity.
2. The private foundation can meet the qualifying requirements of the Internal Revenue Code for public-charity status, within a twelve-month period beginning with its first taxable year and continuing for the next sixty months.
3. The private foundation can change into a supporting organization for a public charity through an amendment to the article of

incorporation and the bylaws (trust instrument), allowing it to keep its name and continue in its general purpose but relinquishing some of its independent control. To be a supporting organization it must:

- Be responsive to the needs of the charity it supports by either having officials of the charities elect or appoint the officers of the supporting organization or giving assurances that these officers will maintain a close relationship with the official representatives of the charities.

- Operate as an integral part of a supported charity by engaging in activities that the charity would otherwise have carried on and paying substantially all its income to the public charity.

But what of private foundations that continue to function as such? The IRS regulations on them are complex and detailed. In the following discussions the basics will be explained, so that your private foundation can operate more economically by staying within the confines of the federal tax laws.

5 ▪ 11
PAYING THE PIPER

To curb a variety of abuses identified with the use of private foundations over the years, the Federal Tax Reform Act of 1969 included many restrictions, requirements, and penalties for private foundations.

A 2 percent excise tax is levied on the net investment income of all domestic private foundations, including operating foundations, in excess of their gross investment income plus net capital gains over allowable deductions. Allowable deductions are ordinary and necessary expenses paid or incurred for the production or collection of gross investment income or for the management, conservation, or maintenance of property held for the production of such income, except that only straight-line depreciation and cost depletion are allowable.

To get a clearer picture of what this means, look at the definitions of these two terms:

Gross investment income is the total amount of income from interest, dividends, rents, and royalties received by a private foundation from all sources. It does not include any unrelated trade or business income, but it does include interest, dividends, rents, and royalties derived from assets devoted to charitable activities. Consequently, interest received on a student loan would be includable in the gross investment income of a private foundation making the loan.

Net investment income is the amount by which the sum of gross investment income and the net capital gain exceeds the allowable deductions.

In computing the tax on net investment income, you must include any capital gains and losses from the sale or other disposition of property held for investment purposes or for the production of income. However, any gain or loss from such sale or disposition used for exempt purposes of the foundation (even if incidental income has been derived from such property) is excluded from the computation of this tax.

5 ▪ 12
THE WOES OF SELF-DEALING

Certain specified transactions engaged in directly or indirectly between a private foundation and one or more disqualified persons are taxed. The taxes are imposed on the disqualified persons and in some cases on the foundation manager. Disqualified persons with respect to a private foundation are:

1. Any substantial contributor to the foundation, in the form of a person alone or with spouse, or a corporation (but never a government unit or qualified public charity), who contributes or bequeathes a total amount of more than $5,000 to the foundation, if the amount is more than 2 percent of the total contributions and bequests received by the foundation before the close of the tax year in which the contribution or bequest is received. Once a person or corporation is pegged a substantial contributor to a private foundation by the IRS in any year, he or she remains one for all later years.

2. A foundation manager who is an officer, director, or trustee of the foundation, and any foundation employee who has responsibil-

ity for the prohibited act. Independent contractors (such as lawyers, accountants, and investment managers and advisers) acting in their professional capacity are not officers and, therefore, are not included. If the IRS asserts the initial tax against a foundation manager, it must prove by clear and convincing evidence that the violation was knowing and willful and not due to reasonable cause.

3. The owner of over 20 percent of the total combined voting power of a corporation, the profits interest in a partnership, or the beneficial interest in a trust or unincorporated business, if any one of these itself is a substantial contributor.

4. A member of the family of a substantial contributor, foundation manager, or 20 percent owner. This term includes an individual's spouse, ancestors, lineal descendants and their spouses, but not a brother or sister.

5. A corporation, partnership, trust, or estate if more than 35 percent of voting power, profits, interest, or beneficial interest is owned by any of the above disqualified persons.

6. A related private foundation with respect to another foundation, but only for purposes of excess business holdings rules. Moreover, it must effectively be controlled directly or indirectly by one who controls the other foundation or else be the recipient of contributions substantially all of which were made by disqualified persons to the other foundation.

7. Government officials only with respect to the tax on self-dealing. They include only elective U.S. officials, U.S. and state civil servants, and a state public officeholder dealing with policy-making. Not included are positions of public employment.

In understanding what transactions constitute prohibited self-dealing, be aware of the following.

- For sanctions to be imposed against self-dealing three elements are required: a private foundation, a disqualified person, and some act of self-dealing between the two.
- Whether a self-dealing transaction turns out to be a plus or a minus to the foundation is immaterial.

- A self-dealing transaction does not include a transaction between a private foundation and a disqualified person when the disqualified person's status arises only as a result of the transaction.
- A self-dealing act can be direct or indirect. An indirect act generally is a transaction between a disqualified person and an organization controlled by a private foundation.
- A tax is imposed automatically on any disqualified person, except for a government official participating in a prohibited act whether or not that official knows it to be an act of self-dealing.

The following acts are generally penalized acts of self-dealing:

1. A sale, exchange, or lease of property. This includes a bargain sale of stock or other securities by a disqualified person to a foundation and the sale of incidental supplies to a foundation by a disqualified person, no matter what he paid for them. Also included is the transfer of real or personal property subject to a mortgage or lien from a disqualified person to a foundation. The leasing of property constitutes self-dealing only if the disqualified person charges the foundation for it.

2. The lending of money or other extension of credit but generally not including interest-free loans to the foundation, or when the proceeds from a loan are used exclusively for exempt purposes.

3. The furnishing of goods, services, and facilities, but not if they are furnished without charge or are available to the public on as favorable a basis.

4. The payment of compensation or reimbursement of expenses, if excessive.

5. Use by, or benefit for, or transfer to a disqualified person of the foundation's assets or income (but not including an incidental benefit).

6. A foundation agreement to make any payment to a government official, except an agreement to employ such official if he is leaving government service within ninety days.

Indirect self-dealing does not include the above acts of self-dealing if:

- The transaction results from a business relationship established before it involved an act of self-dealing.
- The transaction is at least as favorable to the foundation-controlled organization as an arms-length transaction with an unrelated person.
- A severe economic hardship for the controlled organization would result if the transaction took place with someone other than the disqualified person.

Some other exceptions to the tax are:

1. Often when a transaction between a foundation and a disqualified corporation occurs pursuant to a merger, redemption, recapitalization, liquidation, or other corporate organization, reorganization, or adjustment.

2. Certain transactions between government officials and an organization receiving a private foundation award, scholarship, grant, annuity, or gift.

3. Transactions involving $5,000 or less, if the price is fair and the transaction is part of a normal retail business self-dealing. The same is true of certain pledges, performance of certain banking functions, and incidental benefits from the transfer or use of a foundation's income or assets.

4. Indemnification of foundation managers against liability for contesting private foundation taxes may also escape the tax on self-dealing.

5 ▪ 13
THE TAX ON SELF-DEALING

For bona fide acts of self-dealing, an excise tax is imposed on disqualified persons and the foundation manager. The tax base, which is the amount involved, is the greater of the amount of money and property value given or the amount received, at the time the self-dealing took place. In terms of personal services, the amount involved is limited to excess compensation.

The foundation manager pays a tax if he participated willfully, knowingly, and without reasonable cause, but only so long as a tax has been levied against a disqualified person. A participating foundation manager is one who is silent or inactive when he has a duty to speak or act. On the other hand, if he opposes the act in a manner consistent with his responsibilities, he is not considered to have participated. For him to participate "knowingly" means actual knowledge of the facts of the act, awareness of the possibility of an illegal act, and negligence in finding out if the act was forbidden.

The self-dealing tax usually applies to acts engaged in after 1969, but complicated transitional rules exempt certain preexisting commitments.

5 ▪ 14
TAXES ON FAILURE TO DISTRIBUTE INCOME

A private foundation (other than a private operating foundation) not created before May 27, 1969, and required to accumulate income must distribute all its adjusted net income (or a minimum percentage of its assets, if higher) for its exempt purposes in the year received or in the next year. If it does not distribute income currently, it is subject to a tax on its accumulations. If you have thoughts of avoiding income distribution by investing in growth stocks or nonproductive land, forget it. Your minimum investment return, if higher, substitutes for adjusted net income.

Your foundation's income must be distributed as qualifying distributions, including distributions to private operating foundations, public charities, direct expenditures for a charitable purpose, and expenditures for assets used for charitable purposes. Not considered qualifying distributions in most cases are those to private nonoperating foundations and to organizations controlled by certain disqualified persons.

The qualifying distributions must be made to the extent of the greater of adjusted net income or minimum investment return within one year after the year in which the income was earned. Adjusted net income is the foundation's gross income less the ordinary and necessary expenses to produce income, expenses related to exempt interest and the taxes on unrelated business income, and investment income. The minimum investment return (less any unrelated business tax or investment tax) is the basis for figuring the minimum payout if it exceeds the foundation's adjusted net income. Generally, it is 5 percent of the combined fair market value of the foundation's assets not used to carry out its exempt functions. The values of quoted securities are determined monthly, while those of other assets are determined at the time and in the manner prescribed in the Internal Revenue Code.

Some explanations of terms may be useful at this point.

Combined fair market value of all foundation assets includes:

- The average of the foundation's monthly cash balances (exclusive of cash held for charitable and related activities).
- The average of the fair market values on a monthly basis of securities with readily available market quotations.
- The fair market value of all other assets for the period of time they are held by the foundation during the tax year. Not included are assets excluded from computation of the minimum investment return or those used for exempt purposes.

Assets not taken into account in determining minimum investment return are:

- Any future interest of a foundation in the principal or income of any real or personal property.
- The assets of an estate until they are distributed to the foundation or the estate is considered terminated for federal income tax purposes.
- Any pledge of money or property to the foundation.
- Any present foundation interest in any trust created and funded by another person.
- Any assets used in a trade or business not substantially related to the foundation's exempt purpose for which most of the work is performed without pay.
- Any assets used or held for use for exempt purposes.

Assets used for exempt purposes are those actually used by the foundation to carry on the charitable, educational, or similar function giving rise to the exemption. This does not include assets held for the production of income or for investment, although the income from those assets may be used to carry out an exempt purpose. Assets that are used for exempt purposes are:

- Administrative assets to the extent they are devoted to or used directly in the administration of exempt activities.
- Any real estate or portion of a building used by the foundation directly in exempt activities.
- Physical facilities that, under the facts and circumstances, serve a useful purpose in exempt activities.
- Any interest in a program-related investment or in a functionally related business.
- Reasonable cash balances necessary to cover the exempt activities.
- The foundation's leasing of property at no cost or low cost as part of an exempt program.

If your failure to make required payouts results from an incorrect asset valuation made in good faith, you can avoid the tax by promptly making deficiency distributions. Although payouts ordinarily must occur in the year your foundation receives the income or the year after, it may set aside funds up to five years for major projects, if they can be better accomplished by a set-aside than by immediate payment. These set-asides must have advance approval by the IRS. The law also provides that any excess qualifying distributions may be carried forward for a period of five tax years immediately following the tax year in which the excess was created.

Payouts normally reduce undistributed income of the preceding year first, then of the current year then corpus. Your foundation may elect to apply a payout that is in excess of the undistributed income of the immediately preceding year to that of an earlier year. For example, a new foundation has income of $200,000 in 1976 with no distribution that year, and its 1977 income is also $200,000. A payout of $200,000 in 1977 wipes out the 1976 tax, while a payout in 1977 of $400,000 eliminates taxes for both years. If we assume no 1977 payout, the 1978 payout of $200,000 would eliminate the 1977 tax. A larger payout would reduce the 1976 tax if the taxpayer made such an election; otherwise the excessive payment would be applied to reduce the 1978 tax.

5 ▪ 15
TAXES ON EXCESS BUSINESS HOLDINGS

As a private foundation, you are limited in the amount of your business holdings. The IRS has set a 20 percent limit on the combined holdings of a private foundation and all its disqualified persons of the voting stock (or beneficial interest or profits interest for partnerships or joint ventures) in a business enterprise (including a real-estate investment trust). Your foundation cannot hold any interest in a sole proprietorship. By business enterprise we mean the active conduct of a trade or business, including any activity that is regularly carried on for the production of income from the sale of goods or the performance of services that under the Internal Revenue Code constitutes an unrelated trade or business.

Two exceptions to the 20 percent limit rule explained above are:

1. Your foundation can hold any percentage of nonvoting stock if all disqualified persons do not own more than 20 percent of the voting stock. Convertible nonvoting stock and stock with contingent voting rights are nonvoting stock until the conversion or contingency has occurred.
2. Your foundation's permitted holdings are 35 percent if the voting stock of the corporation in question is under the effective control of one or more nondisqualified persons.

Five years are given to dispose of excess holdings resulting from gifts or bequests.

This tax on excess business holdings does not apply to holdings in either a functionally related business or in a trade or business deriving at least 95 percent of its gross income from passive sources (such as dividends, interest, annuities, royalties, certain rents, certain income from sales, exchanges, and other dispositions of property).

A functionally related business may be:

1. A trade or business substantially related in its conduct to the exempt function or purpose of the private foundation.
2. A trade or business that performs substantially all its work for the foundation without pay.
3. A business operated by the foundation primarily for the convenience of its members.
4. A business consisting of the selling of substantially donated merchandise.

5 ▪ 16
TAXES ON INVESTMENTS THAT JEOPARDIZE CHARITABLE PURPOSES

Making speculative or risky investments may subject a foundation and its manager to an excise tax. This tax will apply to investments of either income or principal and applies separately to the foundation and to any foundation manager who knowingly participated in making the investment.

Investment in program-related activities, such as high-risk, low-income housing or low-interest student loans, is not the type that jeopardizes the foundation's purpose. On the other hand, if a foundation manager fails to exercise ordinary business care and prudence in making an investment under the facts prevailing at the time of the investment, it is considered to be a jeopardizing investment.

Jeopardizing investments are generally those that show a lack of reasonable business care and prudence in providing for the short- and long-term financial needs of the foundation for it to carry out its function.

They may be investments in commodity futures; securities on margin; working interests in oil and gas wells; short sales; and warrants, "puts," "calls," and "straddles." Remember, though, that no category constitutes an absolute violation. Whether the investment jeopardized the carrying out of exempt purposes is determined on an investment-by-investment basis, taking into account the foundation's portfolio as a whole. Such a determination is made at the time the investment is made. Therefore, if it is proper when made, it will not be considered otherwise even if it later results in a loss.

5 ▪ 17
TAXES ON TAXABLE EXPENDITURES

An excise tax is imposed on your foundation and its manager for so-called "taxable expenditures." Here are a few examples.

1. To influence the outcome of any public election, or to carry on directly or indirectly certain voter registration drives, except for expenditures by broad-based, nonpartisan organizations for political activity in broad areas over several elections (such as the League of Women Voters).

2. To influence legislation through lobbying directed to the general public or by contacts with legislators, except for discussions of broad social and economic problems, nonpartisan research, requested technical advice, and decisions affecting the powers, duties, tax-exempt status, or deductibility of contributions to private foundations.

3. In the form of a grant to an individual for travel or study. Excepted are grants to bring about a particular objective, produce a specific report, or improve the musical, artistic, scientific, or other skill of the grantee; taxfree (excluded from gross income) fellowships and scholarships; and taxfree prizes and awards. To be excepted, advance approval of the general program by the IRS is necessary. Furthermore, the foundation is required to exercise responsibility over the expenditure by the grantee.

4. To another private nonoperating foundation, unless the granting foundation exercises "expenditure responsibility."

5. Made for any purpose that would not support a charitable deduction if the grantor were taxable.

5 ▪ 18
THE OVERALL PICTURE

To get an overall picture of the tax penalty rates on private foundations and their managers, refer to Table 1.

Table 1. Tax penalty rates.[a]

Internal Revenue Code Section	Initial Taxes		Additional Taxes	
	Foundation	Foundation Manager	Foundation	Foundation Manager
Sec. 4941 (self-dealing)	5% of "amount involved"[b]	2½% (maximum $10,000)	200% of "amount involved"[b]	50% (maximum $10,000)
Sec. 4942 (undistributed income)	15% of "undistributed income"	—	100% of "undistributed income"	—
Sec. 4943 (business holdings)	5% of value of excess holdings	—	200% of value of excess holdings	—
Sec. 4944 (speculative investments)	5% of amount of jeopardy investments	5% (maximum $5,000)	25% of amount of jeopardy investments	5% (maximum $10,000)
Sec. 4945 (taxable expenditures)	10% of amount of improper expenditure	2½% (maximum $5,000)	100% of amount of improper expenditure	50% (maximum $10,000)

[a] These taxes are reported on Form 4720 with Form 990PF (or Form 1041-A by nonexempt charitable trusts).
[b] Imposed on "self-dealer," not foundation.

5 ▪ 19
FOREIGN FOUNDATIONS

Special rules apply to foreign private foundations. They are subject to an annual tax of 4 percent of their gross investment income derived from U.S. sources (instead of tax on net investment income). However, if a treaty exists between the United States and the foreign country in which the foundation resides that exempts certain items from gross investment income, those items will not be taken into account in computing the tax.

If the foreign foundation has received at least 85 percent of its support (other than gross investment income) from sources outside the United States, it will be exempt from the special taxes for private foundations. However, if it engages in a prohibited transaction it may lose this exemption. A "prohibited transaction" is any act or failure to act (except regarding minimum investment return requirements) that would subject the foundation or a disqualified person of the foundation to a penalty if the foreign foundation were domestic in nature.

5 ▪ 20
STATE REGULATION

The state, too, must regulate the foundation on behalf of the public. Although there is still no workable uniform legislative act for control, the states have effected a wide variety of legislation relating to private foundations—some worthwhile, some not. To be effective, state legislation of private foundations should at least meet the following basic criteria:

- That all private foundations be registered with a designated state officer who specifically has the responsibility for supervising them.
- That all private foundations be required to submit regular reports regarding their financial activities.
- That a legislative act provide effective enforcement provisions.

All the above criteria have to do with increasing the effectiveness of the supervisory power of the state government over private foundations. Because of the limited nature of state supervision, federal supervision through the tax laws has been the primary means of control of foundations.

5 ▪ 21
TRUSTS

What about that commonly considered alternative to the private foundation—the charitable trust? If you have any thoughts of avoiding the restrictions on private foundations by operating your organization as a nonexempt charitable trust, forget it. The law imposes many of the private foundation requirements and restrictions on such trusts.

- It may not engage in acts of self-dealing.
- It may not have excess business holdings.
- It may not make prohibited speculative investments.
- It may not make any prohibited expenditures.

If it does any of the above, it loses its charitable deductions, and contributions to it thereafter are not deductible by the donor. In fact, even if a charitable trust meets the requirements for one of the exclusions that classifies it as a public charity, it will not be treated as a charitable organization for purposes of exemption from tax. Accordingly, the trust is subject to the excise tax on its investment income under rules that apply to taxable foundations rather than to tax-exempt foundations. That is, it is subject to 2 percent tax on net investment income only to the extent that the sum of the tax plus a tax on unrelated business income, applied as if the foundation were tax exempt, exceeds the income tax liability for the year.

For example, a taxable charitable trust owed an income tax of $10,000 in 1977. If the trust were tax exempt, it would have a $4,000 liability for tax on net investment income and a $7,000 liability for tax on unrelated business income. The nonexempt trust is liable for $1,000, the amount by which the sum of the tax on net investment income and the tax on unrelated business income ($11,000) exceeds the amount of income tax owed ($10,000).

Note these definitions:

Charitable trust refers to a nonexempt trust with all of its unexpired interests devoted to charitable purposes that is treated as a taxable private foundation, if a charitable contribution deduction has been allowed.

Taxable private foundation refers to an organization exempt as a private foundation as of 1969 but later determined to be nonexempt in the Internal Revenue Code. Even though it may function as a taxable entity, it will continue to be treated as a taxable private foundation unless its status is terminated under Section 507.

If a charitable trust is created by will, it is treated as a private foundation as of the decedent grantor's death. But where a revocable trust becomes irrevocable upon the grantor's death and distribution has to be made of all net assets to beneficiaries or held by the trustee in trust, the trust is not treated as a private foundation for a reasonable period of settlement.

If a charitable trust seeks exemption from federal income tax as a charitable organization, it will be considered organized on the day it first becomes subject to the section of the Internal Revenue Code dealing with the application of private foundation rules to certain nonexempt trusts. It becomes subject to this section on the first day it has amounts in trust for which a deduction was allowed under Internal Revenue law. For instance, A creates a living trust under which B gets 50 percent and C 50 percent of the trust's income for ten years. At the end of that period, the corpus is to be distributed to D. B, C, and D are all charitable organizations and A is allowed a charitable deduction for the value of all interests placed in trust.

The trustees, however, did not give notice to the IRS that they were applying for recognition of tax-exempt status. Therefore, the trust is not tax exempt. It is a charitable trust within the meaning of this section from the date of its creation.

If the nonexempt trust is one that has a noncharitable income beneficiary and a charitable remainder, or vice versa, it is a split-interest trust. It will be subject to private foundation taxes imposed on self-dealing, excess business holdings, investments that jeopardize charitable purposes, and taxable expenditures. Take note that these taxes apply only to amounts transferred in trust beginning May 27, 1969, for which a charitable deduction was allowed. But amounts payable to income beneficiaries are taxed only if a charitable deduction was allowed for the income interest.

Remember, too, that other amounts in trust may also be taxed if those for which a charitable deduction was allowed are not properly segregated from other amounts. In addition, taxes on excess business holdings and investments that jeopardize charitable purposes do not apply if the charity is only an income beneficiary and the beneficial interest of the charity in the trust is less than 60 percent of the value of the trust property and if the only interest of a charity in the trust is that of a remainderman.

5 ▪ 22
KINDS OF GRANTS

The primary function of a private foundation is charitable giving. Some examples of the more common foundation grants are those for research, fellowships and scholarships to individuals, information gathering for educational and professional purposes, operational or sustaining types to organizations or institutions, "seed-money" types to get an endeavor off the ground, cultural programs, relief, to rescue a project, demonstration or social-action programs, and building or other capital purposes.

Why do foundations (or charitable trusts) hold a unique position to make grants? For one thing, unlike a college or private business, they rarely incur monetary obligations and therefore do not need to be concerned with liabilities. Each year they can start anew with their giving. Unlike a unit of government, they do not answer to a constituency for their actions. This should make them freer to conceive and implement new and creative ideas for a better way of life. It should also make easier the undertaking of controversial ideas.

5 ▪ 23
GRANTS TO INDIVIDUALS

For IRS purposes private foundation grants, as we know, are ordinarily taxable expenditures when they are made to an individual for study, travel, or like purposes. They include prizes, awards, scholarships, fellowships, internships, program-related investments, loans for charitable purposes, and payments to exempt organizations for their exempt purposes. Normally, not included as grants are salaries or other payments for personal services performed for the foundation.

On the other hand, a grant to an individual for these purposes is not considered a taxable expenditure if:

1. The grant is awarded on an objective and nondiscriminatory basis, according to a procedure approved in advance by the IRS. For the grantmaking procedure to be approved in advance, it must provide that:

- The group from which the grantees are selected is reasonably related to the purposes of the grant and is sufficiently broad to constitute a charitable class.
- The criteria used in choosing grant recipients are related to the purpose of the grant (such as prior academic performance, financial need, performance on college boards, teachers' recommendations, and selection committee's personal interviews).
- The selectors of recipients are not in a position to gain privately, directly or indirectly, if certain grantees are picked over others.
- Periodic reports (at least once a year) are made to the foundation to decide whether the grantees have performed as intended.
- If periodic reports are not made the foundation will investigate and take corrective action.
- The foundation will keep all records pertaining to grants to individuals.

Requests for approval of grantmaking procedures are to be submitted to the district director.

2. The IRS is shown to its satisfaction that one of the following is true.

- The grant is a scholarship or fellowship type that is excluded from gross income and is to be used for study at an educational institution with a regular faculty and curriculum and a campus for a regularly attending student body.
- The grant is a prize or award grant that is excluded from gross income, so long as the recipient is chosen from the general public.
- The grant's purpose is to achieve a specific objective, produce a report, or improve a skill or talent of the grantee.

If a grant is made to an individual for purposes other than those described above, it is not a taxable expenditure, even if the code's requirements are not met. Therefore, the following foundation grants to individuals are not taxable expenditures:

- Those made in recognition of past achievements (for example, winning a student competition).
- Those not intended to finance future activities of a grantee.
- Those for which no conditions were imposed on the way awards may be spent by the recipients.

Renewal of a qualified grant is not treated as a grant to an individual subject to the code's taxable expenditure requirements if:

- The grantor has no information that the original grant is not being used for a purpose other than that for which it was made.
- The reports expected under the terms of the grant have been furnished.
- Any additional criteria and procedures for renewal are nondiscriminatory and objective.

No grant will be considered to have been made by a private foundation to an individual if:

1. The grant is made to another organization that in turn makes payments to the individual, and the foundation does not earmark the use of the grant for any named individual and there is no agreement whereby the grantor has any part in selecting the individual grantee.
2. The grant is made to a public charity, which uses it to make payments to a qualified individual, and the grant is made for a project to be undertaken and controlled by the public charity.

5 ▪ 24
GRANTS TO ORGANIZATIONS

Grants to organizations, which include loans and program-related investments, are taxable expenditures unless they are made to qualified public charities or unless the private foundation exercises expenditure responsibility over the grant.

Expenditure responsibility is the exertion of all reasonable efforts and establishment of adequate procedures by the foundation:

- To make sure the grant is spent solely for the purpose for which it was made.
- To get complete reports from the grantee organization on how the funds are spent.
- To make complete detailed reports on the expenditures to the IRS.

To meet the expenditure responsibility requirement, the following should be done:

1. A pre-grant inquiry should be made regarding the identity, prior history and experience, activities, management, and practices of the grantee organization. The results of the inquiry should give reasonable assurance that the grantee will use the grant as intended.

2. The grantee organization must make a written commitment:

- To repay any amount not used for the purposes of the grant.
- To submit annual reports to the grantor foundation on how the funds are spent and the progress being made.
- To keep financial records and make its books available to the grantor at reasonable times.
- Not to use the funds in any manner that would result in a taxable expenditure if made directly by the foundation.

Unless certain remedies are met (according to the IRS) any diversion of grant funds for a use not specified in the grant, failure to make the required reports by the grantee, or failure on the grantor's part to do what is required will result in the grant's being treated as a taxable expenditure.

On each expenditure responsibility grant, the foundation must make a report each year (along with the annual return) for any portion of the grant that remains unspent by the grantee. The report must include for each grant the name and address of the grantee, the date and amount of the grant, its purpose, amounts spent by the grantee, whether the grantee has diverted any funds from the grant's purpose, dates that grantee's reports were received, and results and date of verification of grantee's reports by grantor.

In this context, the types of expenditures that are not normally treated as taxable expenditures are:

1. Those to acquire investments that generate income for the purpose of furthering the aims of the organization, and the reasonable expenses related to these investments.
2. The payment of taxes.
3. Expenses that are allowable deductions in computing the unrelated business income tax.
4. Any payment that is a qualifying distribution.
5. Any allowable deduction in arriving at taxable net investment income.
6. Reasonable expenditures for evaluating, acquiring, and disposing of program-related investments.
7. Business expenses made by the recipient of a program-related investment.

A private foundation generally cannot make a grant to an organization not described in Section 501(c)(3) of the Internal Revenue Code. Any amounts it pays or incurs for nonexempt purposes are subject to the tax on taxable expenditures. Activities subject to the tax are those that, if they were a substantial part of the organization's total activities, would cause the loss of tax exemption.

5 ▪ 25
SUMMATION

As you have seen, the federal and state governments regulate foundations through tax laws. By requiring the filing of certain information periodically and by imposing penalties, abuses are curtailed. At the same time, grants are encouraged that will be most beneficial to society at large.

6
Federal Income Tax Exemption

6 ▪ 1
EXEMPTION BENEFITS

Certain nonprofit organizations are granted exemption from taxation, though, as we shall see, they may be taxed on income from businesses they conduct. Federal income-tax exemption may also include exemption from certain federal excise and employment taxes.

If your organization is exempt under federal law, it may further qualify for exemption from state and local sales, use, property, and other forms of tax. What's more, qualifying charitable organizations are eligible to attract deductible charitable contributions from individual and corporate donors.

Finally, many public charities are the likely subject of grants from private foundations. Why? Because a foundation may distribute funds to such organizations to satisfy mandatory payout requirements without having to assume expenditure responsibility for the grants. In fact, federal agencies often only make grants to or enter into contracts with nonprofit, tax-exempt organizations, and often only public charities.

6 ▪ 2
ALTERNATIVE BENEFITS

Althogh most organizations will find exemption the surest route to tax saving, other alternatives are available:

1. Operating an organization (profit or nonprofit) so that its deductions equal or exceed its income in any taxable year. Cooperatives function in this way to avoid income taxes. Organizations that lose their tax-exempt status and those that cannot qualify as tax exempt may find it desirable to become a cooperative.

2. Operating an organization so that its income and deductions are matching, but not as a cooperative. If an organization is a social club or other membership organization operated to furnish goods or services to its members, Section 277 of the Internal Revenue Code (dealing with deductions incurred by certain nonexempt membership organizations) provides that expenses are deductible to the extent of income from members and institutes or trade shows primarily for the members' education.

3. Operating an organization merely as a conduit for the expenditure of a fund established for a specific purpose, such as being simply an administrator of a trust fund.

4. Operating an organization as an unincorporated association and arguing nonentity status for tax purposes. The success of this approach is dubious; the IRS has the authority to treat an unincorporated entity as a taxable corporation. Nonetheless, political campaign committees were successful at this until 1974, when the IRS ruled that they are to be treated as taxable corporations, even though contributions remain nontaxable.

In short, to be exempt from federal income taxation, an organization generally must make an affirmative effort to be recognized as exempt from tax, operate as a cooperative, legally marshal deductions against income, or seek a change in the law. Otherwise, it is almost certain to be liable for tax.

6 ▪ 3
FINDING YOUR PLACE

Your nonprofit organization may become exempt from federal income tax if it applies for an exemption as one of those organizations described in applicable Internal Revenue Code definitions that permit exemption. The exempt category that encompasses your organization depends on the nature and purpose of your nonprofit organization. Table 2 on the following pages provides quick reference to the major categories and a brief explanation of each.

Once you have located the category that fits your future, you will want to examine in greater detail what it requires and what it offers your organization. This will help you to know what to look for in your relationship with the IRS.

Section 501 of the Internal Revenue Code pertains to nonprofit organizations and their tax exemptions. In the following paragraphs you will get a closer look at the more important subsections of Section 501 and how they could affect your organization.

6 ▪ 4
SECTION 501(c)(3)

Subsection 501(c)(3) is the subsection that affects the largest number of nonprofit organizations. It pertains to those that qualify for federal income tax exemption by meeting these requirements:

1. They must be organized and operated exclusively for at least one of the following purposes: charitable, religious, educational, scientific, literary, prevention of cruelty to children or animals, testing for public safety, or fostering national or international amateur sports competition. These entities are eligible:
- A corporation (including associations and joint stock and insurance companies) or community chests, funds, or foundations meeting the requirement.
- Funds and foundations in the form of trusts that need not be created by the community.
- State-owned organizations when they are not acting as official state agencies.

Table 2. Organization reference chart.

Section of 1954 Internal Revenue Code	Description of Organization	General Nature of Activities	Form Number	Annual Return to be Filed	Contributions Allowable
501(c)(1)	Corporations organized under act of Congress (including federal credit unions)	Instrumentalities of the United States	No form	None	Yes, if made for exclusively public purposes
501(c)(2)	Title-holding corporations for exempt organizations	Holding title to property of an exempt organization	1024	990[a]	No[b]
501(c)(3)	Religious, educational, charitable, scientific, literary, testing for public safety, fostering of certain national or international amateur sports competition, and prevention of cruelty to children or animals organizations	Activities of nature implied by description of class of organization	1023	990 or 990-PF[a]	Generally, yes
501(c)(4)	Civic leagues, social welfare organizations, and local associations of employees	Promoting community welfare; charitable, educational, or recreational	1024	990[a]	Generally, no[b,c]
501(c)(5)	Labor, agricultural, and horticultural organizations	Educational or instructive, the purpose being to improve conditions of work and to improve products and efficiency	1024	990[a]	No[b]
501(c)(6)	Business leagues, chambers of commerce, real-estate boards, and so on	Improvement of business conditions of one or more lines of business	1024	990[a]	No[b]

501(c)(7)	Social and recreation clubs	Pleasure, recreation, social activities	1024	990^a	No^b
501(c)(8)	Fraternal beneficiary societies and associations	Lodge providing for payment of life, sickness, accident, or other benefits to members	1024	990^a	Yes, if used for Section 501(c)(3) purposes
501(c)(9)	Voluntary employees' beneficiary associations [including federal employees' voluntary beneficiary associations formerly covered by Section 501(c)(10)]	Providing for payment of life, sickness, accident, or other benefits to members	1024	990^a	No^b
501(c)(10)	Domestic fraternal societies and associations	Lodge devoting its net earnings to charitable, fraternal, and other specified purposes. No life, sickness, or accident benefits to members	1024	990^a	Yes, if used for Section 501(c)(3) purposes
501(c)(11)	Teachers' retirement fund associations	Teachers' association for payment of retirement benefits	No form	990^a	No^b
501(c)(12)	Benevolent life-insurance associations, mutual ditch or irrigation companies, mutual or cooperative telephone companies, etc.	Activities of a mutually beneficial nature similar to those implied by the description of class of organization	1024	990^a	No^b
501(c)(13)	Cemetery companies	Burials and incidental activities	1024	990^a	Generally, yes
501(c)(14)	State-chartered credit unions and mutual reserve funds	Loans to members. Exemption as building and loan associations and cooperative banks repealed by Revenue Act of 1951, affecting all years after 1951	No form	990^a	No^b
501(c)(15)	Mutual insurance companies or associations	Providing insurance to members substantially at cost	1024	990^a	No^b

Code section	Type of organization	Activities	Application form	Annual return	Deductible contributions
501(c)(16)	Cooperative organizations to finance crop operations	Financing crop operations in conjunction with activities of a marketing or purchasing association	No form	990[a]	No[b]
501(c)(17)	Supplemental unemployment benefit trusts	Providing payment of supplemental unemployment compensation benefits	1024	990[a]	No[b]
501(c)(18)	Employee-funded pension trust (created before June 25, 1959)	Payment of benefits under a pension plan funded by employees	No form	990[a]	No[b]
501(c)(19)	Post or organization of war veterans	Activities implied by nature of organization	1024	990[a]	Yes
501(c)(20)	Group legal services plan organizations	Employers providing personal (nonbusiness) legal services for employees for tax years ending before 1/1/82	1024	990[a]	No
501(d)	Religious and apostolic associations	Regular business activities. Communal religious community	No form	1065	No[b]
501(e)	Cooperative hospital service organizations	Performing cooperative services for hospitals	1023	990[a]	Yes
501(f)	Cooperative service organizations of operating educational organizations	Performing collective investment services for educational organizations	1023	990[a]	Yes

[a] For exceptions to the filing requirement, consult the instructions for Forms 990 and 990-AR.

[b] An organization exempt under a subsection of Code Section 501 other than (c)(3) may establish a charitable fund, contributions to which are deductible. Such a fund must itself meet the requirements of Section 501(c)(3) and the related notice requirements of Section 508(a).

[c] Contributions to volunteer fire companies and similar organizations are deductible, if made for exclusively public purposes.

- An organization controlled by one individual or, if a trust, created by a sole or controlling trustee.
- A public library organized under state law as a separate entity not empowered to impose taxes.
- A public hospital corporation granted the power of eminent domain (power to take private property for public use).

The Red Cross, YMCA, Girl Scouts, Veterans of Foreign Wars, American Legion, parent-teacher associations, old-age homes, American Heart Association, C.A.R.E., and United Fund are just a few examples of Section 501(c)(3) organizations.

2. Such an organization must allow no part of its net earnings to inure to the benefit of individuals or private shareholders. To meet this requirement, your organization must not be organized or operated for the benefit of private interests, such as the creator of the organization or his family, shareholders of the organization, persons controlled by private interests, or persons with a personal interest in the organization's activities.

A case in point is the denial of charitable status to the Horace Heidt Foundation. Although the foundation provided housing, medical assistance, and musical instruction to those featured on the Horace Heidt shows, the operation of the foundation was held to lead to private gain for Mr. Heidt in his capacity as an employer.

Activities or dealings between an organization and a private individual that are considered private inurement are:

- The sale, exchange, or leasing of the organization's property for the use or benefit of a private individual.
- The furnishing of goods, services, or facilities to private individuals as a primary purpose.
- The payment of dividends to any stockholders.
- Payment of compensation, expenses, or reimbursement of expenses that are considered unreasonable or excessive.
- A reversionary interest trust, in which the principal reverts to the settlor or his or her estate at the trust's termination, resulting in inurement of investment gains over the life of the trust to the creator's benefit.
- The lending of money if it is not repaid on a timely basis, not

financially advantageous to the organization, or not in keeping with its purposes.

- Certain tax-avoidance schemes. A typical scheme would be the transfer of a person's business assets to a controlled nonprofit entity, from which that person would continue to operate the business as an employee of the transferee organization. His or her sole purpose is to avoid taxes. The IRS views such a practice as an attempt to reduce personal federal income taxes while still enjoying the benefits of one's earnings.

Activities that produce only an incidental and/or unintended benefit to a private individual are not considered private inurement—as decided on a case-by-case basis.

3. A Section 501(c)(3) organization must not engage to any extent in political campaigns for or against any candidate for public office.

4. Finally, it must not attempt to influence legislation (to lobby) as a substantial part of its activities. If it does, it will be dubbed an "action" organization and will not qualify for exemption.

The types of legislative activities prohibited are:

- Presentation of testimony at public hearings held by legislative committees.
- Publication of documents advocating specific legislative action.
- Correspondence and conferences with legislators.
- Appeals to the general public to contact legislators or take other specific action with regard to legislative matters. This practice is referred to as "grass-roots" lobbying.

Note that the IRS will find it irrelevant that legislation advocated would advance the charitable purposes for which your organization was created. At the same time, the IRS will only hold your organization responsible for legislative activities if they are undertaken by the organization itself. Therefore, the legislative activities of a student newspaper would not be attributable to the sponsoring university. During the course of anti-Vietnam War efforts on college campuses during the 1960s, the principle was established that such efforts, which included legislative activities by students and faculty, were not official acts of the particular institution.

This prohibition on legislative activities does not mean, however, that your organization cannot engage in nonpartisan analysis, study, and research. It certainly can as long as it does not advocate the adoption of legislation or legislative action to implement its findings. Performing educational activities, instead of promoting activism, is the key to qualification.

The IRS spells out for you the types of activities that can make yours an "action" organization.

1. Where a substantial part of the organization's activities is directed at influencing legislation by propaganda.
2. Where its primary objective can be attained only by legislation or the defeat of it.
3. Where it advocates or campaigns for the attainment of its primary objective rather than engaging in nonpartisan research and so on and making the results thereof available to the public.

Past decisions indicate that the IRS looks at all the activities, facts, and circumstances surrounding an organization before it determines that it does fit these "action" categories. It has admitted that terms such as "exclusively," "primarily," and "substantial" present difficult conceptual problems and can better be resolved on the basis of the facts of a particular case. The IRS has gone one step further in clarifying what constitutes an "action" organization: It has ruled that attempts to influence legislation imply an affirmative act and something more than a mere passive response to a legislative committee invitation.

6 ▪ 5
A LOOPHOLE TO LOBBYING

At present the IRS does allow an alternative to the traditional restrictions on lobbying for some Section 501(c)(3) organizations. For tax years beginning after Dec. 31, 1976, a public charity—other than a church (or an auxiliary, convention, or association of such)—may elect to replace the "substantial part of activities" test

with an expenditure limit for the purpose of influencing legislation. Private foundations and support organizations are prohibited
from making such an election.

The rules of this newer provision define "influencing legislation"
as any attempt to influence any legislation through a move to affect the opinions of the general public (grass-roots lobbying), and
through communication with any employee or member of a legislative body or any government official or employee who may participate in the formulation of legislation (direct lobbying).

These activities are not considered "influencing legislation":

- Making available the results of nonpartisan analysis, study, or
  research.
- Providing technical help in response to a written request by a
  government body.
- Appearing before or communicating with any legislative body
  regarding a possible decision of that body that might affect your
  organization's existence, powers, and duties, tax-exempt status,
  or the deduction of charitable contributions to it.
- Communicating with a government official or employee other
  than the communications described above as influencing legislation.
- Communicating between your organization and its bona fide
  members, except when the communications directly encourage
  the members to influence legislation or directly encourage them
  to urge nonmembers to do so.

A public charity electing to come under these provisions by filing Form 5768 will not lose its exempt status unless it normally (on
an average over a four-year period) makes lobbying nontaxable
expenditures for the purpose of influencing legislation in excess of
150 percent of the amount allowed for each tax year, or normally
makes grass-roots expenditures in the attempt to affect the opinions of the general public in excess of 150 percent of the amount
allowed.

The amount that is allowed for lobbying nontaxable expenditures for any tax year is the lesser of $1 million or 20 percent of the

first $500,000 of an organization's expenditures for an exempt purpose, plus 15 percent of the next $500,000, 10 percent of the next $500,000, and 5 percent of any remaining expenditures. For the grass-roots nontaxable expenditures in any tax year, a separate limitation is imposed—25 percent of the foregoing amounts. These two limitations may be separately elected.

The term "exempt purpose expenditures," while not including fund-raising activities, refers to the total amounts paid or incurred by the organization to accomplish its exempt purposes. These include administrative expenses paid or incurred and amounts paid or incurred for influencing legislation, whether or not such legislation promotes the organization's exempt purposes.

There are some caveats to consider if your public charity makes the election:

- It can lose its exempt status by abusing its expenditure limitations and engaging in substantial lobbying activities.
- If its exempt status is lost, it cannot convert to a social welfare organization, exempt under Section 501(c)(4).
- If your organization has elected either one or the other of the limitations, but exceeds one of them, it becomes subject to an excise tax of 25 percent of the excess lobbying expenditures. When both limitations are elected, the greater of the two excesses will be taxed.
- If you have a situation in which two or more Section 501(c)(3) organizations are members of an affiliated group and at least one of the members has elected the latest lobbying provisions, the calculations of lobbying and exempt-purpose expenditures must be made by including the expenditures of the entire group. If these expenditures do exceed the permitted limits, each of the electing members must pay a proportionate share of the penalty excise tax, while the nonelecting members are treated under the preexisting law.

There are two tests for determining that two organizations are "affiliated": The first is if one organization is bound by the other's decisions on legislative issues pursuant to its governing instrument; and the second is if the governing board of one includes enough representatives of the other (called an "interlocking directorate") to prevent or cause action on legislative issues by the first organization.

- An electing organization must remember to disclose in its annual information returns to the IRS the amount of its total lobbying expenditures, together with the amount it was allowed to spend without becoming subject to the 25 percent excise tax. This information must also be provided by an electing organization that is a member of an affiliated group for both itself and the entire group.

6 ▪ 6
ORGANIZING

A charitable, religious, or similar organization will be considered organized exclusively for one or more exempt purposes only if its articles of organization—the corporate charter, articles of association, or trust instrument by which it is created—limit its purposes to those described in Section 501(c)(3) and do not expressly empower it to engage in activities not in furtherance of its exempt purposes, except as an insubstantial part of its activities. In construing the terms of an organization's articles, the law of the state in which the organization is set up is controlling. If your organization should contend that the terms of its articles have a meaning different from that generally accepted, it must establish such meaning by clear and convincing reference to relevant court decisions, by state attorney generals' opinions, or by other evidence of applicable state law.

The requirement that your organization's powers and purposes must be limited by its articles will not be satisfied if such limitation is contained only in the bylaws, or by mere statements of your officers that you intend to operate only for exempt purposes, or by the fact that your actual operations are for exempt purposes.

Articles of organization that state that your organization is formed exclusively for, say, scientific purposes within the meaning of Section 501(c)(3) of the Internal Revenue Code of 1954 do correctly limit its purposes. On the other hand, if your organization's articles state that the organization is formed to engage in research, without further description or limitation, its purposes will not be properly limited, since all research is not scientific within the meaning of Section 501(c)(3).

If your articles state that the organization is formed for "charitable purposes" with no further description, such a statement usually is sufficient, since the term "charitable" has a generally accepted meaning. However, if the terms "benevolent" and "philanthropic" are used, the articles will not be sufficient. Since "benevolent" and "philanthropic" have no generally accepted legal meaning, the stated purposes allow activities (under the laws of the state) that are broader than those intended by the exemption law.

The assets of Section 501(c)(3) organizations must be permanently dedicated to an exempt purpose and must not be distributed to members or private individuals for any other purpose. To meet both this requirement and the organizational test, the articles of organization should include a provision that the organization's assets will be distributed for a Section 501(c)(3) exempt purpose or to the federal, state, or local government for a public purpose in the event of dissolution.

Even when reliance is placed upon your state law to establish permanent dedication of assets for exempt purposes, your organization's application for exemption is likely to be processed faster if its articles include such a provision. If your organization does not include this provision and relies instead on the operation of law, it will be necessary for your counsel to submit a brief, outlining either the state statute that governs or the judicial decision relied upon, with a clear assurance that the assets will be distributed only for a Section 501(c)(3) purpose.

6 ▪ 7
EXAMPLE OF INCORPORATION

Look now at this sample of articles of incorporation shown in Exhibit 6. It will aid you and your attorney in meeting IRS requirements.

EXHIBIT 6

Articles of Incorporation of _____

The undersigned, a majority of whom are citizens of the United States, desiring to form a Nonprofit Corporation under the Nonprofit Corporation Law of _____ , do hereby certify:

First: The name of the Corporation shall be _____ .

Second: The place in this State where the principal office of the Corporation is to be located is the City of _____ , _____ County.

Third: Said corporation is organized exclusively for charitable, religious, educational, and scientific purposes, including, for such purposes, the making of distributions to organizations that qualify as exempt organizations under Section 501(c)(3) of the Internal Revenue Code of 1954 (or the corresponding provision of any future U.S. Internal Revenue Law).

Fourth: The names and addresses of the persons who are the initial Trustees of the corporation are as follows:

_____	_____
_____	_____
_____	_____
Name	Address

Fifth: No part of the net earnings of the corporation shall inure to the benefit of, or be distributable to, its members, trustees, officers, or other private persons, except that the corporation shall be authorized and empowered to pay reasonable compensation for services rendered and to make payments and distributions in furtherance of the purposes set forth in Article Third hereof. No substantial part of the activities of the corporation shall be the carrying on of propaganda, or otherwise attempting to influence legislation, and the corporation shall not participate in, or intervene in (including the publishing or distribution of statements) any political campaign on behalf of any candidate for public office. Notwithstanding any other provision of these articles, the corporation shall not carry on any other activities not permitted to be carried on (a) by a corporation exempt from federal income tax under Section 501(c)(3) of the Internal Revenue Code of 1954 (or the corresponding provision of any future U.S. Internal Revenue Law) or (b) by a corporation, contributions to which are deductible under Section 170(c)(2) of the Internal Revenue Code of 1954 (or the corresponding provision of any future U.S. Internal Revenue Law).

(If reference to federal law in articles of incorporation imposes a limitation that is invalid in your state, as in California, you may wish to substitute the following for the last sentence of the preceding paragraph: "Notwithstanding any other provision of these articles, this corporation shall not, except to an insubstantial degree, engage in any activities or exercise any powers that are not in furtherance of the purposes of this corporation.")

Sixth: Upon the dissolution of the corporation, the Board of Trustees shall, after paying or making provision for the payment of all the liabilities of the corporation, dispose of all the assets of the corporation exclusively for the purposes of the corporation in such manner, or to such organization or organizations organized and operated exclusively for charitable, educational, religious, or scientific purposes, as shall at the time qualify as an exempt organization or organizations under Section 501(c)(3) of the Internal Revenue Code of 1954 (or the corresponding provision of any future U.S. Internal Revenue Law), as the Board of Trustees shall determine. Any such assets not so disposed of shall be disposed of by the Court of Common Pleas of the county in which the principal office of the corporation is then located, exclusively for such purposes or to such organization or organizations, as said Court shall determine, which are organized and operated exclusively for such purposes.

In witness whereof, we have hereunto subscribed our names this _____ day of _____ , 19___.

_____

_____

_____

6 ▪ 8
THE RIGHT OPERATION

To be "operated" exclusively for one or more exempt purposes means to engage primarily or substantially in activities that accomplish the purposes qualifying as "exclusively charitable" within the meaning of Section 501(c)(3). In a 1945 decision, the Supreme Court stated a general rule that the presence of a single nonexempt purpose, if substantial in nature, will destroy the exemption regardless of the importance or number of truly exempt purposes. But in 1973 a public parking facility built and run by private businesses and professional people to attract shoppers to the center city was given charitable status. Why? A district court ruled that, although the business activity of the facility was similar to what others partake in for profit, it was carried on only because it was necessary for the attainment of a public end.

From similar case decisions, the trend seems to be that your organization can still meet the operational test if it operates a trade or business as a substantial part of its activities, so long as its primary purpose is a qualified exempt purpose and the trade or business it operates is substantially related to that primary purpose.

If a deficiency exists in your organization's operations that causes failure of the operational test, it cannot be cured by language in your governing instrument.

In essence, to meet the operational test, your organization is required to engage in activities that serve a public, rather than a private, interest. If your organization is not presently tax exempt, but would like to obtain exempt status, its charter must be amended at the beginning of the tax year for which the exemption is sought.

6 ▪ 9
MOTIVES

Which specific purposes are likely to be sustained as qualifying Section 501(c)(3) purposes?

1. An educational organization may be one in which the term "educational" includes much more than formal schooling. In its broad sense it refers to the instruction or training of an individual

for the purpose of improving or developing his capabilities and the instruction of the public on subjects useful to the individual and beneficial to the community.

Your difficulty here may be in establishing a distinction between an educational activity and a trade or business. For instance, in the world of commerce, operation of a restaurant, bookstore, radio station, or publishing company is a trade or business. However, such operations, when run by a university, may qualify as exempt educational organizations. In *American Institute for Economic Research* v. *United States* (1962), the court determined that the answer depends on whether the commercial purpose is primary or incidental to the exempt purpose.

Another important distinction to consider is the difference between "education" and "propaganda," the latter not being an exempt purpose. An educational organization can advocate a particular viewpoint so long as it presents a sufficiently full and fair exposition of the pertinent facts to permit a person or the public to form an independent opinion. But it cannot make mere presentations of unsupported opinion its principal function.

2. A religious organization may be a church, convention, or association of churches with duties that include the conduct of religious worship and the ministration of priestly-type functions. In practice, you will find that the courts are quite reluctant to pass on the question of what is a "church" for fear of impinging upon the guarantees of the First Amendment. Therefore, in *United States* v. *Kuch* (1968), the court was very careful in explaining its decision that the Neo-American Church was not "religious." Only because it was faced with an extreme factual setting could it make a distinction between religious activities and personal codes of conduct that lack spiritual import.

The Neo-American Church's main precept stated that since psychedelic substances were the "true Host of the Church," it was the religious duty of all members to partake of the sacraments on regular occasions. The church bishops were called "BooHoos"; its symbol was a three-eyed toad; it had official songs like "Puff, the Magic Dragon," a church key in the form of a bottle opener, and a catechism and handbook giving the members the right to practice their religion even if they were "a bunch of filthy, drunken bums."

The court based its decision on the absence of any "solid evidence of a belief in a supreme being, a religious discipline, a ritual, or tenets to guide one's daily existence."

More often than not, though, exemption will be denied to a religious group not on the basis of not being religious, but on other issues, such as allowing its net income to inure to the benefit of private individuals or conducting itself as an action organization.

3. A scientific organization, whether engaging in scientific research or disseminating scientific knowledge, must be able to show that it carries on either in the public interest. This means that one of the following applies.

- The results of such research (including copyrights, patents, processes, or formulas) are made available to the public on a nondiscriminatory basis.
- The research is directed toward benefiting the public.
- The research is conducted for the United States, any of its agencies or instrumentalities, or a state or political subdivision thereof.

4. A prevention of cruelty to children or animals organization either protects children from working in unfavorable working conditions or at hazardous occupations in violation of state law or tries to secure humane treatment of laboratory animals. The IRS will want a detailed description of its purposes and proposed activities.

5. Public safety testing organizations, which test consumer products to determine whether they are safe for use by the general public, have been given Section 501(c)(3) status by act of Congress. Therefore, an organization that tested boating equipment and set up safety standards for products used by the boating public was ruled exempt. However, this was not the case for an organization that clinically tested drugs for commercial pharmaceutical companies. The basis for denial was that the testing principally served the private interests of the manufacturer, and a drug is not a consumer product until approved for marketing by the Federal Drug Administration.

6. Amateur sports organizations that foster national or international amateur sports competition can be Section 501(c)(3) organi-

zations, so long as no part of their activities involves the provision of athletic equipment or facilities. The IRS will want a detailed description of your purposes and proposed activities.

7. Cooperative educational service organizations must be organized, controlled by, and comprised solely of members that have Section 501(c)(3) status or are a certain type of state educational institution. Their purpose must be to hold, commingle, and collectively invest and reinvest in stocks and securities, turning over all income, less expenses, to their members.

8. Cooperative hospital service organizations are charitable organizations that must both

- Be organized and operated solely for two or more exempt member hospitals on a cooperative basis.
- Perform only the services specified in Internal Revenue Code Section 501(e) on a centralized basis for their members—purchasing, warehousing, data processing, billing and collection, food, clinical, industrial engineering, communications, printing, laboratory, record center, and personnel (selection, training, testing, and education) services. In order to qualify, these services must constitute exempt activities if performed by a participating hospital on its own behalf.

6 ▪ 10
NEW KINDS OF CHARITIES

The purposes of organizations qualified for exemption under Section 501(c)(3) are not only numerous, but today more and more varied. Traditionally, a charitable organization has worked for the relief of poverty; the advancement of religion, education, and science; the promotion of health and social welfare; the lessening of the burdens of government; and the development of the arts. More recent charitable endeavors include the following:

1. Public-interest law firms that:
- Must be representative of a broad public interest (such as protection of the environment), not a private one.
- May accept fees for services rendered but only under IRS procedures. The IRS allows them to retain only up to 50 percent of fees awarded and still keep their tax-exempt status.

- Cannot sponsor a program of illegal activity, disruption of the judicial system, or violation of the canons of ethics.
- Must have boards or committees responsible for their programs and policies [not to include their employees, those who litigate on their behalf, or any organization that is not Section 501(c)(3)].
- Cannot operate to create identification or confusion with a particular private law firm.
- Must not make any type of arrangement to provide a deduction for the cost of litigation for the private benefit of a donor.

2. Local economic development corporations, whose primary purpose is to alleviate poverty through means not thought charitable until recently, such as investment in local business, business counseling, and encouragement of national businesses to open plants or offices in economically depressed areas.

3. Professional standards review organizations, which are qualified groups of doctors that set up mandatory cost and quality controls in connection with medical treatment given in hospitals, are financed under Medicare and Medicaid, and monitor such care.

This type of organization was conceived as part of a larger effort in the federal government to curb the rising costs of health care and generally to improve the quality of this country's medical care. The requirements of their statutory authorization are:

- They must be nonprofit and be reimbursed by the federal government for administrative costs.
- The members must be licensed practitioners of medicine or osteopathy.

Although promoting health and social welfare and lessening the burdens of government constitute charitable purposes and are characteristic of this type of organization, its status as a Section 501(c)(3) charitable organization had not been ruled on by the IRS as of this writing.

Wholly owned state or municipal government instrumentalities that are separate entities will qualify under Section 501(c)(3) if they are in fact "clear counterparts" of Section 501(c)(3) organizations. This in turn depends on whether their purposes and powers are within the scope of that section. If they have any enforcement or regulatory powers—even if they are in the public interest—they will not qualify.

Charitable U.S. organizations in foreign countries, while otherwise qualifying under Section 501(c)(3), carry on part or all of their charitable activities in foreign countries. They will still qualify if the beneficiaries of their assistance are outside the United States.

In this grouping we can include "friend" organizations, formed to solicit and receive contributions in the United States and to expend them on behalf of a charitable organization in another country. Typical kinds of support would be program or project grants, scholarship or fellowship grants, and provision of equipment or materials.

6 ▪ 11
SECTION 501(c)(2) TITLE HOLDERS

Section 501(c)(2) applies to title-holding companies organized exclusively to hold title to property, to collect income therefrom, and to turn over all the income (less expenses) to another tax-exempt organization. This means no accumulation of income by the title-holding company. However, the IRS has allowed it to retain some income each year to apply to any indebtedness on property it holds. The retention is treated as if the parent organization received income and made a capital contribution to the holding company.

If you wish to qualify as a title-holding company, your company must not only be a corporation, but it must also have a corporate charter that limits its activities to those described above. In addition, it must furnish evidence that the organization for which title is held does in fact have exempt status. Proof of such status would be a copy of a determination letter issued by the IRS.

6 ▪ 12
SOCIAL WELFARE UNDER SECTION 501(c)(4)

Section 501(c)(4) deals with social welfare organizations, such as civic leagues and volunteer fire companies. If your organization is not organized for profit and is operated exclusively for the promotion of social welfare through the betterment of the community as a whole, you can obtain recognition of exemption status under this section.

Your social welfare organization may be exempt under Section 501(c)(3) as a charitable type as long as it is not an "action" organization. However, if it takes on such activist endeavors as minority and civil rights or current social problems through legislative activities, it is likely to be considered an "action" group. As such, it will qualify instead under Section 501(c)(4); that is, if it does not involve itself in political campaigns.

Some of the legislative activities allowed are:

- Drafting of proposed legislation.
- Presentation of petitions for having legislation introduced.
- Circulation of material concerning legislation.
- Informing the public on controversial subjects even though it is advocating a particular viewpoint. This is because an informed citizenry is deemed by the IRS to be beneficial to the community.

For social welfare status, the IRS is very careful to distinguish between groups that actively participate in a political campaign for or against candidates (no matter how objectively) and those acceptable organizations that more passively try to stimulate public interest in improved government and better campaign practices.

Other general characteristics that a social welfare organization must have and regulations it must follow are:

- Its primary purpose must be to further the common good and general welfare of the people of the community by promoting civic betterment and social improvements. Furthermore, it should submit evidence with its application that it is organized exclusively for such purpose.
- It must be organized and operated on a nonprofit basis.
- It must not as its primary activity operate a social club for the benefit, pleasure, or recreation of its members.

Let us consider a couple of examples to illustrate the social welfare classification.

The IRS has said that a trust that was formed to provide group life insurance only for members of an association did not qualify as a social welfare organization. On the other hand, a consumer credit counseling service that helps families and individuals with financial problems was held to qualify, since its objective and activities contributed to the betterment of the community as a whole by checking the rising incidence of personal bankruptcy in the community.

It may be possible that your community (homeowners') association can qualify under Section 501(c)(4), if evidence can be provided that it serves all the residents of the community A community is defined as a geographical unit with a reasonably recognizable relationship to an area usually identified as a government subdivision or a district or unit thereof.

In addition, the community (homeowners') association must not engage in activities that are directed to the exterior maintenance of private residences; and use of the common areas it owns and maintains must be extended to the general public and not restricted to its members.

If your organization is one of those specifically described below, your application for exemption and accompanying statements should include the following information.

- For a volunteer fire company, evidence is needed to the effect that its members are actively engaged in fire fighting and other disaster assistance.
- For an organization devoted to crime prevention activities, evidence of a program of prevention and suppression of crime, such as encouraging the efficiency of a municipal police force, should be submitted.
- For an organization devoted to industrial development of a community, it can demonstrate its social welfare purpose by showing it has leased plant facilities to incoming industries primarily for the purpose of relieving unemployment in a chronically depressed area.

6 ▪ 13
THE BEST OF BOTH WORLDS

Although there are some similarities in the concepts of Section 501(c)(3) charitable organizations and social welfare organizations under Section 501(c)(4), there is a principal distinction between the two. Whereas the charitable organizations are prohibited from influencing legislation as a substantial part of their activities, social welfare groups (while not treated as strictly regarding legislative activities) cannot attract charitable contributions that are deductible for income, gift, and estate tax purposes. The only exceptions are donations to volunteer fire companies, as long as they are made for exclusively public purposes, and donations to social welfare groups organized to build a stadium and lease it to a school district, which eventually receives title.

What about your organization getting its cake and eating it too, by engaging in legislative activity under Section 501(c)(4) while attracting contributions as a Section 501(c)(3) organization? With some maneuvering the Section 501(c)(3) organization can spin off the legislative activity it desires into a separate organization that would qualify under Section 501(c)(4). By contrast, the Section 501(c)(4) entity can attract deductible charitable contributions for a particular purpose by making that purpose the subject of a separate organization that qualifies under Section 501(c)(3).

To ensure such separate tax treatment, care should be taken to organize and operate the two sister groups as independent and self-supporting entities, not to commingle funds, and not to have completely identical boards of directors and personnel. In addition, if the two share office space and some personnel, they should do so under an arrangement whereby one reimburses the other for an allocable portion of shared expenses. Your lawyer can create contractual evidence of separateness.

6 ▪ 14
ORGANIZATIONS UNDER SECTIONS 501(c)(5) AND 501(c)(6)

Section 501(c)(5) deals with organizations that qualify for exemption as labor, agricultural, or horticultural entities. To qualify, they must show that they will not allow their net earnings to inure to the benefit of any member.

If yours is a labor organization, it is an association of workers (usually in the form of a labor union, council, or group) organized to protect and promote the interests of members by bargaining collectively with their employers to secure better working conditions, wages, and similar benefits. Your articles of association or accompanying statements submitted with your exemption application should include information that establishes that your purpose is to carry on the normal functions of labor unions.

Exemption will not be denied if payment of sick, accident, death, and similar benefits to its individual members with funds contributed by its members is made with the objective of bettering the conditions of the members. On the other hand, exemption will be denied to a group controlled by private individuals that provides weekly income to its members in the event of a lawful strike by their union in return for an annual payment by the members.

The general political activity of labor unions has generated considerable controversy, but the courts seem to reject the idea that such activity under Section 501(c)(5) jeopardizes their exemption.

Agricultural and horticultural organizations and certain fisherman's groups (with activities ranging from raising livestock, forestry, harvesting crops, maintaining aquatic resources, and cultivating useful or ornamental plants) are designed to encourage the development of better products through a system of awards. They use income from gate receipts, entry fees, and donations to meet the necessary expenses of upkeep and operation. If yours is such an organization, your primary purpose must be shown in your application for exemption to relate to techniques of production, betterment of conditions of those engaged in agriculture or horticulture, improvement of the grade of products, or development of efficiency.

If, however, the activities are directed toward improvement of marketing or other business conditions, the organization must qualify as a business league or such under Section 501(c)(6). The activities that demonstrate such purposes are as follows:

- The exhibition of livestock, farm products, and the like.
- The promotion of various cooperative agricultural, horticultural, and civic activities among rural residents by a home bureau or a state and county farm.
- The guarding of the priority of a specific breed of livestock.
- The negotiation with processors for the price to be paid to members for their crops.
- The testing of soil and furnishing of the results to community members to educate them in soil treatment.

Conversely, exempt status will not be granted to an organization whose principal purpose is to provide a direct business service for its members' economic benefit.

Contributions to Section 501(c)(5) entities are not deductible as charitable contributions on a donor's federal income tax return. However, such payments may be deductible as business expenses, provided they are ordinary and necessary in the conduct of the donor's trade or business.

Section 501(c)(6) pertains to organizations formed as nonprofit business leagues, chambers of commerce, real-estate boards, or boards of trade. Applications for exemption for these organizations must show

- That your organization is not organized to make a profit or to engage in an activity ordinarily carried on for profit, and that no part of its net earnings will inure to the benefit of any private shareholder or individual.
- That it will be devoted to the improvement of business conditions of one or more lines of business (as opposed to the performance of particular services for individual members).
- That the conditions of a particular trade or the interests of the community will be advanced.
- That all the members of the organization have a common business interest.
- That membership is voluntary.

Examples of activities that illustrate a common business interest are:

- Promotion of the business community's interest by educating the public in the use of credit.
- Operation of a trade publication primarily for the benefit of an entire industry.
- Encouragement of the use of goods and services of an entire industry.
- Promotion of higher business standards and better business methods.
- Encouragement of uniformity and cooperation by a retail merchants' association.
- Provision of information and opinions to government agencies' efforts to influence legislation pertinent to the members' common business interests.
- Attraction of conventions to a city in the interest of the business economy throughout a community.

As with Section 501(c)(5) organizations, contributions are not deductible as charitable donations, but may be deductible as trade or business expenses if they are ordinary and necessary to the conduct of the taxpayer's business.

6 ▪ 15
SOCIAL CLUBS UNDER SECTION 501(c)(7)

Section 501(c)(7) is appropriate for a club organized substantially for pleasure, recreation, and other like nonprofitable purposes. Such a club is supported by membership fees, dues, and assessments, where there is no shifting of income in its operation. Typical social clubs are country clubs, sports clubs, garden clubs, dinner clubs, hobby clubs, variety clubs, and college sororities and fraternities operating chapter houses. Regulations that must be met for a social club to qualify are these:

- Only 15 percent of its total outside income can be used to provide outside services (facilities) to nonmembers.
- No more than 35 percent of its income can come from investments and outside services.
- Income cannot be received from the active conduct of any busi-

nesses not ordinarily carried on by these organizations within the 15 percent or 35 percent allowances.

- No part of the organization's net earnings may inure to the benefit of any individual with a personal interest in the organization's activities.
- The application should evidence that personal contact, commingling, and fellowship exist among the members (fellowship not being necessary between each member but in the sense of constituting a material part in the life of the organization). This means that a federation of clubs will not be exempt.

Those not exempt are clubs operated to help their members in their business endeavors through study and discussion of problems at weekly luncheon meetings. The social aspects in such a case are only incidental to the business purpose of the club. Nor would an automobile club qualify due to the commercial nature of services to its members.

How the tax exemption applies to social clubs is unique. Instead of being taxed on their unrelated business income, as is common with respect to other Section 501(c) organizations, the IRS isolates the exempt function income of social clubs and then taxes the balance of their income. "Exempt function income" is defined as gross income from dues, fees, charges, or similar amounts paid by members in connection with the purposes constituting the basis for a social club's exemption.

Note that a dividends-received deduction will not be allowed in computing the taxable income of the clubs.

Social clubs will be denied exemption if their charters, bylaws, governing instruments, or other written policy statements provide for discrimination against any individual on the basis of race, color, or religion, and they will lose their exemption if they:

- Engage in selling or leasing club property, products, or facilities to the public as a business.
- Lease property to members on a long-term basis.
- Sell property for the primary purpose of making a profit and distributing the proceeds to the members.

Since private inurement can disqualify a social club, a club should be very careful not to let nonmembers' use of facilities bring in too much revenue, resulting in a personal advantage to the members. This can be avoided by contributing such profits to charity. And dealing between a club and its members can add up to private inurement. Such would be the case for a club that regularly sells liquor to its members for consumption off the premises.

6 ▪ 16
FRATERNAL BENEFICIARY SOCIETIES UNDER SECTION 501(c)(8)

Section 501(c)(8) applies to fraternal beneficiary societies that operate either under the lodge system (defined as the carrying on of activities under an organizational form made up of local, largely self-governing branches chartered by a parent organization), or for the exclusive benefit of the members of a fraternity that itself operates under the lodge system. Necessary to their operation is the provision of life, accident, health, or other benefits to its members or their dependents. These insurance features must conform with state insurance law.

To qualify for exemption both the fraternal purposes and members' benefits must be shown to be present.

6 ▪ 17
EMPLOYEE BENEFITS UNDER SECTION 501(c)(9)

Section 501(c)(9) recognition as a voluntary employees' benefit association entails (a) being a voluntary association of employees; (b) providing for payment of life, health, accident, or other benefits to members, their dependents, or designated beneficiaries; and (c) not allowing any of its earnings to inure to the benefit of any private individual or shareholder except in the form of scheduled benefit payments.

Moreover, each year it must be established that no more than 10 percent of an association's total membership is composed of persons other than employees.

6 ▪ 18
DOMESTIC FRATERNAL SOCIETIES UNDER SECTION 501(c)(10)

Section 501(c)(10) requires an organization to

- Be a domestic fraternal type.
- Operate under the lodge system.
- Devote its net earnings exclusively to fraternal, charitable, or other such purposes.
- Provide for the payment of life, health, accident, or other benefits.

6 ▪ 19
ORGANIZATIONS UNDER SECTION 501(c)(12)

Section 501(c)(12), relating to benevolent life-insurance associations and mutual or cooperative telephone companies, requires that

- At least 85 percent of income be collected from association members for the sole purpose of meeting expenses and losses.
- These associations be organized and operated on a mutual or cooperative basis.
- All their income be used solely to cover losses and expenses (any excess to be returned to members or kept for future losses and expenses).

A cooperative telephone company meeting the 85 percent requirement will earn its exemption even if nonmembers pay a higher rate than members. If it fails to meet the 85 percent test but is classified under this section, it cannot qualify for exemption as any other Section 501(c) organization.

Of the various groups qualifying under this section, only the benevolent life-insurance associations and the like must have a purely local character: their business activities must be confined to a particular district or community.

6 ▪ 20
CEMETERY COMPANIES UNDER SECTION 501(c)(13)

Section 501(c)(13), pertaining to cemetery companies, requires that these companies not be operated for profit and that they be owned by and operated exclusively for the benefit of lot owners who hold their lots for actual burials, not for resale. They should also show that they are nonprofit and that their activities are to own cemeteries, sell lots therein, and maintain all lots in a state of repair and upkeep befitting a proper final resting place.

Since no part of net earnings can inure to the benefit of private individuals, the sale of flowers, markers, vaults, and monuments for use in the cemetery is allowed so long as any profits made are used to maintain the cemetery as a whole.

A perpetual care organization that receives, maintains, and administers funds it receives from a nonprofit tax-exempt cemetery will be exempt (even though it owns no land used for burial) if it devotes the income from such funds exclusively to the perpetual care and maintenance of the cemetery as a whole.

6 ▪ 21
MUTUAL INSURANCE COMPANIES UNDER SECTION 501(c)(15)

Section 501(c)(15) allows an exemption for mutual insurance companies that meet the following requirements:

- The gross amount received during the taxable year from gross investment income is not over $150,000.
- The only purpose is to supply insurance, substantially at cost.
- Policyholders can be members to the exclusion of others.

The rights of members include

- Choosing management.
- Receiving the return of premiums exceeding amounts needed to cover expenses and losses.
- Holding common equitable ownership.

6 ▪ 22
CROP FINANCING ORGANIZATIONS UNDER SECTION 501(c)(16)

Section 501(c)(16) permits exemption if a corporation is organized by a crop financing cooperative to finance ordinary crop operations of members or other producers as long as the cooperative itself is exempt. An exemption will be granted if all the following conditions are met.

- The corporation accumulates a required or reasonable reserve.
- The dividend rate of the capital stock of the corporation is limited to the legal interest rate of the state of incorporation or 8 percent per annum, whichever is greater.
- Most of the stock is owned by the association or its members.

6 ▪ 23
UNEMPLOYMENT COMPENSATION TRUSTS UNDER SECTION 501(c)(17)

Section 501(c)(17), dealing with a trust or trusts forming part of a plan providing for payment of supplemental unemployment compensation benefits, requires a conformed copy of such plan to be attached to the application. The types of benefits allowed are those paid to an employee because of the employees' involuntary separation from employment (even if temporary) resulting directly from a reduction in force, discontinuance of a plant or operation, or other such conditions and those of sickness and accident that are subordinate to the unemployment compensation benefits.

Neither the corpus nor the income of the trust may be diverted to any other purpose. Moreover, neither the terms of the plan nor the actual benefit payments may discriminate in favor of the company's officers, stockholders, supervisors, or highly paid employees.

6 ▪ 24
WAR VETERANS' ORGANIZATIONS UNDER SECTION 501(c)(19)

Section 501(c)(19), pertaining to war veterans' organizations (including an auxiliary unit or society thereof and a trust or foundation established for it), allows an exemption if the following is true:

- Seventy-five percent of the membership are in fact war veterans.
- Ninety-seven and a half percent of the members are present or past members of the armed services, war veterans, cadets, and spouses, widowers, or widows of any of the above.
- The post or organization was organized in the United States or in any of its possessions.
- No part of its net earnings inures to the benefit of any private individual.

These organizations must be operated exclusively for such purposes as:

- Helping any of the above-mentioned persons.
- Providing care, assistance, and entertainment to hospitalized service members or veterans.
- Promoting the social welfare of the community, and conducting programs for charitable, religious, and similar purposes.
- Sponsoring patriotic-type activities.
- Providing recreational and social activities for their members, and insurance benefits for their members and dependents.

6 ▪ 25
LEGAL SERVICES ORGANIZATIONS UNDER SECTION 501(c)(20)

Section 501(c)(20) deals with group legal services plans and provides exemption only for tax years ending before Jan. 1, 1982. A separate written plan of an employer must be for the exclusive benefit of the employees, their spouses, or dependents. It gives them specified benefits consisting of personal legal services either through prepayment of, or through provision in advance for, legal fees in whole or in part by the employer.

6 ▪ 26
THE OTHER 501'S

Section 501(d) covers religious or apostolic associations and corporations not otherwise exempt under Section 501(c) and actively engaging in business. To be granted exemption, they must maintain a common treasury and their members must reap a common benefit from the business operation. Each individual member must include in his gross income on his tax return his entire pro rata share of the organization's net income, whether or not that share is distributed. The IRS will treat this amount as a dividend received. A return must also be filed by the exempt organization showing its gross income, receipts, disbursements, and other pertinent information.

Section 501(e) covers cooperative hospital service organizations. They must be organized and operated on a cooperative basis for two or more exempt member hospitals. To qualify, they must perform services that would qualify as exempt activities if performed by a participating hospital on its own behalf.

Section 501(f) covers cooperative educational service organizations. These must be composed only of state educational institutions or educational groups under Section 501(c)(3) and operated for the purpose of investing commingled funds contributed by the member organizations in stocks and securities. All the income therefrom, less expenses, must be turned over to the organization's members.

6 ▪ 27
GAINING YOUR EXEMPTION

These are the steps to tax exemption:

1. Your organization must file an Application for Recognition (of exemption) with its IRS district director. Section 501(c)(3) types must file Form 1023. Other Section 501's file Form 1024.

2. Until your application is approved you must file regular income tax returns and pay the taxes due. When you become exempt you can file a refund claim. You will then be refunded all taxes paid from the time your organization was organized.

3. But you must give notice to the IRS that you have applied for recognition of exempt status. If no notice is given, the IRS will not consider your organization exempt prior to filing and no taxes will be refunded. While the application is pending you must file a Form 990, the principal information return for exempt organizations. You must indicate that you are filing this in belief that your organization is exempt and will be approved as exempt.

4. A ruling or determination letter will be issued by the IRS declaring your organization exempt. In some instances, it is possible to receive a letter or ruling approving exemption even before your organization begins operating. This can be done if the proposed activities of the organization can be described in sufficient detail to allow the IRS to determine that it meets the requirements of the Internal Revenue Code section under which it is claiming the exemption. Just a statement that your organization will operate in furtherance of its purposes will not do the trick. Instead, the activities in which it expects to engage must be described fully. This means the following information should be included:

- The standards, procedures, or other means planned for carrying out its activities.
- Its expected sources of funds, which should include an explanation as to whether they are from public or private sources; the nature of the support—such as grants or contributions; and the nature of the venture or revenue-producing enterprise if income is anticipated to come from fund-raising events, rentals, ticket sales, or other business or investment sources.
- The nature of the organization's contemplated expenditures. If they are for the furtherance of purposes, as opposed to administrative and general operating expenses, an explanation should be included as to how the receipts will be selected.

6 · 28
HOW LONG DOES ALL THIS TAKE?

The effective date of exemption varies according to the circumstances or conditions.

If your organization's activities are those required by statute from the date of formation until the time a ruling or determination letter is issued by the IRS, the effective date will be the date the organization was formed. Until a ruling or determination letter is received, be sure to file a tax return on Form 990. On this form indicate that you believe your organization to be exempt under Section 501(a) of the Internal Revenue Code, but that the IRS has not as yet recognized the exemption.

If your organization must substantially amend its charter or change its activities in order to qualify, its exemption will become effective only as the IRS ruling or determination directs.

Section 501(c)(3) organizations may have fifteen months from the end of the month during which they were formed to file Form 1023 and still receive retroactive tax-exempt treatment. If an application is received later than this, exemption will be recognized only from the date on which the application is received.

6 ▪ 29
WHO NEED NOT FILE?

Excluded from this filing requirement are:

1. Churches, interchurch organizations of local units of a church, conventions or associations of churches, or integrated auxiliaries of women's or men's organizations.
2. Any subordinate organizations (other than private foundations) covered by a group exemption letter.
3. Any other class of organization that the commissioner from time to time excludes from this requirement.
4. Any organization not a private foundation having annual gross receipts normally of not more than $5,000. Your organization will meet this test if during your first tax year the gross receipts were $7,500 or less; during its first two years it had a total of $12,000 or less in gross receipts; or having been in existence at least three years, the total gross receipts during the immediately preceding two years, plus the current year, are $15,000 or less.
5. Certain nonexempt charitable trusts.

6 ▪ 30
LOOKING INSIDE THE APPLICATION

If your organization must file, the Application for Recognition is one of the most important documents in the process. To be effective it must include these statements demonstrating the intent of your organization:

▪ The organization is organized and operated not for the benefit of private interests but exclusively for one or more of the purposes qualifying under its appropriate section.

- No part of its net earnings will inure to the benefit of private shareholders or individuals.
- It will not attempt to influence legislation as a substantial part of its activities (unless it elects to come under the provisions that allow for certain lobbying expenditures) or participate to any extent in a political campaign for or against any candidate for public office.

Each application for exemption must:

- Be filed with the district director for the key district in which the organization's principal office is located.
- Be signed by either a principal officer, an employee specifically authorized to sign, or an agent or attorney specifically appointed to sign with a power of attorney. If the application is filed on behalf of a trust, the trustee authorized to act must sign.

Each Application for Recognition must be accompanied by

- The organization's enabling instrument and its bylaws.
- A classified statement of receipts and expenditures, and a balance sheet for the current year and the three immediate prior years, or, if less, the years of its existence.
- A statement of proposed activities and purposes.
- If its name has been officially changed by amendment of its enabling instrument, a conformed copy of such amendment.
- A completed Form SS-4, Application for Employer Identification Number (if your organization does not already have such a number), since every exempt organization must have an employer identification number (even if it has no employees).
- Any additional information necessary to clarify the nature of the organization, such as copies of publications, advertising placed, distributed written material regarding proposed legislation, and copies of contracts, leases, or agreements into which the organization has entered.

Every attachment to the application should show the name and address of the organization, the date, an identifiable heading, and that it is in fact an attachment to the application form. In unusual situations, additional attachments must be included with the applications. For example, if your organization issues capital stock, you should provide the following additional information:

- The class or classes of stock.
- The number and par value of shares.
- The consideration for which it was issued.
- Whether your certificate of organization authorized dividends on any class of stock.
- Whether any dividends have been paid.
- A copy of the stock certificate.

If your organization expends any of its funds in a foreign country, you must attach a statement to your application for recognition that includes:

- How and by whom recipients are or will be selected.
- Names of recipients and purposes for which the funds are or will be spent.
- How much control your organization has or will have over the expenditure of the funds donated and whether there is, or will be, any required reporting of these expenditures to your organization.
- What contributions are, or will be, solicited by your organization and earmarked for specific foreign distributees.

6 ▪ 31
IF THE IRS TURNS YOU DOWN

There is a process for appeal if an adverse determination letter or ruling is issued. Such an appeal is filed at the key district office, then normally goes to the regional office for a decision. However, it can go as high as the national office, if that office accepts it for consideration. You will be given thirty days in which to make your appeal from an adverse ruling notification from the district office and, if applicable, from the regional office. If no appeal is filed within that period, the adverse ruling will become final.

The appeal process is not the only road open to your organization for remedying controversies. Once it has exhausted all the administrative remedies available to it or 270 days have passed since it asked for a determination of the issue in question, it can file a petition for declaratory judgment with the U.S. Tax Court or U.S. Court of Claims. But this only applies to adverse determinations regarding Section 501(c)(3) organizations and others to which contributions can be made and those that are not private foundations or private operating foundations.

Procedural limitations also apply to a petition for declaratory judgment. The petition must be filed by the organization whose exemption or classification as a private foundation is at issue, and it must be filed within ninety days after the date the IRS has sent a notice of its determination by certified mail.

6 ▪ 32
KEEP ON FILING

It is necessary for exempt organizations to file an annual information return (again on Form 990 or 990-PF for private foundations) once exempt status has been established. The filing must be done by the fifteenth day of the fifth month after the close of your organization's accounting period. If it is not, your exemption will be lost. For exceptions to those needing to file, check IRS Publication 557.

A $10 a day fine will be charged for each day a private foundation is late in filing (not to exceed $5,000) unless it can be shown that the failure to file was for reasonable cause. If a private foundation has assets of at least $5,000 at any time during the tax year, it must also file an annual report on Form 990-AR. Remember, this is in addition to, not in lieu of, Form 990-PF.

6 ▪ 33
IF YOU'VE GOT A SECRET

An approved application for recognition of exemption, along with any supporting papers submitted, will be available for public inspection. If it happens that any of the information submitted relates to a trade secret, patent, style of work, process, or apparatus, you may make a request to the commissioner that such information be withheld from public inspection.

6 ▪ 34
OTHER TAX BENEFITS

All kinds of nonprofit organizations are eligible for extraordinary tax treatment outside the 501 umbrella:

1. *Feeder organizations.* Feeder organizations are independent organizations that as their primary purpose operate a trade or business for profit and are denied exemption even though all their profits go to organizations exempt in themselves. But there are exceptions:

- When the operation is the rental of real property and personal property rented with it (with certain limitations).
- When substantially all the work of the business is done for the exempt organization without compensation.
- When the operation of the business is to sell merchandise received as donations by an exempt organization.

As for subsidiaries of tax-exempt organizations, they themselves will be exempt if they carry on activities considered exempt when performed by their parent organizations.

2. *Farmers' cooperatives.* Section 521 exempts farmers', fruit growers', or like associations organized and operated on a cooperative basis for the purpose of marketing products of members or other producers and returning to them the proceeds of sales, less the necessary marketing expenses, on the basis of either the quantity or value of products furnished by them or purchasing supplies and equipment at actual cost plus necessary expenses.

3. *Shipowners' protection and indemnity associations.* Section 526 exempts receipts of shipowners' mutual protection and indemnity associations not organized for profit, no part of the net earnings of which inures to the benefit of any private shareholder. They are subject to tax on their taxable income from interest, dividends, and rents.

4. *Political organizations.* Section 527 controls political organizations, including party, committee, association, fund, or other organizations organized and operated primarily for the purpose of directly or indirectly accepting contributions or making expendi-

tures, or both, for an "exempt function." An "exempt function" is a function of influencing or attempting to influence the selection, nomination, election, or appointment of any individual to any federal, state, or local public office or office in a political organization, or election of presidential or vice-presidential electors.

Political organizations are subject to regular corporate tax on their "taxable income," which is their gross income, less "exempt function income" and direct expenses, subject to certain modifications. "Exempt function income" means:

- Contributions of money or other property.
- Membership dues or fees or assessments from a member of the organization.
- Proceeds from a political fund-raising or entertainment event.
- Proceeds from the sale of political campaign materials (not received in the ordinary course of any trade or business) to the extent such an amount is segregated for use only for an exempt function of a political organization.

Any Section 501(c) organization that expends any amount during a tax year for a political organization's exempt function must include in its gross income for the year an amount equal to the lesser of its net investment income for the year or the aggregate amount so expended during the year for the function.

An unincorporated campaign committee is not exempt from federal income taxation and must file tax returns showing as gross income the interest, dividends, and net gains from the sale of securities and related deductions.

5. *Homeowners' associations.* Section 528 deals with homeowners' associations that are formed as part of the development of a real-estate subdivision, condominium project, or cooperative housing project, and enable their members (individual homeowners and the like) to act together in managing, maintaining, and improving the areas in which they live. The purposes of such associations are:

- Administration and enforcement of covenants for preserving the physical appearance of the development.
- Ownership and management of common areas.
- Exterior maintenance of property owned by members.

The exemption is elective for condominium management and residential real-estate associations. Only "exempt function income" (any amount received as membership dues, fees, or assessments from association's members) escapes taxation.

To qualify:

- The association must be organized and operated to provide for the acquisition, construction, management, maintenance, and care of association property.
- At least 60 percent of the association's gross income for a tax year must consist of exempt function income.
- At least 90 percent of the annual expenditures of the association must be to acquire, construct, manage, maintain, and care for or improve its property.
- No part of its net earnings inures to the benefit of any private shareholder or individual.
- Substantially all the dwelling units in the project, subdivision, or the like must be used as residences.

Activities not constituting private inurement are:

- Acquiring, constructing, or providing management, maintenance, and care of association property.
- Rebating excess membership dues, fees, or assessments.

Taxable income includes payments by nonmembers for use of the association's facilities, subject to a specific $100 deduction and deductions directly connected with the production of gross income (other than exempt function income).

Note that this exemption is not allowed for cooperative housing corporations under Section 216(c). Instead, they get a deduction for depreciation with respect to property leased to a tenant-stockholder even though the tenant-stockholder may be entitled to depreciate his stock in the corporation, to the extent that the stock is related to a proprietary lease or right of tenancy that is used by the tenant-stockholder in a trade or business or for the production of income.

6. *States, political subdivisions, and instrumentalities.* Section 115 exempts entities that exercise an "essential government function" when the income thereby generated accrues to a state or political subdivision thereof.

This tax exemption is the result of the docrine of intergovernmental immunity (not any Internal Revenue Code provision)—a doctrine implicit in the U.S. Constitution that the federal government will not tax the states. The general principle is that the United States cannot tax instrumentalities that a state may employ in the discharge of its essential government duties.

This tax exemption also extends to integral parts thereof, like instrumentalities, agencies, and political subdivisions, the District of Columbia, and any territory.

6 ▪ 35
THE FEDERAL SUBSIDY

Tax exemption and privilege are the motivation behind many nonprofit organizations and the reasons that still others can survive and fulfill their benevolent purposes. Comply with the rigorous rules our legal system has intricately developed, and your organization may gain and preserve this lifeblood.

7
Unrelated
Business
Taxable Income

7 ▪ 1
TAXING THE TAX-EXEMPTS

Your tax-exempt organization, even if it follows all the stringent requirements of the Internal Revenue Code, may not escape federal taxation altogether. All tax-exempt organizations—except for government instrumentalities, certain religious and apostolic organizations, farmers' cooperatives, and shipowners' protection and indemnity associations—must file Form 990-T with the IRS and pay the tax due on income from any trade or business or debt-financed income unrelated to the purposes entitling them to exemption, if they've earned $1,000 or more of such income during the course of a year.

Before income earned by your organization is treated as an "unrelated" trade or business income, four tests must be met.

1. The income must come from an activity that is a trade or business.

2. The trade or business must be regularly carried on by your organization.

3. The conduct of the trade or business must not be substantially related to the achievement of your organization's tax-exempt purposes (other than providing funds to carry out those purposes). The use of any income generated by an activity of an exempt organization is irrelevant to a decision as to whether the activity constitutes a related or unrelated activity. In addition, the issue of relatedness in no way is affected by whether or not the activity is profitable.

4. The trade or business must be conducted regularly. A business activity is considered to be carried on regularly by your organization if, for instance, it conducts the activity one day each week on a year-round basis. Conversely, a sandwich stand operated by a hospital auxiliary for only two weeks at a state fair would not be such a trade or business, nor would an occasional dance given by a charitable organization to which the public is admitted for a charge. To be carried on regularly, an activity must demonstrate both frequency and continuity and must be pursued in a manner similar to comparable commercial activities of nonexempt organizations.

7 ▪ 2
WHEN IS BUSINESS "RELATED"?

Whether or not a trade or business activity is substantially related to your organization's exempt purpose is rarely clear-cut. Such decisions are necessarily made on a case-by-case basis: What is your organization's real purpose? What is it trying to accomplish and does the activity in question contribute importantly to the accomplishment of its exempt purpose?

To determine whether it contributes importantly, you should consider the size and extent of the activity in relation to the nature and extent of the exempt function the activity intends to serve. If it is being conducted on a scale larger than necessary, the gross income attributable to that portion in excess of the needs of the exempt function is income from an unrelated trade or business.

Let's reduce the theory to specifics.

A halfway house organized to provide room, board, therapy, and counseling for persons discharged from alcoholic treatment centers that operates a furniture store to give full-time employment to its residents and applies the profits to the operating costs of the halfway house will not be subject to the unrelated business income tax.

An exempt organization organized and operated for the prevention of cruelty to animals will be subject to the unrelated business tax on income it derives from providing pet boarding and grooming services for the general public.

An agricultural organization whose primary purpose is to promote better conditions for cattle breeders and to improve the breed generally will engage in an unrelated trade or business if it regularly sells cattle to its members on a commission basis.

An exempt hospital that leases its adjacent office building and furnishes certain office services to a hospital-based medical group for a fee will not be engaging in an unrelated trade or business.

What generalizations can we make? Few indeed. But we do know that these are some of the more important activities excluded from the definition of unrelated trade or business and therefore outside the tax's application:

1. A business in which substantially all of the work is performed without pay, such as an orphanage operating a second-hand clothing store with volunteers.

2. A trade or business conducted by charitable, religious, or educational organizations, universities, and state colleges primarily for the convenience of their members, officers, employees, patients, or students, such as a restaurant or a laundry run by a college to launder dormitory linen and students' clothing.

3. The selling of merchandise substantially all of which has been received as gifts or contributions, such as thrift shops.

4. Public entertainment activities at fairs and expositions conducted by nonprofit charitable, social welfare, labor, agricultural, and horticultural organizations that regularly conduct, as a substantial exempt purpose, both an agricultural and educational fair or exposition if one of the following requirements is met:

- The activity is conducted in conjunction with an international, national, or local fair or exposition.
- The activity is carried out under a state law that allows it to be conducted only by that type of exempt organization or by a government entity.
- The activity is conducted under a state law that allows it to be held for not more than twenty days a year and allows the organization to pay a lower percentage of the revenue from such activity than is required from other organizations.

5. Convention and trade show activities applying to labor, agricultural, and horticultural organizations and business leagues that regularly conduct shows as a substantial exempt purpose, if all the following requirements are met:

- The activity is conducted in conjunction with an international, national, state, regional, or local convention or show.
- There is promotion and stimulation of interest in and demand for the industry's products and services in general.
- The show is designed to promote that purpose through the nature of the exhibits and the extent to which the industry's products are displayed.

6. Hospital services provided by a tax-exempt hospital to other exempt hospitals if:

- The services are consistent with the recipient hospital's exempt purposes.
- The recipient hospital's facilities serve no more than 100 inpatients.
- The services are at a cost not to exceed their actual cost (which can include straight-line depreciation and a reasonable amount for return of capital goods used to provide such services).

7 ▪ 3
SOME SPECIAL CASES

Perhaps your unrelated business income falls under a special rule. Income from a regularly carried on activity that is an integral part of a larger endeavor in furtherance of an exempt purpose will be taxed as unrelated business income if the activity is the soliciting, selling, or publishing of commercial advertising. Such income is taxable to the extent that it exceeds expenses directly related to the advertising. However, if the editorial portion of the publication is carried on at a loss, the loss may be offset against the advertising income from the publication. To help you determine whether such advertising endeavors are to be considered as carried on regularly, here are some examples:

- The sale of advertising by volunteers of an exempt organization that raises funds for an exempt symphony orchestra and publishes an annual concert book distributed at the orchestra's annual charity ball is not a regularly carried on activity.
- Conversely, the sale of advertising over a four-month period by paid employees of an exempt organization that raises funds for the exempt symphony orchestra and publishes a weekly concert program distributed free at symphony performances is a regularly carried on business.

Income from a commercial activity that makes use of a facility necessary to the conduct of an exempt function or that has exploited the goodwill and other intangibles resulting from an exempt activity will be considered gross income from an unrelated trade or business unless the commercial activity itself contributes importantly to the accomplishment of an exempt purpose.

The unrelated business income of churches is taxable, except for religious orders and the schools run by them receiving income from a trade or business carried on before May 27, 1959, under a license issued by a federal regulatory agency, if less than 10 percent of the income is used annually for unrelated purposes.

If the source of a title-holding company's income is related to the exempt functions of the organization receiving its income, that income will not be subject to the unrelated business income tax if both the holding company and the exempt payee organization file a consolidated return. Keep in mind, though, that the title-holding company will be subject to the tax if one of its parent organizations is subject to the tax.

Social clubs are taxed for unrelated business income on all of their gross income (less deductions) except their exempt function income. Thus, they are taxed on their investment income but not on fees, dues, charges, and the like paid by club members for club facilities and services rendered to them, their dependents or guests, or investment income set aside for charitable, religious, or educational purposes.

Voluntary employee benefit associations receive the same tax treatment as social clubs with an additional exclusion: investment income can be set aside to provide for payment of life, sickness, accident, or other benefits.

Insurance income of veterans' organizations will not be subject to the tax if income set aside for life, accident, or health benefits is actually used for benefits, charitable purposes, or administration costs.

A tax-exempt foreign organization will pay a tax on unrelated business income if the income is derived from sources within the United States, although not effectively connected with the conduct of a trade or business within the United States, or the income is effectively connected with the conduct of a trade or business within the United States, whether or not such income is derived from sources within the United States.

7 ▪ 4
DEBT-FINANCED PROPERTY

Unrelated business income includes a part of the income from property acquired through debt financing. Such debt-financed property is property such as corporate stock, rental real estate, and tangible personal property that is financed by debt at any time during the tax year and held by an exempt organization to produce income (rents, royalties, dividends, and interest), rather than for its exempt purposes.

For example, real estate acquired through the assumption of outstanding mortgages on them by an exempt organization whose purpose is to preserve, restore, and exhibit buildings of historical or architectural significance will constitute debt-financed property when they are leased at fair rental value for uses bearing no relationship to the buildings' historical or architectural significance and will not accommodate viewing by the general public.

The rules governing unrelated business income provide that if your exempt organization has income from debt-financed property the use of which is unrelated to an exempt purpose, such unrelated debt-financed income must be treated as unrelated business income subject to tax in the same proportion as the property continues to be financed by the debt. Thus, if a business property is acquired and the purchase price is subject to an 80 percent mortgage, then 80 percent of the income and deductions generally must be taken into account in computing unrelated business taxable income. Further, if a capital gain is later realized from the sale of such debt-financed property, it is taxed in the same proportion.

But take solace. Property will not be treated as debt financed in the following cases:

1. Property when at least 85 percent of its use is related to an organization's exempt purposes. Consider the case of a medical clinic leased by an exempt hospital to an unincorporated association of physicians and surgeons. The lessee agreed to use the space to provide all the hospital's outpatient medical and surgical services and to train all the hospital's interns and residents—purposes substantially related to the lessor's exempt purposes. The rents received are not unrelated debt-financed income.

Bear in mind that related use does not include the organization's need for income or funds or the use it makes of the profits derived. And if the organization devotes less than 85 percent of the use of the property to its exempt purposes, only the portion actually used to further the exempt purposes will avoid debt-financed property treatment.

2. Property to the extent that its income is already subject to tax as income from the carrying on of an unrelated trade or business, such as rents from personal property and passive income from controlled organizations. However, if there is any gain on the disposition of the property that is not included in income from an unrelated trade or business, that gain is includable as gross income derived from debt-financed property.

3. Property owned by an exempt organization to the extent that it is used by related exempt organizations in furtherance of their

exempt purposes. An exempt organization is related to another when:

- One is an exempt holding company and the other receives profits from it.
- One has (at least 80 percent) control of the other.
- More than 50 percent of the members of one are members of the other.
- Each is a local organization directly affiliated with a common state, national, or international organization that is also exempt.

4. Property to the extent that its income is derived from its use in a trade or business exempt from unrelated business taxable income because it deals with research activities, is carried on by unpaid volunteers, is carried on primarily for the convenience of its members, patients, students, officers, or employees, or sells only donated merchandise.

5. Property that comes under the "neighborhood land rule," whereby the income from it is exempt from the debt-financed property rules in the following situations:

- When newly acquired land in the neighborhood of other land owned by an exempt organization will be used by the organization for some exempt purpose within ten years of its acquisition. Neighborhood property is that which is contiguous to the exempt-purpose property or within one mile of it.
- When church-owned land is used by the church for an exempt purpose within fifteen years after acquisition regardless of whether or not the land is in the neighborhood of other church property.

If income-producing property is debt-financed property only when there is an acquisition indebtedness attributable to it, just what is acquisition indebtedness? With respect to debt-financed property, it means the unpaid amount of:

- Any indebtedness incurred by your organization in acquiring or improving property.
- Any indebtedness incurred before or after such acquisition or im-

provement that would not have been incurred except for the acquisition or improvement. If incurred afterward, the indebtedness must have been reasonably foreseeable at the time of the acquisition or improvement, as determined by the facts and circumstances of each situation.

Note these points about acquisition:

1. Where property is acquired subject to a mortgage, the mortgage is acquisition indebtedness even if your organization does not assume it or agree to pay the indebtedness. An exception to this involves mortgaged property received from a bequest, devise, or gift. Such indebtedness will not be treated as acquisition indebtedness during the ten-year period that follows the date the property is received.

2. Acquisition indebtedness will not arise out of a refinancing, renewal, or extension of an existing debt (which includes any modification or substitution of terms of an obligation) to the extent the outstanding principal amount is not increased. If the principal amount of a modified obligation should exceed the outstanding principal amount of the preexisting indebtedness, the excess will be treated as a separate indebtedness.

3. An obligation insured by the Federal Housing Administration to finance the purchase, construction, or rehabilitation of low- or moderate-income housing and an obligation to make certain annuity payments are also excepted from acquisition indebtedness.

In computing unrelated debt-financed net (taxable) income, apply the following fraction to your total gross income and to the deductions attributable to the property:

$$\frac{\text{Average acquisition indebtedness for the tax year}}{\text{Average adjusted basis of property for the time held in tax year}}$$

The same percentage is generally used to find the allowable portion of the deductions directly connected with the property or its income. When only a portion of property is debt financed, you must allocate its basis, income, indebtedness, and deductions properly to determine how much income or gain is debt financed.

7 ▪ 5
SPECIAL OFFSETS

Unrelated business taxable income is computed much the same as the taxable income of a taxable entity, but with these exceptions and limitations:

1. Dividends, interest, and annuities are excluded.

2. Royalties, whether measured by production or by gross or net income from property, are excluded.

3. Rents from real property generally and from personal property leased with real property, if such rents are no more than 10 percent of the total rents from all leased property, are excluded. If rent attributable to personal property is over 50 percent of the total rent, none of the rent is excluded. Not included in this exclusion are rents involving the rendering of personal services, such as hotel room rentals.

4. Capital gains and losses from the sale, exchange, or other disposition of property are excluded except for inventory and property held primarily for sale to customers in the ordinary course of business.

5. Income is excluded from research grants or contracts conducted:

- For state and local governments and the United States, its agencies, and instrumentalities.
- By hospitals, colleges, or universities.
- By a research organization that makes the results freely available to the general public.

The extent of the exclusion depends on the nature of the organization and the type of research conducted.

6. All income from labor, agricultural, or horticultural organizations, if the income is used to establish, maintain, or operate a hospital, retirement home, or the like for the exclusive benefit and use of the aged and infirm members of the organization, is excluded.

7. A special deduction of $1,000 is allowed in computing unrelated business taxable income, regardless of the number of unrelated businesses in which an organization is engaged. This is true except in the case of a diocese, religious order, or convention of

churches that may claim the $1,000 deduction or the gross income derived from an unrelated trade or business, whichever is less. If a local unit of such files its own separate tax return, it gets the deduction rather than the national body.

8. A charitable contributions deduction is allowed for organizations taxed at corporate rates, up to 5 percent of the corporation's unrelated business taxable income. Any excess may be carried over to the next five taxable years. A trust is also allowed such a deduction but in the same amounts as allowed for individuals.

9. A net operating loss deduction is allowed in computing unrelated business taxable income, but any carryback or carryover is permitted only from a tax year for which an organization is subject to the tax.

7 ▪ 6
SOME SPECIAL SITUATIONS

A special rule applies to controlled organizations, those in which at least 80 percent of the directors or trustees of the organization are either representatives of, or directly or indirectly controlled by, the controlling organization (or at least 80 percent of the stock is controlled, in the case of a stock organization). By this rule, any interest, rents, royalties, and annuities (so-called "passive" income) received by an exempt controlling organization from an 80 percent controlled subsidiary are taxed as unrelated business taxable income. If control is gained or lost during the tax year, the controlling organization will be taxed only for that part of the tax year it has control.

In a similar vein, suppose that your organization is a subsidiary of a tax-exempt parent organization and it operates a trade or business. Since an organization primarily operating for the purpose of carrying on a business or trade for profit is not tax exempt, even a feeder organization that turns its income over to an exempt organization is not exempt if it is operated for the primary purpose of carrying on a trade or business that would be considered unrelated if regularly carried on by the parent.

If the feeder organization cannot prove that it is nonoperating, its entire income will be taxable. On the other hand, if the organization can prove that its activities are an integral part of the parent's activities and that its carrying on of a trade or business is not its primary function, the organization may be exempt and the income from such trade or business will be taxed as unrelated business income.

7 ▪ 7
PAYING YOUR TAX

All organizations subject to this tax are taxed at corporate rates, except for trusts. Exempt trusts are taxable at trust rates, and the deduction normally allowed for a personal exemption cannot be claimed. Whereas corporations subject to unrelated business income tax must file their income tax returns (Form 990-T) on or before the fifteenth day of the third month following the close of the tax year, trusts must file on or before the fifteenth day of the fourth month, and foreign organizations with no place of business in the United States must file on or before the fifteenth day of the sixth month.

Be aware that your organization may also be subject to a minimum 15 percent tax if it has both unrelated business income and items of tax preference, including gain on the sale of debt-financed property. Tax preference items are taxed at a flat 15 percent rate after deducting the greater of a $10,000 exemption or the regular tax deduction, defined in Section 56(c) of the Internal Revenue Code. For purposes of the minimum tax, only income and deduction items enter into the determination of unrelated business taxable income. Form 4624, which lists tax preference items, must be attached to your organization's income tax return.

7 ▪ 8
TAX CREDITS

Before you sign that check, your organization may be able to take advantage of certain tax credits available to those filing Form 990-T. The limitations on the credit are computed on the basis of your unrelated business taxable income. These tax credits—dollar-for-dollar reductions in your tax liability—are available:

- A credit equal to 20 percent of salaries and wages paid or incurred in an unrelated trade or business for employees hired under a work incentive program.
- A 10 percent investment credit for qualified property that must be used predominantly in an unrelated trade or business placed in service during the year.
- A credit for tax on special fuels and other taxes described in Form 990-T.

7 ▪ 9
PROTECTING YOURSELF

The congressional motive behind taxing unrelated business income is self-evident. To do otherwise would grant an unfair competitive advantage to a commercial enterprise only because it happens to be conducted by an organization whose other purposes may be altruistic. It also would inequitably deprive the treasury's coffers of their just extraction.

Yet the line separating related and unrelated commercial activities is imperceptibly thin. Before crossing it unwittingly, seek out legal counsel and plan your income-generating activities with a sensitive awareness of these sticky principles.

8
Other Benefits

8 ▪ 1
STATE EXEMPTIONS

Federal tax exemption is only one of many privileges probably available to your nonprofit organization. For one, a federal exemption invariably triggers all these state exemptions:

1. *Organization taxes* (also called incorporation fees or initial fees). These are imposed on a corporation before it can begin operation within a state. Since the amount of the tax is usually determined by the value of the organization's capital stock (upon which dividends may be paid), your nonprofit organization can usually escape such fees or taxes, as it would be uncommon for it to issue such stock. Remember that these are not filing fees, owed for the filing of a certificate of incorporation with the secretary of state. If your organization is a corporation, it will be necessary to pay such a filing fee.

2. *Franchise tax.* This is an annual tax imposed for the privilege of doing business within a state, whether or not the privilege is exer-

cised. Although charitable organizations are almost universally exempt and other nonprofit groups are usually exempt, some may not be so fortunate. For instance, if your organization is an agricultural or marketing association, it will probably not be exempt.

3. *State income tax.* This is a tax from which all nonprofit organizations are generally exempt. States that impose a corporate income tax usually exempt most nonprofit corporations. In states that impose an income tax on individuals, a deduction for their charitable contributions will generally be allowed (often closely following the rules for federal income tax deductions). In New York, trusts and other unincorporated organizations that are nonprofit and exempt from federal income tax are also exempt from the state income tax on unincorporated businesses and from the personal income tax.

Most states are influenced by the federal code. For instance, a California statute follows the federal example by making the unrelated business income of religious bodies subject to income taxation.

4. *Sales and use taxes.* Sales to, or for the use of, charitable organizations are not subject to a sales or use tax in many states. In some cases, sales by charities are exempt as long as no private individuals benefit from the profit. However, if a charitable organizaion is engaged in business, its sales to noncharitable entities are usually subject to the sales tax.

5. *Property taxes.* As long as a charitable organization's property is used for charitable purposes, it usually will be exempt from real property taxes. Normally, if it happens that only a portion is used for charitable purposes, only that portion is exempt. In some states, a parcel of property is either entirely tax exempt or entirely taxable, with no partial exemption allowed. This broad exemption, more frequently available to charitable associations and corporations than to trusts, usually extends to property taxes on personal property as well.

To be exempt from property taxes, an organization must meet the test of charitability on the day the tax is due. It will meet this test even if the property is not actually used for charity on that day, but is being made ready for such use on that day.

The trend in property tax exemptions seems to be moving in two directions. On the one hand, to encourage and promote nonprofit activities, state courts and administrative authorities strongly support tax exemptions. A case in point involves housing for the elderly.

It is generally acknowledged that caring for poor, elderly people is a worthy cause that should be of government concern. Therefore, a charitable organization that provides housing for the poor elderly is serving a government purpose and as such deserves tax-exempt status. Nonprofit organizations, called "nonprofit building organizations," that put up public housing for the elderly with FHA-insured loans at low interest rates have gained increasing popularity. With government encouragement, such housing has appeared nationwide. There have been many such instances in which tax exemptions and tax incentives are employed to address such community problems as urban housing.

On the other hand, some state courts and administrative authorities are justifiably critical of tax exemptions granted to nonprofit organizations that do not serve a worthy cause. A case in point involves homes for the elderly who are not poor. In many cases, steep entrance fees are required of prospective tenants and rents are at healthy rates. Many courts do not see such commercial ploys as charitable, and will deny tax exemption.

Some churches, too, have met adverse reaction in their efforts to gain property tax exemption. The churches in the United States have, of course, been large holders of exempt real property; the church building and grounds immediately surrounding it have traditionally been exempt. But in a 1969 case, *Christward Ministry* v. *County of San Diego,* where the Christward Ministry was a nature-worshiping group whose members insisted they needed the vast acreage of natural beauty surrounding them as a barrier from commercial property in order to worship properly, the appeals court ruled that property to be tax exempt. It explained that the property was being used for religious purposes since the church members believed it was necessary to their faith.

In the years since *Christward Ministry,* it has increasingly been argued that such tax exemptions erode a necessary tax base, particularly for local governments. The states' main source of revenue is the sales tax, but the property tax is the principal source of revenue for local governments. The property tax levied by a municipality, a county, and often a township, school district, and some special districts may be based upon the assessable value of property in a geographic area. Because of the large number of tax exemptions granted to nonprofit organizations, some critics contend that the local communities and the taxpayers supporting community operations end up servicing the tax-exempt properties. This philosophy may signal a new direction in property tax exemption.

6. *Gift and death taxes.* In general, transfers made to charity are not subject to state inheritance or estate taxes.

7. *Miscellaneous taxes.* Nonprofit charitable organizations are often the subject of other tax relief, such as special state tax provisions dealing with motor vehicles they own and exemptions from the requirements of unemployment compensation funds.

8 ▪ 2
POSTAGE RATES

Another major perk enjoyed by certain nonprofit organizations is the special postage rates for which you may be able to apply. These rates pertain to second- and third-class mailings.

To qualify for special third-class postage rates, your organization must not be organized for profit, and none of its net income may benefit any private stockholder or individual, and it must be a religious, educational, scientific, philanthropic (charitable), agricultural, labor, veterans', or fraternal organization. These organizations must meet a standard of primary purpose in terms of organization and operation. To qualify as a religious organization, your primary purpose must be one of the following:

1. To conduct religious worship as a church, temple, or synagogue.
2. To support the religious activities of nonprofit organizations whose primary purpose is to conduct religious worship.
3. To perform instruction in, to disseminate information about, or otherwise to further the teaching of particular faiths or tenets.

To qualify as an educational organization the main purpose must be:

1. The instruction or training of an individual for the purpose of improving or developing his capabilities.
2. The instruction of the public on subjects beneficial to the community.

You will not jeopardize your educational status by advocating a particular position or viewpoint, so long as you present a sufficiently full and fair exposition of the pertinent facts to allow an individual or the public to form an independent opinion or conclusion. But you will lose your educational status if your principal function is merely the presentation of unsupported opinion.

The following examples may assist you in deciding whether your organization is educational:

1. An organization (a primary or secondary school, a college, or a professional or trade school) that has a regularly scheduled curriculum, a regular faculty, and a regularly enrolled body of students in attendance at a place at which the educational activities are regularly carried on.
2. An organization that presents public discussion groups, panels, lectures, forums, or other similar programs. These programs may be on radio or television.
3. An organization that conducts a course of instruction by correspondence or through radio or television.
4. Organizations such as museums, zoos, planetariums, and symphony orchestras.

To qualify as scientific, your primary purpose must be one of these:

1. To conduct research in the pure, applied, or natural sciences.
2. To disseminate systematized technical information dealing with pure, applied, or natural sciences.

To qualify as charitable, your organization must be organized and operated for purposes beneficial to the public. Examples of such purposes are the advancement of religion, education, or science; relief of the poor and distressed or the underprivileged; lessening of the burdens of government; and the erection or maintenance of public buildings, monuments, or works. Also included is the promotion of social welfare by groups designed to accomplish any of the aforementioned purposes, or to eliminate prejudice and discrimination, lessen neighborhood tensions, defend human and civil rights secured by law, or combat juvenile delinquency and community deterioration.

A charitable organization that advocates civil or social change or gives opinions on controversial issues in the carrying on of its primary purpose will not be precluded from qualifying as charitable if it is an "action" organization. The U.S. Postal Service defines an action organization as one engaging in:

- Direct or indirect intervention in any political campaign on behalf of, or in opposition to, any political candidate.
- Attempts to influence legislation by contacting, or urging the public to contact, legislators for the purpose of supporting, proposing, or opposing legislation, or advocating either the adoption or the rejection of legislation.

If your nonprofit organization's primary purpose is the betterment of the conditions of those engaged in agricultural pursuits, the improvement of the grade of their products, and the development of a higher degree of efficiency in agriculture, it will qualify in this category. Other activities permitted are:

1. The furtherance and advancement of agricultural interests through educational activities.
2. The holding of agricultural fairs.
3. The collection and dissemination of information or materials relating to agricultural pursuits.

To qualify as a nonprofit labor organization, your primary purpose must be the betterment of the conditions of workers. This group includes, but is not limited to, organizations in which the employees or workmen participate, and whose main purpose is to deal with employers concerning grievances, wages, hours of employment, labor disputes, working conditions, and the like. Labor unions and employees' associations are examples.

A fraternal group must meet all of these criteria to qualify:

1. Its primary purpose must be to foster brotherhood and mutual benefits among its members.
2. Its organization must be under a lodge or chapter system, with a representative form of government.
3. It must follow a ritualistic format.
4. It must be made up of members who are elected to membership by vote by the members.

This type includes the Elks, the Knights of Columbus, the Masons, and college sororities and fraternities.

Veterans organizations are simply nonprofit organizations of veterans of the U.S. armed services, or an auxiliary unit or society thereof, or a foundation or trust for, any such organization or post.

Organizations that do not qualify for special postage rates, even though they may qualify as nonprofit, include automobile clubs, social and hobby clubs, service clubs (such as Kiwanis or Rotary), business leagues, professional associations, political organizations, chambers of commerce, citizens' and civic improvement associations, mutual insurance associations, trade associations, and associations of rural electric cooperatives. State, county, and municipal governments are also ineligible. On the other hand, if a separate and distinct government organization meets the criteria for any of the prescribed categories, it is eligible for special bulk mailing rates. A "charitable"-type government organization is not eligible, since its income is usually not derived primarily from voluntary contributions or donations.

To apply for special postal rates:

1. Your eligible nonprofit group must fill out an application on Form 3624, Application to Mail at Special Bulk Third-Class Rates for Qualified Nonprofit Organizations or Associations, and

file it at the post office at which mailings will be deposited. You must include with the application evidence that your organization is nonprofit and, if available, a certificate of exemption from federal income tax. Such exemption, although not required, will be considered as evidence of qualification, but it will not be controlling.

2. Form 3624, together with any supporting papers, is sent to the U.S. Postal Service's center, where the postmaster will approve or deny the application.

3. If additional information or evidence is requested for a decision, failure to furnish it will be reason enough to deny the application.

4. An appeal of an adverse decision may be made in writing by the applicant to the postmaster where the application was filed. He will forward it through the prescribed chain of command.

5. Until final action is taken on the application, you will be eligible for the special rates as long as you deposit with the postmaster an amount sufficient to cover the additional postage at the higher rates if your application is denied.

6. If your group becomes disqualified, approval can be revoked. After the postmaster notifies you of the pending cancellation, you are allowed fifteen days within which to file a written appeal.

If your nonprofit organization puts out a mailable publication, it may qualify for second-class rates. It will qualify if your publication is one of an institution or society listed below, and it contains only its publisher's own advertising, and under no conditions the advertising of other persons, institutions, or concerns:

1. A publication published by a regularly incorporated institution of learning, or by a regularly established state institution of learning supported somewhat by public taxation.
2. A bulletin issued by a state board of health, a state industrial development agency, a state conservation or fish and game agency, or a state board of public charities and corrections.
3. A publication put out by any public or nonprofit private elementary or secondary institution of learning or its administrative or governing body.

4. Program announcements or guides published by a nonprofit educational radio or television station or by an educational radio or television agency of a state or political subdivision thereof.

These may contain the advertising of others:

1. A publication published under the auspices of a fraternal or benevolent society organized under the lodge system and having a bona fide membership of not less than 1,000 persons.
2. A publication put out under the auspices of a trade union or published by a strictly professional, historical, literary, or scientific society, or by a church or church organization.

However, the following conditions must prevail:

- The publication cannot be published or designed primarily for advertising purposes.
- It must be originated and published to further the objects and purposes of the society in question.
- The circulation must be limited to copies mailed to members who pay, either as a part of their assessments or dues or otherwise, not less than 50 percent of the regular subscription price; to other actual subscribers; to exchanges; and to 10 percent of such circulation as sample copies.
- When members pay for their subcriptions as a part of their dues or assessments, individual subscriptions or receipts are not necessary.

The basic qualifications the publications of these institutions and societies must meet are:

1. The publishers must decide the number of issues they will publish each year and adopt a statement of frequency showing the regular intervals the issues will appear. The frequency for publishing cannot be less than four issues each year. Publishers can change the number of issues scheduled and adopt a new statement of frequency by filing an application for second-class reentry on Form 3510. (An application for reentry must be filed at the U.S. Post

Office of original entry, accompanied by two copies of the publication showing the new name or frequency.)

If your publication fails to maintain its schedule of frequency, the postmaster will inform the publisher and request compliance. If that fails, or if the publication is discontinued, the postmaster will report all the facts to the Office of Mail Classification for a determination as to whether proceedings should be instituted to revoke the second-class privilege.

2. The publications must be issued and mailed at the regular business office of the publication.

3. They must be made up of printed sheets, not reproduced by processes that are in imitation of typewriting.

4. Those that are designed primarily for advertising purposes or for free circulation do not qualify for second-class privileges. The same is true for those designed primarily for circulation at nominal rates. A nominal rate may be a price so low that it is not a material consideration, or it may be a reduction to the subscriber under a premium offer.

5. They must have a legitimate paid subscription list.

6. They must be originated and published to disseminate information of a public character, or else they must be devoted to literature, art, or another cultural field.

A publication must show its second-class mailing privilege clearly by following these requirements:

1. Copies of publications must be identified as second-class mail by having printed on one of the first five pages the name of the publication (shown on the front), the date of issue, the statement of frequency, the issue number, the subscription price, and the name of known office of publication and ZIP Code. Also necessary is a second-class imprint, reading "Second-class postage paid at _____ ."

2. If a publication is mailed at two or more offices, the imprint must read "Second-class postage paid at _____ and at additional mailing offices."

3. Finally, a "notice of pending application" is required if copies

are mailed before the application is approved. It must read "Application to mail at second-class postage rates is pending at _____."

Remember, an application must be filed by the publisher before a publication can be mailed at second-class rates.

To apply for second-class mailing privileges:

1. An application is filed on Form 3501 for second-class privileges for a qualified publication at the post office nearest the regular business office. For a publication of an institution or society that does not meet the basic qualifications, file Form 3502.

2. Nonprofit organizations may apply to the postmaster for special second-class rates, with a written request for such rates filed at the post office where the publication of such an organization has original second-class entry. Evidence must also be submitted to establish the organization's nonprofit status and to show that it falls within one of the qualifying categories for third-class bulk rates.

3. Any foreign publications of the same general character as domestic publications entered as second-class mail can be accepted by the Postmaster General, on the publishers' application (Form 3501-A) for transmission through the mail at the same rates as if published in the United States.

4. Publishers of educational, religious, or scientific publications designed for use in school classrooms or in religious instruction classes can apply to the postmaster for the special classroom rate. Evidence must be submitted showing that their publications are of such character and for the uses stated.

5. Publishers of publications with the purpose of promoting the science of agriculture can apply for a special science of agriculture rate to the postmaster. Not only must they submit evidence of character and use stated, but also that more than 70 percent of the copies distributed by any means for any purpose during a twelve-month period are to subscribers living in rural areas.

6. A procedure called "exceptional dispatch" can also be applied for by a publisher. The purpose of this is to deliver copies of a second-class publication at the publisher's expense and risk from the post office of original entry to other post offices or elsewhere.

Applications for exceptional dispatch may be filed jointly with those for original entry, reentry, or special rates, but no form is provided. Applications will be approved or disapproved by the postmaster at the office of original entry on the basis of whether the exceptional dispatch will improve service.

7. Publishers or news agents (who resell purchased publications or have publications consigned to them) cannot mail at the second-class rates until their application is approved by the director, Office of Mail Classification, Rates and Classification Department. But postage at the applicable third- or fourth-class rates may be paid in money (and not by stamps affixed) on mailings made while an application is pending. If the pending application is approved, the publisher will receive the difference between the third- or fourth-class rates and the second-class rates.

8. Set fees are charged and must accompany applications for second-class entry, reentry, additional entry, or registration as a news agent. The amounts can be learned from your postmaster. If your application is not approved, no part of the fee is returned.

9. The director of mail classification not only has the authority to grant or deny an application, he may also suspend or revoke a second-class entry, subject, though, to an appeal and hearing if requested by the publisher.

8 • 3
SPECIAL TREATMENT

By no means is the nonprofit organization automatically the recipient of government largesse. Like federal tax exemption, state and local tax exemption and postage privileges are benefits that your organization may enjoy only after affirmatively establishing your entitlement to them. The need for careful and conscientious planning and skilled and experienced advice again becomes self-evident.

9
Charitable
Fund Raising

9 ▪ 1
READY FOR REGULATIONS?

If yours is a fund-raising organization, you certainly don't sit back and wait for donors to come to you. Undoubtedly, you go after gifts aggressively, just as any public charity does—by means of solicitation. Solicitation is not yet regulated on the federal level, but it is the subject of widely varying state statutes and innumerable city and county ordinances.

Why the need for regulations? The answer lies in the notorious abuses in this area, such as insufficient disclosure of meaningful information to prospective donors, excessive administrative and fund-raising costs, and insufficient portions of the proceeds going for charitable purposes.

Unlike regulations for private foundations, there is no requirement:

1. That public charities distribute a minimum portion of their funds annually for charitable purposes.

2. That they disclose to potential contributors what portion of their funds is actually devoted to charitable purposes.
3. That they have common requirements with regard to registration, licensing, periodic reporting, disclosure of financial information, and limitations on the compensation paid to fund raisers.
4. That they have uniform accounting standards imposed by law.

Presently, about two-thirds of the states do have some form of statute requiring a charitable organization soliciting contributions within the jurisdiction to register, be licensed, and report to a government authority. The more stringent laws provide that the attorney general can, upon his own motion or upon any person's complaint, investigate a charity. If necessary, he can subpoena records and seek injunctive relief. Moreover, cities and counties within many of these states have comparable ordinances. Consequently, before you send out solicitors and begin your fund-raising operations, ask your attorney to check your particular jurisdiction to know what, if anything, is legally expected of your organization.

In addition, there may be other statutory impediments that must be faced by your organization soliciting gift support. Some of them are cited below.

1. *A state's nonprofit corporation act.* This will have registration and annual reporting requirements for foreign corporations (those incorporated in one state but operating in another) that transact business within the state. If you are such a foreign corporation, check to see if the solicitation of contributions is considered a business transaction in the state (as in Iowa and Kansas) in which you are operating. If it is, there will be considerable reporting for you to do.

2. *A state's insurance law.* Such a law (like New York's) may have a requirement that a charitable organization writing charitable gift annuity contracts must obtain a permit to do so and thereafter file annual statements.

3. *A state's law prohibiting fraudulent practices.* For instance, Ohio's Charitable Trust Act gives the state's attorney general unqualified investigative power over charitable groups.

4. *A state's "blue sky" statute.* A statute's regulation of securities offerings may be applicable to offers to sell and sales of interests in, and operation of, pooled income funds. Moreover, such statutes may also apply to charitable remainder annuity trusts and unitrusts.

9 ▪ 2
TOWARD A GENERAL UNDERSTANDING

The terms and requirements of regulatory statutes vary widely from state to state. And the requirements imposed by interpretive rules accompanying the statutes vary even more, as do the enforcement efforts among the states.

Because of the variety of laws enacted from state to state, a universally accepted solicitation statute just doesn't exist. But you will be headed in the right direction if you rely upon the general features embodied in most satutes.

1. It will define the pivotal terms in uses, including "contribution," "solicitation," "person," "charitable" (usually broader than the IRS definition), "professional fund raiser," and "professional solicitor." Also, it will name the particular state agencies involved in its administration and enforcement.

2. A charitable organization not specifically exempted from the statute will be required to apply to a certain state official for a permit or license to solicit (usually thirty days in advance of operation). The application will ask for:

- Your organization's exact name.
- The name it will use to solicit contributions.
- Its principal address or that of the person having custody of its financial records.
- The names and addresses of its trustees, directors, officers, executive staff, and state agent.
- The place and date your organization was set up and its form.
- The purposes for which it was organized and those for which the solicited contributions will be used.
- Its federal tax-exempt status.
- All the methods it will use to make solicitations.

- Certification that it has never been enjoined from making solicitations.
- Its fiscal year.

It will also be asked to furnish copies of its contracts with professional fund raisers.

3. The license or permit your organization receives will usually expire one year after the date of issuance. It may be renewed by filing a renewal application and supporting information within a specified period. Many states require this annual renewal in addition to an annual report. If there has been any violation, the statute will authorize the enforcement agency to suspend or even revoke the license.

4. If an annual report is required, it must include a financial statement covering the preceding accounting period, and it must be prepared to conform to accepted accounting standards (which vary considerably from one statute to another).

5. Once your organization is licensed, all the documents it has filed and will file are normally required to be open to public inspection. The accurate and detailed books and records it must keep will be open to the inspection of the enforcement agency.

6. The professional fund raiser acting on behalf of a licensed charity will usually be required to register or obtain a license from the appropriate state agency before setting out on his or her mission. Normally, he or she will also be required to file a bond in an amount anywhere from $15,000 to $100,000. The statute will usually define the fund raiser as one who, for pay, conducts, plans, manages, carries on, acts, or advises as a consultant in connection with the soliciting of contributions on behalf of a charity, but doesn't actually solicit the contributions.

7. A professional solicitor in the employ of the professional fund raiser must register with the appropriate state agency. The solicitor will be defined as one who, again for pay, either plans, manages, carries on, acts, or advises as a consultant (but is not qualified as a fund raiser) or solicits contributions for or on behalf of a charity either personally or through employees or agents employed for that purpose.

8. What can a professional fund raiser or solicitor be paid? For

statutes that have a ceiling on the amount of compensation allowed, that amount varies considerably —from 15 percent to 35 percent of the funds collected.

Such a ceiling seems to make for a twofold problem:

- The professional fund raiser may regard the percentage method of pay as unethical and will therefore provide his services for a stated fee only.
- A charity just starting a solicitation program normally will have much higher fund-raising costs than it will in future years when it and its program become more established.

9. Many statutes require the appointment of a state official to act as a state agent for professional fund raisers and solicitors (as well as for foreign organizations). Such an agent may be served process in a proceeding brought under a statute.

10. Some states have adopted a provision to alleviate the confusion arising from the different statutes among the states. The provision enables the appropriate state official to enter into a reciprocal agreement with his counterpart in other states to

- Exchange information about charities and professional fund raisers and solicitors, and accept filings from them from other states where the information required is similar.
- Grant exemptions to organizations granted such under other states' statutes that are substantially similar.

Here again there is a wide variance as to what groups are considered exempt under the various statutes. Be sure to check for an exemption for your organization in each state you enter before going through the trouble of meeting solicitation statute requirements.

11. A list of prohibited acts is frequently included in a statute. Included are such acts as:

- Using another person's name without his consent (except for an official of the charity for which the solicitations are made).
- Using a name, symbol, or statement so similar to one used by another charitable organization that it might confuse or mislead the public.
- Using or exploiting a license so that the public believes it to constitute an endorsement by the state.
- Misleading someone into believing that the solicitation is

being conducted by a charitable organization with the proceeds used for charitable purposes when this is not true.

- Using solicited funds for purposes other than those for which the funds were collected.

12. Many of the statutes invest the state's attorney general with specific powers in connection with its administration and enforcement. These often include authorization to investigate the conduct and operations of charities and their fund raisers and solicitors subject to the statute, with the power to issue orders with the force and effect of a subpoena. The attorney general may also have an express power to bring a legal action in court to enjoin an offender who engages in any violation of the statute or uses in a solicitation effort any device or scheme to defraud or make a false pretense, promise, or deception to obtain a donation.

13. Violations of these statutes are usually treated as misdemeanors. However, when an offense is willful and repeated, it can be elevated to a felony.

If your organization participates in the solicitation of contributions, be prepared for stiffer and more extensive regulation. The alleged misdeeds of some charities—with their unscrupulous and fraudulent operators—have brought an increase in public attention to the activities of charitable organizations. The consumerism movement appears to be making donors more concerned and sophisticated about the uses to which their charitable dollars are put—with emphasis on public accountability and disclosure. The result of this movement has been to see an increase in state and local government regulation and a desire for further regulation by local, state, and especially the federal government of the processes of soliciting charitable contributions.

9 ▪ 3
FROM STATE TO STATE

Most nonprofit organizations don't confine their soliciting to their home state. They seek donations from sources everywhere. When you solicit in another state you are usually considered to be doing business in that state as a "foreign" entity.

When applied to associations or corporations, foreign means nonresident, and a foreign organization is one that carries on activities in a state other than the one in which it was formed or incorporated. It does not acquire citizenship in another state for federal jurisdictional purposes merely by registering in that state. To gain citizenship the organization must reincorporate in that state. Whether it is better to reincorporate or simply to register in each state in which activities are carried on depends on the individual situation. It is often advisable to incorporate local branches, then affiliate them under the charter and bylaws of the parent organization.

A corporation that does not elect to become a citizen of another state, but desires to expand its activities elsewhere, must register and be licensed by that state before conducting any business there. If an unincorporated association is considered to have the ordinary attributes of a corporation, it too will be required to be registered and licensed. For registering and licensing procedures, be sure to look to the laws of the state in which you want to conduct your activities.

If a foreign organization fails to register and be licensed in a foreign state, it may be subject to injunctions and penalties by the states. This is particularly true for the making of contracts and the solicitation of contributions. The penalties can range from $250 to $10,000, plus fees that should have been paid, plus interest. Five years is often the period for the statute of limitations.

The biggest penalty is that the foreign organization's local contracts will be unenforceable in the state courts or, in some cases, completely void. And any filing done after a contract is made normally does not make the contract valid. However, in some states, organizations can file later, pay a penalty, and then sue in the local courts to enforce their contracts.

One aspect of this is uniform in all the states: Failure to register formally as a foreign corporation cannot cause that organization to be punished by injunction against all its activity in the state. Injunction by the attorney general is authorized, however, when unlicensed activities are carried on.

Many nonprofit regulatory agencies simply do not have the

money or manpower to enforce many of the laws now in effect. This has been particularly unfortunate where effectively unregulated foreign organizations have spent an unconscionably large part of their budgets on their fund-raising activities and administrative costs. For instance, the *Reader's Digest* reported that none of the $218,000 raised on a 1972 telethon for the Foundation for Research and Education in Sickle Cell Diseases actually went to that organization. Some states and municipal governments have taken steps to eliminate charitable waste by limiting the percentage a charity may spend on fund-raising and administrative costs.

Two trends can be detected today in nonprofit foreign organizations. First, they have expanded in numbers, in the number of states in which they operate, and in the amount of public donations they collect. Second, there is still not adequate state supervision and regulation to protect the public and even the good names of reputable nonprofit organizations.

9 ▪ 4
OUT-OF-STATE REGULATIONS

To give you a general idea of what is required in registration as a foreign corporation, the following are some typical statutory rules:

1. It may carry on no activities (except for purely interstate activities) in the state unless it first files a certificate of authority with the secretary of state. Since the states cannot regulate "interstate" business, a state's taxation of foreign activities in purely interstate activities conducted within its jurisdiction by foreign organizations is in most instances unlawful.

2. In order to earn this certificate, the foreign organization must do the following:

- Give the secretary of state a statement signed by its officers of its name, state of incorporation or formation, office address within the state, and the activities (authorized by its charter) that it proposes to carry on.
- Designate the secretary of state as its agent for the service of legal process within the state.
- Attach to the certificate a document by the authorizing officer in the home state that it is an existing entity in its own state.

3. To be licensed the organization can conduct only those activities it is allowed to conduct as a domestic organization. If these activities require administrative approvals domestically, certificates of administrative approvals from the "foreign" state will also be necessary.

4. Its name must be distinctive. Therefore, if it is similar to that of a local organization, a certificate giving the local group's consent must be annexed.

Once the statement is filed and the fees, ranging from $50 to $100, are paid, the secretary of state issues a certificate of authority.

9 ▪ 5
CHANGING YOUR MIND

If you decide to discontinue activities as a foreign organization, you can file a certificate to that effect with the department of state, firing the secretary of state as your agent. Local statutes will prescribe the form of the certificate. To discontinue activities as a means of avoiding existing contract rights, claims, or pending action is, of course, illegal. In fact, some states require a formal certificate of surrender of authority, showing that all taxes, fees, and workmen's compensation benefits have been paid.

Keep in mind, too, that holding property in a state, even for investment purposes, may be considered doing business in that state.

One final caveat about the common practice of discontinuing activities in a foreign state without filing a certificate of surrender of authority. The result is a continuation of the state regulatory rights that could come back to haunt you someday.

9 ▪ 6
YOUR DONOR'S MOTIVES

Your donor may have a noble desire to give to your charitable cause in order to help those in need, and that is praiseworthy. But that person may also have another personal motive that can be realized at the same time—tax savings in the form of a charitable contribution deduction. Our tax laws actually encourage charitable giving. For instance, a person who gives to charity pays no gift tax or, if applicable, capital gains tax; that person receives a deduction on his or her income or estate tax; and may even be fortunate enough to make a profit on the gift.

For a gift to result in a charitable deduction, it must be itemized on Schedule A, Form 1040, and the gift must be made to or for the use of one of the following qualified organizations:

1. The United States or one of its states or possessions for public purposes.
2. A corporation, trust, community chest, fund, or foundation organized and operated exclusively for religious, charitable, scientific, literary, or educational organizations, so long as its income does not inure to the benefit of any individual and provided no substantial part of its activities consists in carrying on propaganda or attempting to influence legislation.
3. An organization operated for the prevention of cruelty to children or animals or to foster national or international amateur sports competition (as long as no part of its activities involves the provision of athletic facilities or equipment).
4. A domestic fraternal society operating under the lodge system, provided that the contribution is to be used exclusively for one or more of the charitable purposes described in Item 2 above.
5. A war veterans' group, including auxiliaries, posts, trusts, and foundations.
6. A nonprofit volunteer fire company or a civil defense organization created under federal, state, or local law.
7. A nonprofit cemetery company, provided the funds are irrevocably dedicated to the perpetual care of the cemetery as a whole, rather than a particular lot or mausoleum crypt.

IRS Publication 78 lists the organizations (described in Section 170(c) of the Internal Revenue Code) with IRS rulings that contributions to them are deductible, and gives the limits on deduction.

9 ▪ 7
GUIDING THE DONOR

Guiding a would-be donor to contribute to your organization most tax-effectively is a good way to ensure that his gift is as large as it really can be. And getting the greatest possible tax benefits from one's donation boils down to two simple considerations: What is the best way to make a charitable donation? When is the best time to make it?

Should your donor make a gift directly to charity, create a charitable trust, or establish a foundation? This is determined by considering the donor's particular financial situation and personal desires. What is that person's current income and prospects for future income, the nature of the donor's assets, the size of his or her estate, age and health, needs of spouse and family, and nature of the proposed charitable purpose?

Should the donor give while still alive or in the will? Casting aside personal considerations and looking at it solely from a tax point of view, that person should decide on the basis of whether it is better to save income or estate taxes. If the individual gives during his or her lifetime, income taxes are saved; if after death, estate taxes are saved. Yet it may be possible to arrange matters so that both income and estate tax deductions are allowable for the same gift.

9 ▪ 8
LIFETIME GIVING—ONLY FOR THE RICH?

Generally, lifetime charitable giving is not significant to the person in the lower income tax brackets. Since that person saves little, he or she is probably better off with a plan that provides an estate tax deduction. On the other hand, the high-bracket taxpayer may be wiser in making gifts during his or her lifetime. As a rule, the income tax bracket is higher than the estate tax bracket. Therefore, the savings will be greater. Furthermore, the income tax dollars saved increase spendable income and so, too, the ultimate estate. The donor may save even more if the state or locality taxes his or her income and allows a charitable deduction.

Table 3 below shows the out-of-pocket costs of a $100 deductible contribution at different levels of taxable income. As one's tax rate goes up, the actual cost of giving goes down. The tax rates in effect as we go to press have been used (disregarding the earned income ceiling and the zero bracket amount).

Table 3. Cost of a $100 contribution.[a]

Taxable Income	Single Person	Married Person	Taxable Income	Corporations
$ 6,000	$79	$81		
8,000	76	81		
12,000	73	78		
16,000	69	75		
20,000	64	72		
24,000	60	68	To $25,000	$83
28,000	55	64		
32,000	55	61		
36,000	50	58		
40,000	45	55		
50,000	40	50	To 50,000	80
70,000	36	45	To 75,000	70
95,000	31	40	To 100,000	60
110,000	30	38	Over 100,000	54
130,000	30	36		
150,000	30	34		

[a] Based on federal tax savings only.

9 ▪ 9
SIZE OF DONATION

Ask your prospective donor to consider lifetime giving and the income tax approach. All of us make lifetime gifts to charity in some form or another. With some foresight and planning, we can reduce the actual cost of charitable giving or increase the amount of the gift.

Unlike the estate and gift tax laws, which carry no restrictions as to the amount deductible for charitable contributions, the income tax deduction is a limited one. It works like this: An individual is allowed a deduction up to 50 percent of his adjusted gross income, if his gift is made to (not for the use of) a publicly supported organization or public charity, a supporting organization of a public charity, or certain types of private foundations. For instance, a taxpayer whose adjusted gross income is $50,000 may deduct all of a $25,000 gift to such organizations.

Publicly supported organizations include the following:

1. Churches, synagogues, and associations of churches.
2. Tax-exempt educational organizations that have a regular faculty and curriculum and a regular student body attending resident classes.
3. Tax-exempt hospitals and, under particular circumstances, organizations directly engaged in continuous medical research in conjunction with such hospitals.
4. Organizations receiving substantial government or general public support and operating for the sole purpose of holding and administering property for state and municipal colleges and universities.
5. A state, a U.S. possession, or any political subdivision thereof, plus the United States or District of Columbia if the contribution is made for exclusively public purposes.
6. Internal Revenue Code Section 501(c)(3)-qualified organizations that normally receive a substantial part of their support (other than income from their activities) from direct or indirect contributions from government units or the general public. Moreover, the public support received must be from a representative number of persons within the community, and not from a few individuals or families.

If one's gift is to a private foundation, the donor may only receive a deduction up to a maximum of 20 percent of adjusted gross income, but with certain exceptions. The donor may be allowed up to a 50 percent deduction if the gift is made to one of the following:

1. *A private operating foundation.* This type of foundation must spend at least 85 percent of its income directly for the active conduct of the activities that constitute the exempt purpose for which it is organized, and it must meet one of the following tests:
   - At least 65 percent of its assets must be devoted directly to its exempt purpose or to functionally related businesses, or both.
   - Substantially all its support must come from at least five independent exempt organizations or the general public, but only

a maximum of 25 percent from any one exempt organization
and not more than 50 percent from gross investment income.
- Qualifying distributions are normally made by the foundation
  in order to carry on activities that comprise the purpose or
  function for which it is organized and operated. These distributions must equal at least 3.⅓% of its assets (two-thirds of the
  foundation's minimum investment return).

2. *A private nonoperating foundation* (generally a family foundation), provided that it distributes the contribution to a 50 percent
charity within two and a half months of its reporting year. Private
nonoperating foundations are any organizations, other than public
charities or private operating foundations, exempt from federal income tax under Section 501(c)(3) of the Internal Revenue Code.

3. *A community foundation* that pools the contributions it receives
from many people and administers them as a common fund. A gift
to a common fund is kept in a separate account in the donor's
name, and he can designate the charities that are to receive the
benefits of his contribution. Most large cities and many small ones
have them.

Donations to some types of organizations have a 20 percent limitation:

1. Private nonoperating foundations, war veterans' organizations,
   domestic fraternal societies, and nonprofit cemeteries that do
   not qualify for the 50 percent limitation.
2. Contributions for the use of (in trust for) any charitable organization. This includes out-of-pocket expenses incurred on behalf
   of charity or a gift of an income interest in trust to a charitable
   organization.

This 20 percent ceiling acts as a subceiling within one 50 percent ceiling for all donations. In other words, an individual cannot
deduct the 50 percent limit plus another 20 percent of adjusted
gross income. The combined total is limited to 50 percent.

The ceiling on contributions made by corporations (and unincorporated associations) is quite different. A corporation may annually deduct only 5 percent of its net income (not counting the

charitable contribution) for charitable contributions. If a corporation's annual contributions exceed the 5 percent limit, the corporation can carry over and deduct the excess as part of its contributions in the next five years, again subject to the same annual ceiling.

In addition to individuals and corporations (and unincorporated associations), partnerships, estates, and nonexempt trusts are eligible to receive deductions for their charitable contributions. (By definition, private foundations are exempt and therefore receive no charitable deductions.)

Partnerships themselves are not taxpayers and hence receive no benefit at the partnership level. They pass their contributions through to the partners, who deduct them.

Estates and complex trusts are allowed a charitable contribution deduction for any amount of gross income that, under the terms of a will or trust deed, is paid for charitable purposes. No limitation is placed on the amount that can be deducted by either. A complex trust is any trust, other than a simple trust, that may accumulate income or make charitable contributions, or that distributes the corpus (principal) during the taxable year. A simple trust is required to distribute all its income currently and is not authorized to make deductible contributions to charity during the taxable year. But it will not be simple for any taxable year during which it distributes corpus or in which it defines ordinary dividends and interest as corpus.

Estates and certain living and testamentary trusts in existence on Oct. 10, 1969, get a deduction for any amount of gross income that is permanently set aside for charitable purposes. The set-aside deduction is also available to pooled income funds, but only with regard to long-term gain from the sale of capital assets.

For the donor to get the deduction, the charitable contribution generally must come from the gross income of the trust or estate. The trust instrument may specifically determine the income source for the charitable contribution. A provision on this point is controlling and enables the trustees to get the full benefit of the deduction for the amount paid (or set aside). A taxpayer will want his governing instrument specifically to provide that contributions be payable out of ordinary taxable income, not from tax-exempt or long-term capital gains. Local law will fabricate the "intent" if the trust deed is silent on whether the charity payments come from income or principal.

These rules for charitable deductions do not apply to nonexempt charitable and so-called "split interest" (split-interest or annuity) trusts. They are treated as taxable private foundations and generally take their charitable deductions under the rules for individuals.

9 ▪ 10
WHAT TO GIVE

Determining how much to give is only one side of the coin. The kind and form of the gift your donor gives can be very important, since one type may provide a better tax break than another.

The most common gift one can give is cash. Property gifts in kind are another, and often tax-wiser, contribution. Unreimbursed expenses incurred in performing services for a charity may be deductible. And so can certain gifts of property and gifts of partial interests in property or in trust. Let's explore some hypothetical examples.

Your donor's unreimbursed expenses incurred in performing services for your charity may be deductible. Such expenses can include telephone charges, special uniforms, out-of-pocket travel and transportation costs, and costs of meals and lodging while traveling away from home. If the donor uses an automobile, he or she can either take a mileage allowance, plus parking fees and tools, or deduct the car operating and maintenance costs directly attributable to his or her services. But the donor cannot deduct the cost of general maintenance and repair, depreciation, or insurance.

If someone receives a per-diem allowance for performing services to a charity, it is income to that person to the extent that it exceeds the actual travel expenses. Conversely, if the donor's travel expenses exceed the allowance, the excess is deductible.

Also deductible are church or synagogue building fund assessments, pew rents, or periodic dues. However, membership dues to other qualified organizations are deductible only to the extent they exceed the value of the benefits the individual receives for them.

Suppose your donor wants to make a gift of property other than money. Generally, the donor will receive an income tax deduction equal to the fair market value of the property at the time the contribution is made. The fair market value is the price at which the property would have changed hands between a willing buyer and a willing seller.

If the person donates property with a fair market value that is greater than that person's basis in it (appreciated property), he or she may have to reduce the fair market value by all or a portion of such appreciation when computing the deduction. In other words, the donor will get a reduced charitable contribution deduction. The amount of the reduction depends on whether the individual donates ordinary income property or capital gain property.

Ordinary income property is that which, if sold on the date it was contributed, would result either in ordinary income or in short-term gain—inventory, letters given by the one who prepared them or for whom they were prepared, and capital stock held for twelve months or less. Also included is depreciable property to the extent of any gain treated as ordinary income because of depreciation, had the property been sold.

The deduction for such a contribution is limited to the fair market value less the amount that would be ordinary income. Say your donor contributes to your church stock that he or she has held for nine months. The value of the stock is $1,000, but the donor paid only $850. Since the $150 of appreciation would be short-term gain if the donor sold the stock, his or her deduction is limited to $850 (the fair market value less the appreciation).

If your donor owns a retail store and gives merchandise to your charity that costs the business $5,000 and would have been sold for $9,000 in the normal course of business, that donor will only receive a deduction for the $5,000 cost.

Corporations (except Subchapter S corporations) are an exception. They can contribute high markup inventory and property used in a trade or business cost free. If they meet the following conditions, they can deduct the cost of the inventory or property plus half of the appreciation in value. However, the deduction cannot exceed twice the basis of the donated property.

1. The use of the property must be related to the exempt purposes of the donee. This means it must be used solely for the care of infants, the needy, or the ill.
2. The donee does not transfer the property in exchange for money, services, or other property.
3. The donee supplies the donor with a written statement attesting that the use of the property will satisfy Items 1 and 2 above.
4. For property subject to the Federal Food, Drug, and Cosmetic Act, it must completely satisfy the pertinent requirements on the date of transfer and 180 days prior to it.

If you can, discourge gifts of ordinary income or short-term property. This is especially true for gifts of papers and the like where the donor's basis and deduction is negligible. The donor would probably be wiser to leave such items to charity through a will and get a full estate tax setoff, or leave them to his children who in turn can give them to charity and receive a full income-tax deduction.

9 ▪ 11
THE CAPITAL GAIN GAME

Capital gain property is property that would result in long-term capital gain if it were sold at its fair market value on the date it was contributed. The most common types are stocks and bonds. It also includes certain real property (land) and depreciable property used in one's trade or business, and usually held longer than twelve months. Your donor may find gifts of appreciated property to be of particular value. Not only can they cost the donor less than an equivalent gift of cash; in some cases they may result in a profit. Moreover, the greater the appreciation of the property compared to its cost basis, the greater the tax reduction.

If your donor gives long-term capital gain property, he or she will receive a deduction for the full value of the property and will not pay tax on the appreciation in value. Since the sale of such property would be subject to a long-term capital gains tax, a contribution instead may cut the cost of giving. In some cases, it may even be less expensive than selling the property and pocketing the after-tax proceeds.

Your donor, for example, is in a 70 percent federal and state tax bracket. The donor has 1,000 shares of stock that cost $3,000, and after a year the stock has risen to a value of $10,000. If that individual sold the stock, he or she would have a long-term capital gain of $7,000. Assume that the various taxes will produce a cost of 29 percent of any gain. The after-tax receipts will be $7,970 ($10,000 less 29 percent of $7,000). On the other hand, if that person gives the stock to a favorite charity, he or she will save $7,000 in taxes (70 percent of $10,000). It ends up costing the donor $970 ($7,970 less $7,000) to give away $10,000 worth of property.

Although gifts of capital gain property may normally be deducted at their fair market value, some adjustments may have to be made if the property has appreciated in value.

1. If your donor's gift of capital gain property is tangible personal property that your organization puts to a use not related to its exempt purpose, the contribution is reduced by 50 percent of any long-term capital gain appreciation if the donor is an individual, and 62.5 percent if a corporation. If your donor owns tangible personal property that has appreciated substantially in value, like diamonds, coins, or paintings, he or she is drastically limited on the tax savings available unless your charitable organization, other than a government unit, puts the gift to a use related to its exempt purpose. In the case of a government unit, a proper use would be for a purpose or function that would support a charitable contribution deduction.

Technically, the donor can avoid this reduction and treat the property as not being put to an unrelated use if the donor establishes that the property is not being put to an unrelated use or at the time the contribution is made, he or she can reasonably anticipate that the property will not be so used. For instance, if an educational institution uses a painting contributed to it for educational purposes by placing it in its library for display and study by art students, the use is not unrelated. But if the painting is sold and the proceeds are used by the organization for educational purposes, the use is related.

2. If your donor's gift to a 50 percent charity consists of appreciated property that if sold would result in a long-term capital

gain, that donor is allowed a full deduction up to 30 percent of adjusted gross income, unless he or she elects to give up part of the deduction in exchange for bringing the contributed property under the 50 percent ceiling.

With such an election, the donor must reduce the property's fair market value by 50 percent of the appreciation in value that would be long-term capital gain if the property had been sold. This election applies to all 30 percent capital gain property, and it must be made on the donor's original tax return Form 1040 or an amended return filed by the due date for filing the original one.

3. If the gift is to a 20 percent charity, even though the appreciated property is long-term capital gain property, your donor's deduction is computed by subtracting 50 percent (62.5 percent for corporate donors) of the unrealized gain from the market value of the donated property. When computing the charitable deduction to a 50 percent or 20 percent charity, first consider any gifts made to the 50 percent charities. Next consider gifts to 20 percent charities, but only to the extent of the lesser of 20 percent of adjusted gross income or 50 percent of gross income less the contributions to which the 50 percent limitation applies. Any gifts of capital gain property to which the 30 percent limitation applies are considered after all other gifts.

If your church asks your donor to pledge $2,000 to its building program, and he or she pays the pledge in cash, the donor will get a $2,000 deduction. If that person is in, say, a 36 percent bracket, the out-of-pocket cost for the donation is $1,280. If the donor decides instead to satisfy the pledge with stock worth $2,000, the original cost of which was only $500, the contribution would cost less because the donor will have avoided the capital gains tax. If the donor had sold the stock instead, he or she would ordinarily have paid a capital gains tax of $270 on the $1,500 appreciation. By giving the stock to charity, the donor in effect realizes that gain, but pays no tax on it. The happy result is that the $2,000 gift only costs $1,010 ($1,280 minus $270).

4. If the donation is a gift of property that if sold would result in ordinary income or short-term capital gain, the deduction is based on the donor's cost, thus giving that individual no tax savings. This

is true of property such as books, letters, and works of art created by or prepared for the donor and capital stock held for less than a year. Say the individual donates stock that he or she has held for eight months. The value of the stock is $1,000, but originally cost only $850. Since the $150 of appreciation would be short-term gain if the stock were sold, the deduction is limited to $850, the donor's cost.

9 ▪ 12
A CASE IN POINT

Suppose your donor's adjusted gross income was $50,000. During the year he or she gave to a tax-exempt hospital $2,000 in cash and land that had a fair market value of $30,000 with a basis to the donor of $10,000 (the donor had held the land for investment for more than twelve months). In addition, that person gave $5,000 in cash to a private foundation to which the 20 percent limitation applies. Now let us figure the deduction.

Since the donor's allowable contributions to a 50 percent donee organization exceed $25,000 (50 percent of $50,000), the deduction subject to the 20 percent limitation is not allowed. The $2,000 donated to the hospital is considered first. The deduction for the gift of land is not required to be reduced by the appreciation in value (held over twelve months) and is limited to $15,000 (30 percent times $50,000). The $15,000 unused portion may be carried over to later years. Consequently, the deduction is limited to $17,000 ($2,000 plus $15,000). The $5,000 contribution to the private foundation cannot be carried over.

If, however, the donor elects to disregard the 30 percent limitation, the deduction would be $25,000, but he or she would have no carryover. In order to disregard the 30 percent limitation, the donor must elect to reduce the fair market value of the property by 50 percent of the appreciated value. Thus, the deduction for the land would be $20,000 ($30,000 less 50 percent of $20,000). The $20,000 is then added to the $2,000 cash contribution to the hospital. Next the donor deducts $3,000 of the amount donated to the private foundation because the amount applicable to the 50 percent limitation ($22,000) is less than 50 percent of adjusted gross income. The total deduction for the year is $25,000: $2,000 cash to the hospital, $20,000 of property donated to the hospital, and $3,000 cash given to the private foundation.

9 ▪ 13
TRADING ON YOUR FUTURE

Suppose your donor wishes to give your organization only a future interest in property. A contribution of a future interest in tangible personal property will earn the donor no charitable deduction until all intervening interests in and rights to the actual possession of the property either have expired or are held by someone other than the donor or "related" persons. Related persons are

- Members of the same family.
- The donor and a corporation of which the donor directly or indirectly owns 50 percent of the stock.
- The donor, any trust of the donor's creation, and the trust's beneficiaries.
- The donor and an exempt charitable or educational organization controlled directly or indirectly by the donor or a family member.

The amount of the contribution is the value of the future interest when the interest of the donor and of the related party expires. This is true regardless of whether or not there are other outstanding interests that must run out before the future interest is realized by the donee organization. For example, your donor transferred a painting in 1974 to his daughter for life and then to a museum of art, but she irrevocably transfers her life interest to someone else in a later year. Your donor can take a charitable deduction in that later year, but not any sooner. The donor's deduction is the value of the future interest in the painting at the time of the transfer in that year.

9 ▪ 14
REAPING THE PROFITS

What if your donor wants to contribute only the profit on some appreciated property? He or she does it by selling it to your charity at cost. Then the donor deducts the excess of the value over the selling price to the charity. If the bargain sale results in a deductible contribution, the donor will have to pay tax on some portion of the appreciation of the property.

Such a sale is treated as if some of the property were sold for fair market value and the rest given to the charity, with the contributor's cost allocated between the two. To compute the taxable gain, subtract from the bargain price the same percentage of the total cost of the property as the bargain price is of the market value.

Say your donor owns long-term capital gain stock worth $25,000 that cost $15,000, and sells it to your charity for $15,000. Although this gives the donor a $10,000 charitable contribution deduction, he or she also gets a taxable long-term capital gain of $6,000, computed by figuring the selling price over the fair market value times the cost, then deducting the result from the selling price.

$$\frac{\$15,000}{\$25,000} \times \$15,000 = \$9,000$$
$$\$15,000 - \$9,000 = \$6,000$$

If your donor donates a gift consisting of less than his or her entire interest in appreciated property (whether or not made in trust) and is allowed a charitable contribution for a portion of its fair market value, that individual must allocate the adjusted basis between the contributed and noncontributed portions of the property. The rules for gifts of appreciated property are applied to each portion. The donor then applies the appreciated property rules to his or her deduction by allocating his or her basis in the property between contributed and noncontributed portions. The basis of the contributed portion bears the same ratio to the total adjusted basis as the fair market value of the contributed portion bears to the fair market value of the entire property.

Keep in mind, though, that gifts of partial interest in property, not made by a transfer in trust, can be deducted only in certain situations:

- Where your donor contributes an undivided portion of his or her entire interest. If the donor owns 200 acres of land and donates a 50 percent undivided interest to your charity, a deduction is allowed.
- Where your donor contributes a partial interest that would be

deductible if transferred to a trust. For an outright transfer of less than his or her entire interest to a qualified organization, the donor may get a deduction in the same amount he or she would be allowed if that person had transferred the same property in trust for the charity.

- Where your donor donates a partial interest in property for conservation purposes. If the donor transferred a lease, purchase option, remainder interest, or easement on real property to a charity exclusively for conservation purposes after June 13, 1977, or does it before June 14, 1981, the gift is deductible if it is made in perpetuity.

- Where your donor contributes a remainder interest in his or her personal residence or farm.

9 ▪ 15
GIFTS WITH STRINGS ATTACHED

What happens when your donor gives property, but still wants to use it for a while? A perfect example is a gift of a residence or farm to a charity, whereby the donor or the donor's spouse retains the right to use it during his or her lifetime or for a specified period of time. Your donor is Mr. Gentleman Farmer, age 60, an owner of a country estate worth $240,000. He has three wishes: to enjoy his estate during his lifetime; to leave it upon his death to his alma mater; and to make some lifetime charitable gifts. In his 70 percent tax bracket, the savings would mean a lot to him.

First of all, each year he can donate to the college a $30,000 interest in the property, but keep the right to live on it while he is alive. He will earn an annual tax deduction of about $18,000 (the remainder value of property worth $30,000 at the end of the life expectancy of a 60-year-old man). In his 70 percent tax bracket, that means an annual tax savings of $12,600.

But that is not all. As he gets older, he is allowed to donate interests worth less than $30,000 each year. This is true because, as his life expectancy decreases, the proportionate value of the remainder interest going to the college increases. As long as the value of the remainder interest he gives away each year is worth $18,000, he will find himself with $12,600 more of spendable income.

If he would rather retain the right to live on the estate for only a certain number of years (not for life) or if he wants his wife to enjoy it after his death, he can arrange his gifts accordingly. In the latter case, the college will not get possession of the estate until his wife dies. The remainder interests (or value of the charitable gifts) will then be reduced by the joint life expectancies of both of them. But be aware that he may have to pay gift taxes, since he is making a gift to his wife of the value of her survivorship interest in the property. Nevertheless, the income tax savings he realizes because of the charitable deduction may well offset any gift taxes.

The amount of the deduction he will receive for a charitable contribution of a partial interest in his property is the fair market value of the partial interest at the time the contribution is made. If the contribution is a remainder interest in real property, he must take into account depreciation (computed on the straight-line method) and depletion of the property in determining the value. This value must then be discounted further at a rate of 6 percent a year.

9 ▪ 16
A PIECE OF THE ACTION

Turning to contributions of partial interest in trust, those of a remainder or income interest in trust are generally not deductible. However, this exclusion does not apply if your donor's entire interest is transferred in trust and an income interest donated to one qualified donee and the remainder interest to another. Nor will the exclusion apply if the income or remainder interest your donor contributes is his or her entire interest in the property.

But what if either the income interest or remainder interest transferred in trust is payable to a noncharity? If your donor makes a charitable contribution of an income interest in property by a transfer in trust, a deduction will be allowed if the income interest is either a guaranteed annuity interest or a unitrust interest, and if the grantor is treated as the owner of the interest.

A *guaranteed annuity* interest means an irrevocable right under the terms of the trust instrument for your donor to receive payment of a fixed amount at least annually that does not change from year to year. This fixed amount is payable out of the income or the corpus of the trust. The deduction for a gift of such interest is limited to its fair market value on the contribution date.

A *unitrust* interest differs from a guaranteed annuity interest in the amount your donor has a right to receive from the trust. It is a fixed percentage of the net fair market value of the trust assets determined annually. The deduction for this type of gift is limited to its fair market value on the contribution date. This is found by subtracting from the fair market value of the transferred property the present value of all interests in it other than the unitrust interest.

Although the grantor deducts the present value of the charity's income interest in the year of the transfer, he or she gets no deduction later for the trust's charitable payouts. If, before the charity's interest ends, the grantor stops being treated as the owner of the trust (if, for example, the grantor dies), he or she is considered to receive the amount of the contribution deduction minus the discounted value of the amounts actually paid to the charity up to that date.

If it looks as if your charity will not get beneficial enjoyment of the entire income interest directed to be paid, the grantor can deduct only the minimum amount the charity will clearly get. Suppose the grantor transfers $20,000 in trust with the requirement that a guaranteed annuity interest of $4,000 be paid every year for nine years to a hospital and that the residue revert to the grantor. Even though the fair market value (under the regulations) of such an annuity is $27,206.80, he or she is only allowed to deduct $20,-000, the minimum amount the hospital will clearly get.

The trust itself gets no deduction for payouts to charity. As long as the grantor is taxable on its income, no one cares. But even if the trust becomes taxable (owing to the grantor's death, for instance) a deduction, then useful, is still denied.

9 ▪ 17
ENGINEERING INCOME AND WRITE-OFF TOGETHER

What if your donor wants to get a charitable deduction without giving up income? There is a way to leave property to a charitable organization after the death of the donor (or the donor and spouse) in such a way that the donor gets an immediate charitable deduction without a loss of income from the property during his or her lifetime. The basic procedure for accomplishing this goal is one of the following:

- To transfer title to the property to a trust for delivery to a charitable organization and require the trust to pay the donor a given amount for a period of up to twenty years or for life.
- To transfer the property to certain pooled funds your organization can set up that give the donor a life income and then keep the remainder at the donor's death.

This gives the donor an immediate charitable deduction for the present value of the charitable organization's remainder interest in the property.

For a charitable contribution of a remainder interest in property transferred in trust to be deductible, one of the following types of trusts must be employed:

A pooled income fund. It is made up of commingled funds donated by contributors who retain a life income interest in the earnings of the fund. This life income interest may be for the contributor alone or for the life of one or more named beneficiaries alive at the time of the transfer. Such a beneficiary may be the charity that will receive the remainder.

It is maintained by a public charity, and that charity must be the recipient of an irrevocable remainder interest in the donated assets. The term "public charity" refers to schools, churches, hospitals, and other organizations receiving broad support from the general public. The donor keeps or gives to other persons named as beneficiaries the right to the income.

If the charity does not receive the property when the income interest ends (when the life income beneficiary dies), the gift will not qualify as a gift to a pooled income fund. When the charity gets the property at the end of the income interest, an amount corresponding to the value of the donated property is removed from the fund.

The charity may have several pooled income funds and may commingle property received from several donors. If it does so, it must keep detailed accounting records identifying the assets of each pooled income fund. A bank that serves as trustee for more than one pooled income fund may maintain a common trust fund for such funds.

The trust may not receive exempt securities as a contribution to it; and whereas the charity reinvests the property (as trustee), it may not invest in tax-exempt securities.

No donor or beneficiary may be the trustee of the fund. But a donor may be a trustee or official of the charity maintaining the fund. Since the charity maintains the fund, it must have the power to name or remove the trustees.

The donor or named beneficiary must report the annual earnings of his or her share of the pooled income fund. And each income beneficiary must receive the annual income to which he or she is entitled, determined by the fund's rate of return for its tax year and the value of the donated property. A donor can arrange to have the income shared by beneficiaries, or they can be paid consecutively. For instance, the donor may want to receive the income for his or her lifetime, and then have it paid to the surviving spouse. The donor has no gain or loss on his or her contribution to the fund unless he or she receives property from the fund or gives it property subject to debt.

The donor receives a charitable contribution deduction, which is basically the market value of the donated property at the time the contribution is made less the value of the income interests. The donor must support a claim of deduction by a statement attached to his or her return showing the computation of the present value of his or her interest. Treasury tables are used to establish the value of the right to income, taking age, sex, and the fund's rate of earnings into account.

There can be further tax benefit to the donor. If the donor contributes appreciated property held long term to this fund, he or she is not taxed on the appreciation. But the appreciated value of the property is used in figuring the contribution deduction.

The donor's basis and holding period for the transferred property is assumed by the fund. However, when the fund sells donated property held long term by the donor, generally it is not taxed on the gain. Therefore, the value of the property is fully, available for reinvestment, and the fund is taxed only to the extent of undistributed short-term capital gains.

When the income from the fund covers only the donor, there is no estate tax payable upon that donor's death. The value of the property the donor transferred to the fund is included in his or her gross estate since the donor kept the life income, but the estate gets a charitable deduction for the same amount. On the other hand, when the life income is paid to another beneficiary, the value of the income interest is subject to tax in the donor's estate (with the taxable interest being actuarially computed).

If an income interest is given to another person, a gift tax may be payable. However, the donor can use the $3,000 annual gift tax exclusion. Moreover, the unified credit (a combination of the estate and gift taxes) may substantially offset the gift tax.

A charitable remainder trust. Whereas a pooled income fund is offered by a charity to the general public, a charitable remainder trust must be personally set up by the donor. The donor can create such a trust either during his or her lifetime (inter vivos) or by will (testamentary). The donor has the opportunity, within limits, to fix the amount of annual income to be paid to the beneficiaries and the types of investment to be made by the trustees. Since the rules for setting up a charitable deduction are complex, careful planning and drafting should be done by experienced tax counsel.

To receive a deduction for a charitable remainder interest, your donor must have a trust set up either as a charitable remainder annuity trust or as a charitable remainder unitrust. In addition to being exempt from income taxes, both types are irrevocable, so that the trust assets must pass to the charitable remainderman rather than being used by the trust settlor or any of the beneficiaries. Therefore, your donor should be very certain that before setting up such a trust neither the donor nor the heirs will need the assets.

As for the annuity trust, it pays out at least annually a fixed amount (for example, $10,000 yearly regardless of whether income is more or less than $10,000) based on the value of the property at the time of the transfer. The rate cannot be less than 5 percent of the net initial value of the property. The paid-out amount must be paid at least annually to one or more income beneficiaries for life, or for a term not to exceed twenty years. All beneficiaries must be living at the time the trust is created.

The unitrust is more flexible, in that income payments may fluctuate with the value of the trust property. If the fund at the beginning of the year is $100,000, income to the valuation date is $10,000, and unrealized appreciation to that date is $10,000, the total value of the fund is $120,000 on the valuation date. If, say, 5 percent is to be paid to the income beneficiary, the amount payable is $6,000. Although the amount may not be less than 5 percent of the fair market value of the trust assets valued annually, your donor may authorize payment of the fixed percentage or the trust's annual income, whichever is smaller.

If the income is in fact below the fixed rate, the trustee must make up the difference if excess income is earned in a later year. But no invasions of principal are required to make good an income deficiency. As in the annuity trust, the income interest is paid to one or more beneficiaries who are living at the time the trust is created, for life or for a term not exceeding twenty years.

Appreciated securities held long term can be transferred to a charitable remainder trust without the settlor being taxed. Any additional transfers can be made to a unitrust, but not to an annuity trust. Moreover, to the extent the trust income is paid to the beneficiary, it is taxable to that beneficiary; but the trust can invest in tax exempts and provide a taxfree income return.

Should your donor choose an annuity or a unitrust? The answer will depend on the objectives. The unitrust does have some advantages. With its return based on the annual value of the trust principal, it can adjust to inflationary trends. And both the income beneficiary and charitable remainderman share a common interest in the appreciation of the principal. In addition, the trustees may be free to invest in securities or real estate that will benefit both the beneficiary and the remainderman. But there can be a problem in generating enough cash to meet the annual income payment.

Be aware that the trustees of charitable remainder trusts are subject to the same prohibitions and excise taxes as are applied to charitable foundations in establishing and maintaining their exempt status. They must not engage in self-dealing, retain excess business holdings, make investments that might subject them to tax, or make taxable expenditures. These prohibitions should be contained in the trust deed.

9 ▪ 18
A TAX BREAK FOR THE REMAINDER TRUST

As long as a charitable remainder trust adheres to the legal requirements, a charitable deduction will be allowed for the value of the interest that will pass to the charitable remainderman. The estate will deduct the value of the property transferred to the trust, reduced by the value of the income beneficiary's interest. Treasury tables that take the age and sex of the beneficiary into account are used to compute the value of this interest. These tables assume that the trust fund will realize income at the rate of 6 percent a year, even though it may in fact produce more or less income, depending on investment results.

A larger deduction will usually result from a transfer to a unitrust than to an annuity trust if the stipulated payout of income is more than 6 percent. Whether you have an inter vivos or testamentary trust, the deduction is computed the same way. Either method can serve to reduce or even eliminate the federal estate tax, give income to your donor's spouse or other beneficiary for life, and preserve the capital of the fund for the ultimate benefit of your organization and its chosen philanthropies.

Estate taxes may also be reduced sharply or eliminated with the use of a testamentary charitable remainder trust, taking advantage of the "marital" deduction. Your estate-planning donor can bequeath part of the estate to his or her spouse to qualify for the marital deduction and the balance to a charitable remainder trust paying either the annuity or unitrust amount to the spouse for life. Only the actuarial value of the spouse's life income interest is taxable to a decedent's estate, and this may be offset by the unified credit. With the use of such a trust, the spouse has a larger lifetime income because the trust corpus is not reduced by taxes. Also, your charity is provided with a substantial gift on the spouse's death.

If Clyde Clever dies after 1980, leaving outright an adjusted gross estate of $500,000 entirely to his surviving spouse, the maximum marital deduction is $250,000. The federal estate tax will be $70,000 minus the unified credit of $47,000, or $23,888. Mrs. Clever will receive from the estate $476,200 ($500,000 minus $23,-800). If this amount is invested at 5 percent, she will have an annual income of $23,820.

On the other hand, suppose Clyde Clever leaves only $175,000 outright to his spouse and puts the balance in a charitable remainder unitrust. Mrs. Clever is made the lifetime beneficiary of the unitrust amount of 5 percent of the trust assets valued annually. The estate is allowed to deduct the actuarially computed charitable remainder as well as the marital deduction, and the only item taxable to the estate is Mrs. Clever's life income interest.

Because Mrs. Clever is a 65-year-old woman, about $157,000 is subject to federal estate tax, but it is completely offset by the unified credit. Assuming a constant rate of return of 5 percent on the outright bequest to Mrs. Clever and also on the trust corpus of $325,000, she will receive an annual income of $25,000 for life. Of that amount, $8,750 will come from assets qualifying for the marital deduction and $16,250 will come from the unitrust. Moreover, tax on Mrs. Clever's estate of $175,000 is eliminated by the unified credit. Take note, too, that if the value of the unitrust assets increases, Mrs. Clever will get a larger annual payout.

This plan has its merits, but before your donor jumps into it, remember that it assumes that the surviving spouse's needs can be met by the principal sum and the life income left to him or her and that your donor has a serious commitment to pass on the bulk of the estate to charity. If your donor's only beneficiaries are a spouse and your charity, the donor can leave more to the spouse by making the charitable gifts at death rather than through lifetime transfers.

Suppose your donor has an estate of $1 million and a desire to give half to a spouse and the other half to your charity. By giving the charitable half away during the donor's lifetime, the spouse is left with an estate of $500,000. Only half of that, $250,000, will qualify for the marital deduction. An estate tax of $47,000 will be payable on the balance, so that the spouse will receive $453,000.

On the other hand, if your donor leaves half to charity at death, the entire estate passes taxfree and the spouse gets the entire $500,-000. Since there would be a deduction of one-half for the marital deduction and a charitable deduction for the rest, there would be a net taxable estate of zero. Your donor will also leave a larger adjusted gross estate and, therefore, gain a greater marital deduction.

9 ▪ 19
DOUBLING YOUR DONOR'S BENEFITS

Believe it or not, your donor can get both income and estate tax deductions from the same gift. The donor can start by creating a living trust whereby he or she receives an annuity for life with the principal going to charity at death. Every year the donor transfers money or property to the trust and gets an income tax deduction for each year's gifts. When the donor dies the trust will be included in the gross taxable estate because the donor kept the right to the annuity during his or her lifetime.

But do not worry. This property is fully estate-tax deductible. Moreover, by including the charitable trust in the estate, the donor's marital deduction can be greater, which in turn means a reduction in estate taxes. For every dollar of trust property included in the gross taxable estate that passes to charity, the donor can give the spouse an additional 50 cents taxfree.

9 ▪ 20
SHORT-TERM TRUSTS

Short-term trusts are another excellent device for charitable giving. What if your donor wants to make a gift that will surpass the 20 percent or 50 percent limitation on charitable deductions? Your donor may be smart to divert income away from himself or herself and forget about the charitable deduction.

Suppose the contributor wants to donate a science laboratory to a father's alma mater in his memory. The donor has an adjusted gross income of $75,000 and wants to give the college $50,000 a year for the next ten years to finance the project. If the donor simply gives away $50,000 each year, the maximum tax deduction that person can expect will be only $37,500 (50 percent of $75,000). The donor will pay income taxes of $11,000.

On the other hand, if the donor sets up a trust to last at least ten years, funding it with property that will produce an annual income of $50,000 to be paid to the college, he or she will have removed $50,000 from personal taxable income, reducing personal taxes to $6,000. Because the property will revert to the donor, he or she does not get a charitable deduction. Nevertheless, that donor will still have saved $5,000 a year in taxes.

9 ▪ 21
THE CHARITABLE FOUNDATION

The operation of a foundation that your donor creates during his or her lifetime can continue to be controlled by the family after the donor's death. This can be of particular importance in your donor's estate plan if the major asset is a family business. This was true in the case of the Ford family. The taxes on Henry Ford's estate were so large that a choice had to made between selling most of the family stock to raise sufficient funds to pay the tax or making a large charitable contribution in order to reduce the estate tax bill to an amount that could be paid out of other assets of the estate. The solution was to reclassify the Ford common stock into voting common and nonvoting stock. The nonvoting common went to the Ford Foundation, and control of the corporation remained in the hands of the Ford family by the retention of the voting stock.

But what if your donor is not a Ford, a Rockefeller, or a Carnegie? As a small businessman or woman, the donor may still be helped by including a charitable foundation in the estate plan. Since the larger part of the estate will normally consist of the business, unless that business can supply the necessary cash to pay the estate taxes upon the donor's death, the other assets may be eaten up. The family's security will then depend totally on the business. If your donor gives part of the business to a foundation, the estate taxes payable out of the other assets can be reduced, leaving a cushion for the family. Although the foundation ends up owning part of the business, the family will still control it—and charitable objectives will have been met, too.

9 ▪ 22
CHARITABLE GIVING THROUGH INSURANCE

Your donor has several choices for making charitable gifts through insurance:

1. The donor can give away an insurance policy and get an income tax deduction for its value, which will be approximately the cash value of the policy .

2. If the donor names your organization as irrevocable beneficiary, he or she can get an income tax deduction for the premium payments.

3. The donor can retain an incident of ownership—the right, in conjunction with the charity, to surrender the policy or borrow its cash value. In this way the insurance will be included in your donor's gross taxable estate and create a larger marital deduction, a smaller estate tax, and an income tax deduction for the premium payments.

Suppose Mr. Adams and Ms. Brown both have net estates of $500,000, but Ms. Brown takes out a $150,000 insurance policy for her favorite charity. Since Ms. Brown retains an incident of ownership in the policy, her adjusted gross estate is $650,000. She has a $325,000 marital deduction, a $150,000 charitable deduction, a $115,000 net taxable estate, and a $25,200 tax bill.

Without the charitable insurance, Mr. Adams figures his adjusted gross estate to be $500,000. He has a $250,000 marital deduction, a $190,000 net taxable estate, and a $47,000 tax bill. Ms. Brown's estate will owe $22,500 less than Mr. Adams' estate.

4. By creating an insurance trust, your donor can get the same benefit. He or she can make the trust the irrevocable beneficiary and direct that the proceeds be used for charitable purposes. The donor can also name himself or herself as trustee with the power to choose the charitable beneficiaries.

5. If your donor wants to contribute more than he or she nor-

mally can afford, such donor can make a pet charity the beneficiary of a large insurance policy.

Suppose your donor wants to give an impressive and lasting gift, like a new wing for a hospital, but cannot afford to give more than $6,000 a year out of capital. Although $6,000 a year may not seem like much, the donor can use it to build a fund of $500,000 through insurance. Assuming your donor is in a 60 percent tax bracket and the net premium for the first year is $16,725, the donor's actual net cost is only $6,690. The premium will continually decrease over the years. For a fifteen-year period, the annual after-tax premium cost will average out to $5,466 a year. This will buy the donor a charitable gift of $500,000.

6. If your donor names your organization as irrevocable beneficiary of life insurance and you agree to pay an annuity or income to a member of the family out of the insurance proceeds, the donor is providing a guaranteed income for that family member. The donor is then allowed an income-tax deduction for annual premiums to the extent that they are attributable to the remainder of the proceeds kept by the charity.

9 ▪ 23
THE CLOSELY HELD CORPORATION AS CONTRIBUTOR

Owners of closely held corporations can withdraw earnings from their companies taxfree by using charitable contributions. This is how they do it.

By contributing some of his or her corporate stock to a charity, an owner receives a charitable contribution deduction for the value of the stock (say, $10,000), giving the contributor a tax savings. Then, soon after the donor makes the charitable gift, the corporation buys back from the charity the stock the donor contributed for the same $10,000. In effect, the donor now has a tax saving from a charitable deduction made with cash taken out of the corporation taxfree.

Even though this type of maneuvering is prearranged, the courts and, reluctantly, the IRS, have okayed it. But the IRS will treat the deal as a stock redemption resulting in dividend income to the stockholder if the donee is legally bound, or can be compelled by the corporation, to surrender the shares for redemption.

An owner interested in such an arrangement must be careful not to overprice the stock. Otherwise, the IRS could claim the contribution was actually worth less than the price set and cut the charitable contribution down, even in the face of a higher redemption price.

It is unwise to short-circuit this so-called "bail-out" technique. If the corporation first purchased the stock directly from the stockholder in order for the stockholder to contribute the cash to the charity, the IRS could well treat such a corporate payment to the stockholder as an ordinary dividend. Since dividend income would offset a charitable deduction for the same amount, the tax saving would be nullified.

Be aware that both a shareholder and the corporation can make currently deductible contributions. If your donor, a shareholder, has contributed up to his or her limit for the year, the corporation can add its contribution up to its separate limit.

The use of a charitable foundation was another handy device for the owner of a closely held corporation. In addition to getting a charitable deduction out of it, he used it to help his business, the manufacture of scuba-diving equipment. The funds contributed by him, Fred Fish, owner of Fish Gear, Inc., to his foundation, the Fish Foundation, were used to promote scuba diving through scientific research, scholarships to worthy divers, rest homes for water-logged retired scuba divers, and underwater-creature museums.

The charitable gifts bearing the Fish name have important byproducts for Mr. Fish's business. He gets free advertising and the promotion of goodwill among the scuba-diving segment of the consumer market. The use of a private foundation that is one's own personal charity can also be helpful to him as a person willing and able to spread his charitable contribution over several years, so that it can be deducted from his highest income bracket in each year.

The foundation can also be useful in getting the benefits of income-tax deductions and in building up funds to meet specific charitable purposes. If your donor is asked to donate large sums annually to a number of charities, that donor may face a problem. In some years the amount expected from him or her may exceed that person's charitable deduction limit for the year, and in other years the donor may not be able financially to meet these obligations. What is easy to do in a good year becomes difficult in a lean one.

This is a problem that can be solved by the donor setting up his or her own foundation. Your donor can either endow it with a certain amount of property or can annually contribute amounts up to 20 percent of his or her adjusted gross income, the maximum deduction allowed. The donor diverts income from himself or herself and realizes further tax savings from the deductions. Moreover, the foundation's income is received by it taxfree.

But there s a rub: If the foundation does not pay out the income each year for the charitable purposes for which it was created, as we have discussed, it will be subject to tax. The IRS strongly disapproves of the foundation operated as nothing more than a tool for the rich to escape high taxes.

Your donor is free to select the charitable recipients of the fund and can determine the amount and time of payments. Remember, though, the donor receives the charitable deduction when making the contribution to the foundation, not when it pays out to charities.

Alert your donor to these hazards in charitable giving:

Canceled checks to charitable organizations may not be sufficient support for a charitable deduction. If your donor's tax return is examined, he or she may have to substantiate the deduction by furnishing a statement from the charitable donee showing the date, purpose, and amount of the contribution. By these requirements, the IRS hopes to cut down on the number of claims of a full deduction for payments that are in whole or in part actually for a noncharitable purpose.

A good example is the person who pays $80 for benefit tickets that are normally worth $40. Since any payments made for admission to or participation in charity affairs are deductible only to the extent they exceed the fair market value of the benefit received, the contribution deduction is only $40. If the donor pays more than fair market value to a qualified organization for goods or services, only the amount paid in excess of the normal value may be a charitable contribution; if the donor pays $2,000 for an all-expense trip actually worth $1,000, only $1,000 is deductible.

The pledge is full of wrinkles. If your donor makes a pledge of a charitable contribution, he or she can only get the deduction if the contribution is actually made during the taxable year (no matter the accounting method). The contribution will be considered paid in the year the check is put in the mail. If the donor pays with a credit card, the payment will be in the year the charge is made, not when the bill is paid.

The rule for corporations is the same, except that an accrual-basis corporation can still get a deduction this year for payment made on or before the fifteenth day of the third month following the close of the taxable year, if the donation was approved by its board of directors during this year.

If your donor dies before the pledge is paid, the estate will be entitled to the charitable deduction upon its payment of such pledge.

Although a pledge is similar to a debt, do not worry that its payment with appreciated securities could give rise to a tax liability. The IRS does not look at the payment of a pledge as the discharge of a legal obligation.

When pledges are not honored (which is relatively infrequent), resort to legal action is rare. Yet the courts have developed case law holding that a pledge is enforceable when the charity or other donors have acted in reliance on that pledge. This is the reasoning of "promissory estoppel." For instance, a pledge was indeed enforced when it was conditioned on matching funds and the charity initiated a fund-raising project to meet that condition. In most states today, charitable contributions are held to be binding contracts on the theory of promissory estoppel.

Business or investment property now worth less than your donor paid for it is not appropriate for charitable gift giving. The donor is better off selling the property and establishing a deductible loss, and then donating the proceeds and receiving a contribution deduction. Since the charity will receive cash equal to the value of the property, it will not suffer. The donor will have both a loss deduction and the charitable deduction.

A sale of property for less than its fair market value to a qualified donee—called a "bargain" sale—is usually treated as a gift in part and a sale in part. If a charitable contribution deduction results, your donor must allocate the property's basis between the part sold and the part contributed. The basis allocated to the part sold is in the same proportion to the total basis as the amount realized from the charity to the property's fair market value.

Suppose your donor sells stock held over twelve months to a hospital for $48,000 that has a cost basis of $48,000 but a value of $60,000. Because the sales proceeds ($48,000) are 80 percent of the value ($60,000), only 80 percent of the basis or $38,400 offsets the proceeds. The gain is $9,600. Your donor's contribution is $12,000 ($60,000 − $48,000) worth of stock with a basis of $9,600 (20 percent × $48,000). Since the stock is a gift of intangible long-term capital gain property, no appreciated property reductions apply. Therefore, the donor can deduct the full $12,000.

The law does not allow a double deduction if a donee assumes a liability connected with a charitable contribution or if the contributed property is subject to a liability. If your donor pays interest on the liability for a period after the contribution, he or she loses part of the charitable deduction. In addition, if bonds subject to a liability are contributed, the interest paid by the donor taxpayer before the donation is also subtracted from the donation, but only to the extent that it does not exceed the interest receivable on the bond for the period before the donation that the donor did not include in his gross income.

For example, as a cash-basis, calendar-year taxpayer, your donor, in January 1978, gave real estate to charity with a fair market value and adjusted basis of $12,000. The charity assumed an indebtedness on the gift of $8,000 that the donor incurred. On Dec. 31, 1977, your donor prepaid one year's interest on that indebtedness for 1978 in the amount of $960 and took an interest deduction. The gift amount is $4,960 ($12,000 − $8,000 of indebtedness, plus $960 of prepaid interest). In order to determine the charitable deduction, the value of the gift ($4,960) must be reduced by $960 in deducted interest.

9 ▪ 24
THE MECHANICS OF CHARITABLE GIVING

Finally, pass these pointers along to your donor. They will firm up the write-off:

1. Your donor must keep receipts, canceled checks, records, and other evidence to substantiate the deduction.

2. Certain information must be furnished for cash contributions on Form 1040, but additional information is required for contributions of property. Your donor must describe the kind of property donated, the cost and fair market value, the method of determining the fair market value at the time of the contribution, and a statement as to whether or not the amount of the contribution was reduced by any appreciation in value.

3. For each property gift for which your donor claims more than a $200 deduction, the donor will need to attach a statement to his or her return that supplies the following additional information:

- The name and address of the donee and the date of the actual contribution.
- A detailed description of the property and how and when the donor acquired it.
- The cost or other basis, as adjusted, for appreciated property other than securities.
- The amount of the reduction in the value of the contribution of certain appreciated property and how the reduction was determined.
- The terms of any agreement or understanding entered into by the donor (or on the donor's behalf) relating to the use, sale, or other disposition of the property.
- The amount the donor is claiming as a deduction for the tax year as a result of the contribution.

9 ▪ 25
FORTIFY YOUR SOLICITATION PLAN

Without the continuous gift dollar, nearly all charitable organizations would be crippled severely and some would wither away. Yet the complexities surrounding charitable solicitation and charitable contribution deduction are labyrinthine, complexities that render virtually every solicitation and contribution decision a legal decision. As statutory tightening erodes individual and pluralistic charitable endeavors, fortify your organization's solicitation plan with the professional counsel you certainly will need in the years to come.

10
What's Next?

10 ■ 1
THE TREND TOWARD NONDISCRIMINATION

Perhaps the very essence of most nonprofit organizations—the continuing tax deductibility of contributions they receive—is in some doubt. At the same time, the societal trends that influence all of our day-in, day-out behavior affect the evolution of the nonprofit organization in a special way. For both reasons, the course of the nonprofit organization is an uncertain one, and its managers are obliged to keep current about legislative, judicial, and administrative decisions likely to upset that course.

Organizations that operate private schools, for example, should respect the holding in *Green* v. *Connally,* a landmark 1971 case that confirmed the long-standing principle that an organization operating illegally or contrary to public policy is not "charitable" and is therefore denied the benefits of federal income tax exemption. To enforce the *Green* rule, the IRS requires the following information from every private school filing an application for recognition of tax-exempt status:

1. The racial composition of the student body, faculty, and administrative staff as of the current academic year, and a reasonable projection for subsequent years.
2. The amount of scholarship and loan funds to students enrolled and the racial composition of those receiving such awards.
3. The year the school was organized, and a list of its incorporators, founders, board members, and donors of land or buildings, whether organizations or individuals.
4. A statement showing whether the school has an objective of maintaining segregated public or private school education and if so, a statement showing whether any organizers or major contributors are officers or active members of the school at the time the application is filed.

To qualify for federal income tax exemption, a private school must meet the following IRS requirements:

1. It must include a statement in its charter, bylaws, or other governing instrument that it has a racially nondiscriminatory policy toward students and that it does not discriminate against students or applicants on the basis of race, color, and national or ethnic origin.

2. It normally must circulate information that clearly states the school's admission policies and that reaches all racial segments in the community the school serves. This can be accomplished through the newspapers or the broadcast media. Such a statement must also be included in all its brochures and catalogs dealing with student admissions, programs, and scholarships and in other written advertising used to inform prospective students of its programs.

What is a racially nondiscriminatory policy toward students? It is the school's admission of students of any race to all the rights, privileges, programs, and activities generally accorded to students at that school. It also means that the school does not discriminate on the basis of race in administering its admission and educational policies, scholarship and loan programs, and athletic and other school-administered programs.

The IRS considers the existence (or absence thereof) of a racially discriminatory policy with respect to the employment of faculty and administrative staff to be indicative of a racially discriminatory policy (or absence thereof) toward students.

3. An authorized official of each school must certify its racially nondiscriminatory policy annually, under penalty of perjury, on Form 990 or 5578, whichever is applicable. Failure to comply with the guidelines will ordinarily result in the proposed revocation of the exempt status of the school.

4. For at least three years, each school must keep copies of all materials used by or on behalf of the school to solicit contributions. Failure to maintain or produce the required records and information creates a presumption that the school has failed to comply.

But what about a school policy that favors racial minority groups in admissions, facilities, and programs and financial assistance? The well-publicized Bakke case, charging reverse discrimination, has left schools uncertain on how to avoid discrimination in their admissions policies.

A church-related school that teaches secular subjects and generally complies with state law public-education requirements cannot rely on the First Amendment to avoid nondiscriminatory rules. A school that selects students on the basis of their membership in a religious denomination is not considered to be practicing a discriminatory policy, so long as membership is open to all on a racially nondiscriminatory basis.

Other private nonprofit organizations have had their discriminatory practices increasingly challenged, particularly when racial bias has been apparent. The membership policies of private clubs have been exempted from the 1964 Civil Rights Act and the clubs are therefore free to discriminate in their membership policies. Still, to avoid judicial interference, a club's activities must not involve it with "state action" that violates the Fourteenth Amendment. And the private conduct of a club that is racially discriminatory may constitute state action within the meaning of the equal protection clause when the discrimination is enforced or supported by the state. Although in the important 1972 case *Moose Lodge* v. *Irvis,* the Supreme Court tried to restrict the doctrine of state action to instances in which the state encourages and supports discrimination, later cases have broadened that interpretation.

Recently, state action has been found even when government involvement is token.

In *Jackson* v. *Statler,* a 1974 case, state action was extended to include federal tax exemption granted to private charitable foundations when racial discrimination was charged in the hiring and investment policies of a foundation. In this case, it was shown that the 1969 Tax Reform Act called for the IRS to scrutinize and regulate applicants for exemption, constituting a significant government involvement. And since the IRS's rationale for allowing charitable exemptions is based on such organizations serving the public interest, the court considered the foundation as having a public function.

Again, the trend in the federal courts is to apply the concept of state action broadly in cases involving racial discrimination. A "more rigorous standard" has been employed by the courts when the issues are other equal protection claims, such as sex discrimination.

In a 1975 federal court case, the plaintiff wanted to enjoin a private hospital's policy prohibiting the performance of elective abortions. His claim was that the practice was an unconstitutional interference with his economic interests. The court found that federal financial assistance did not constitute state action and bring the "otherwise private facility within the parameters of the Civil Rights Act." In another case, a federal district court did not find state action in the congressional chartering of the Veterans of Foreign Wars or its tax exemption. Consequently, relief was denied to a female plaintiff who was turned down for membership on the basis of sex.

10 ▪ 2
THE TREND TOWARD FREEDOM OF ASSOCIATION

Freedom of association is not an express constitutional right. Yet it is implied from the First Amendment's protection of free expression and so related to it that it is a highly protected right. As other First Amendment rights, the freedom to associate is not absolute. To avoid legislative or judicial intervention, an organization's goals and activities must be lawful. States often use corporate statutes to enforce the legality requirement and are endured as a necessary limitation of associational freedom. In the case of homosexual societies, they were denied incorporation in Ohio (1974) on the ground that "the promotion of homosexuality as a valid life-style [was] contrary to the public policy of the state." It did not matter that homosexual acts among consenting adults was no longer illegal in Ohio. The courts showed that they would consider public policy as an extension of the legality requirement in determining associational and incorporation rights.

Even though courts are careful to protect individuals' freedom to associate, they are just as concerned to protect personal freedoms against associational abuse. Some examples of recently decided association cases follow:

1. The courts have uniformly held that an association cannot deny a member his right to free speech, even if it conflicts with the association's objectives.
2. In tort actions, the courts have held that an association cannot interfere with a member's freedom to contract or pursue his vocation, that association members are liable for negligence if someone is injured on the association's premises, and that association officers may be held responsible for defamation of a nonmember's character if they ratify a libelous act.
3. The courts have recognized the freedom not to associate by upholding a member's right to resign from an organization.

10 ▪ 3
MORE FREE-SPEECH TRENDS

In cases of expulsion and suspension from schools, the trend of the courts has been to require broad notice and hearing standards to satisfy the due process clause. In a 1975 case, when a school board expelled a student for spiking the punch bowl at a school function without notifying the student or his parents of the meeting at which the expulsion was decided, the school board members were not immune from liability for damages. The effect of the decision is to make school board members' immunity dependent on good faith. And the question of good faith turns on what the member knew or reasonably should have known.

In a 1972 case, student freedom of speech was extended further recognition. In denying a university the right to expel a student for distributing on campus a publication containing supposedly "indecent speech" as proscribed by a university bylaw, the court said that universities can enforce reasonable rules governing students, but they cannot act as conclaves immune from the sweep of the First Amendment. In this and similar cases, the trend of the courts is to interpret constitutional freedoms broadly and to regard one's right to education as a proprietary interest.

In instances of exclusion and expulsion of members of organizations, the courts have traditionally taken jurisdiction when the dispute has been on the theories of property, trust, and contract. The big trend, through, is to take jurisdiction in matters of due process when expulsion from an association does harm to a person's pursuit of his profession. In a 1974 case involving the denial of membership in a professional society to a member of that profession, the court held that a private association is required to use substantively fair procedures in an action to exclude applicants from membership. This does not mean, however, that the courts will consider the criteria for membership or the merits of an applicant. Although it was not unequivocally stated, the court's decision implied that it considers professional individuals to have a proprietary interest in their professional societies.

10 ▪ 4
NONPROFITS THAT AREN'T

A striking new development in nonprofit law is the advent of the not-for-profit corporation that mixes business and nonprofit purposes. The New York Not-for-Profit Corporation Law, for instance, permits a not-for-profit corporation to be formed for business purposes. California and Pennsylvania have followed suit, and the Model Non-Profit Corporation Act implicitly condones the mixed-purpose concept by not expressly outlawing it.

Some states allow no business activity whatsoever that does not directly promote the purposes for which the coporation was organized. At the other extreme lies the New York act, which defines a not-for-profit corporation as one in which no part of its income is distributable to its members, directors, or officers. Consequently, so long as "profit" and "nonprofit" income are properly accounted for, nonprofit and exempt status may presumably be maintained, and completely unrelated business profits are allowed to be realized. The trend appears strong that nonprofit organizations will be allowed business activities.

Whether such corporations are granted federal tax exemption depends on the particular circumstances. We know that a business may be federally tax exempt if its operation is part of a qualified program. For instance, the operation of a food market by emotionally disturbed youngsters has been ruled exempt as part of their therapy. Or a retail store may be incorporated as nonprofit for the purpose of rehabilitating ex-offenders there.

The IRS position is that a business activity directly in furtherance of an exempt purpose is permitted; the substantiality of it is less important. What is important is the destination of the income received from the business activity. Therefore, if tax exemption is a main concern of the organizers, none of the corporation's purposes should fall outside the scope of the Internal Revenue Code, and the articles of incorporation should be worded in such a way that indicates each business activity is in direct furtherance of an exempt purpose. Of course, if more than an insubstantial amount of its activities is devoted to other than charitable functions, its exemption will not be preserved.

The state trend to increase the permissible range of nonprofit operation does not broaden federal tax exemption. Moreover, if the organization meets the IRS requirements, any business income it has that is unrelated to its exempt purpose will be taxed. Nevertheless, the not-for-profit business corporation can invest its funds in businesses or securities and make a profit on them. The profit factor is not the crucial one; what is, is the use to which the profit is put.

A number of commentators, however, feel that the lack of tax-exempt status may not always be so important today for these reasons:

1. The exemption was historically desirable because private contributions were the largest source of revenue for nonprofit chari-

table organizations. But with the imposition of the 1969 tax reforms, the development of the corporate foundation as an instrument of business planning, and the increased use of the not-for-profit business corporation, this is less and less often the case.

2. The loss of exemption from federal taxes does not mean the loss of exemption from numerous state and local taxes. Although the two exemptions often converge in practice, they are in fact independent.

3. Although exemption has been emphasized for tax savings, the import of other tax factors, such as the deductibility of various expenses, has been minimized. Other such tax features can be encouraged.

The not-for-profit business corporation has stimulated both praise and criticism. The principal advantages seen in the not-for-profit business corporation are as follows:

1. Public funds and private enterprise can be joined into an effective catalyst for large-scale tasks. Community development projects are one example. They are multimillion-dollar entities, no longer dependent on private contributions for their existence, but having the potential of making large profits while carrying on a necessary public function. Management skills and techniques of the private sector are blended with the power of the public sector to halt environmental pollution and restore central-city areas. On a smaller scale, the principle can be employed to aid in the social or economic rehabilitation of the needy.

2. In New York and Pennsylvania, a capital instrument known as a "subvention" is allowed. A subvention is made up of money or other property received by the corporation and spent for its benefit. Through this device, seed money is provided to the corporation until it becomes financially able, at which time the subventioner may be repaid to the extent that the contribution was not allowed as a tax deduction.

3. The not-for-profit business corporation, by engaging in socially useful enterprises, decreases the burdens the government would otherwise be called upon to carry.

4. A permissive statute like New York's allows great financial flexibility: The not-for-profit business corporation may issue notes, bonds, and other obligations and dispose of its assets without court supervision.

5. The not-for-profit business corporation gives stature and efficiency to the nonprofit sector. For one thing, nonprofit organizations have been notorious for their poor management. Without the profit motive and stockholders to hold them accountable, these traditional nonprofit charitable organizations did not feel compelled to run efficient operations. As long as they were tax exempt and could attract private contributions to keep them sufficiently funded, there was no need to concentrate on business skills and sound management. Business skills and management control techniques make a nonprofit organization more efficient and useful in pursuing a project. As such, the new not-for-profit corporation can be taken more seriously.

But its detractors see many drawbacks to this hybrid corporation.

1. Whereas nonprofit organizations may incorporate for business purposes, it is basic that they cannot operate solely for profit or financial gain; and statutory safeguards exist to ensure that all commercial activity is for other than a profit motive. To tempt nonprofit corporate participants with income that may be generated continuously by these not-for-profit business corporations but that cannot be distributed to them may lead to abuse.

2. With their susceptibility to abuse, close scrutiny is needed for these corporations. Unfortunately, correcting abuses rests with the state attorney general's office—often ineffective and overworked as the public's protector.

3. The business activity that the hybrid corporation undertakes can put it in competition with for-profit business corporations. Even if we put aside possible tax advantages, the nonprofit entity has an unfair advantage owing to the public image of nonprofit status. Moreover, incidental profits, although they do not jeopardize nonprofit status, can be applied to the maintenance or expansion of the not-for-profit corporate functions. This intrusion into the commercial sector is seen as a violation of sound public policy.

4. The subvention is seen as a device that may bring about undue influence problems. With the kind of investment the subventioner has in the corporation, an investment he or she cannot remove at will, the temptation to exert influence on the recipient may be great. The result can be a benefit to the contributor coupled with that contributor's interference with the real nonprofit public goals of the corporation.

The detractors see the blending of the basic principles of nonprofit with profit endeavors as a sure road to abuse and the confusion of objectives. As an alternative, they suggest that business operations of nonprofit organizations be affiliated as distinct for-profit subsidiaries. The proponents of not-for-profit business corporations disagree. They assume that the business corporation is interested in making itself relevant to the needs of society. They see the not-for-profit business corporation as a convenient and valuable vehicle for business planning for the public good: This hybrid corporation can provide the path through which business can become more socially responsible. But can it be trusted to make such a commitment?

10 ▪ 5
SPECIALIZATION

Specialization of nonprofit organizations has grown considerably over recent years. Take a look at these examples of some of the more prominent specialized groups:

Development corporations. These have evolved as a result of government encouragement for the improvement of communities that have been in decline. In states with statutes providing for community improvement corporations and development corporations, these organizations have lending, borrowing, and financing powers much broader than those allowed for other nonprofit organizations. When the use of stock is permitted, the members may have voting power based both on the number of shares they hold and on the amount of money contributed to the corporate loan fund.

Educational corporations. In most states these are normally ruled by a state department of education, with many having their own books of regulations to handle the detailed supervision. These corporations are usually managed by broadly empowered trustees.

Accreditation agencies are also important to schools and colleges to give recognition to students' diplomas. And special types of schools, such as law schools, must get other or additional accreditation.

Labor unions. In addition to being noteworthy as the largest group of unincorporated associations, labor unions should also be mentioned for the special laws working for them and against them. They often enjoy exemption from antimonopoly laws, but labor union negotiations in hospitals are barred in some states. Labor relations in most private nonprofit operations are controlled by the National Labor Relations Act.

Health care organizations. These may include hospital service associations, medical care corporations, and dental care corporations. Examples are Blue Cross and Blue Shield. In many cases, these organizations are governed by the general nonprofit and insurance statutes, and are under the supervision of the state commissioner of insurance.

Cooperatives. Express legislation for these organizations formed for mutual service and help to and among their members exists today in many states. Food producers, marketers, and consumers are especially favored groups, with memberships made up of both individuals and organizations. Local statutes detail their powers, methods of formation and management, and liabilities.

Trade associations. As chambers of commerce, boards of trade, and associations of business organizations, trade associations must operate within the antimonopoly laws. The exchanging and compiling of information they do is legal as long as it does not include the exchange of price, current contract and work, and other information directed at monopolistic practices.

Mutual associations. These are credit unions or bureaus, banking, and mutual insurance organizations governed by very complex local statutes and regulations, combining local insurance or banking law with corporation and administrative law, and even benevolent and fraternal organization law.

Public-interest organizations. These groups have names like Citizens for a Better Environment, Policyholders' Protective Association International, Purchase Power, and Telephone Users Association. Public-affairs groups keep growing in number and are seen by some as an ever-continuing revolt against the extent to which non-elected bureaucrats affect our daily lives. A corporate charter can be obtained in some states only if an organization's purpose does not interfere with the state's public policy, but some states follow the more liberal view that freedom of expression and association and the equal protection clause outweigh any state's purported public policy.

Along with all this specialization have come special laws enacted by a number of states. In keeping with the general laws for non-profit organizations, these too lack uniformity. States like California, Florida, Illinois, Louisiana, Minnesota, New Jersey, New York, Ohio, Texas, and Wisconsin have fairly complete provisions for the main types of specialized organizations. The state statutory systems regarding all nonprofit entities are the most detailed and complete in New York and Ohio.

In terms of funding these organizations, difficulties in obtaining charters can have serious consequences. Such a difficulty may very well make the organization suspect to the IRS. Since obtaining federal tax-exempt status is of primary importance to these groups, they literally cannot afford to lose this tax advantage by failing to get a charter. Just as important is the tax deductibility of contributions these organizations receive. Without the advantage of tax deductibility, the contributions they receive can be neither as large nor as frequent.

We can best understand the importance of the tax exemption for public-interest groups when we consider that most got their starts with grants from organizations like the Carnegie or Ford Foundation to cover costs for the first few years. These foundations serve to get the ball rolling, then leave it to others to keep it going. Like public-interest law firms, if the organization's purpose serves a need and it is tax exempt, it will attract contributors and it will survive.

10 ▪ 6
THE TREND TOWARD ANTITRUST REGULATION

Our economic system is one of free enterprise, and businesses are encouraged to compete freely and to contract independently. Nevertheless, business relationships with both competitors and customers are governed by a battery of federal and state antitrust laws enacted to regulate the marketing and distribution of goods and services and are enforced by the Federal Trade Commission and the Department of Justice.

The Sherman Antitrust Act seeks to ensure the survival of a competitive, capitalist economy. The act bars unreasonable restraints that would threaten open competition and thereby tend to create monopolies. Businesses are specifically prohibited from engaging in activities that would unduly restrain others from competing freely—boycotts, price fixing, tying agreements, and now even fair trading.

The Clayton Act, amended by the Robinson-Patman Act and the Celler-Kefauver Act, guarantees the right of the small business to compete. The act prohibits discrimination by reason of size or economic power, and outlaws tactics such as unjust price discrimination, total requirements contracts, and the monopolistic acquisition of competitors.

The Federal Trade Commission Act defends the public's right to choose among competing goods and services on the basis of their true merit.

To associate nonprofit organizations with antitrust laws almost seems a contradiction in terms. After all, nonprofit organizations are not intended to produce monetary gain. Nonetheless, there has been a rapid growth of these organizations into big business, thanks to the tax advantages afforded them. Here are a couple of antitrust precepts as they now apply to nonprofit organizations:

1. If a questionable activity is within the flow of interstate commerce, it will be considered a federal antitrust violation. Remember, though, that this is not applicable to state antitrust violations.

2. The courts generally agree that nonprofit organizations (unlike the learned professions) are engaged in trade of commerce

within the meaning of the Sherman Act (unlike the learned professions). This means that nonprofit organizations can engage in restraints of trade.

- *Rule of reason.* This applies to actions that fall somewhere between per se violations and restraint of trade, resulting in some "reasonable" restraint of trade. The courts in this matter seem to take a case-by-case approach, either fitting the restraint to the nonprofit purpose or disavowing it from such purpose. To do the latter is to hold the restraint to be a violation.
- *Per se violations.* These evolved from application of the "rule of reason" to numerous similar fact situations involving the same restraints of trade amounting to antitrust violations. When per se violations are found, noneconomic purposes of true nonprofit organizations will not work as a defense.

But don't panic. All kinds of judicial exceptions to the antitrust laws apply to nonprofit organizations.

State and federal government action. Although the federal government cannot be held to violate the antitrust laws, the Supremacy Clause of the Constitution did not make this conclusion obvious for state government action until 1943, when a court determined that state government activities are not within the Sherman Act prohibitions. This means that the state must actively regulate a business seeking antitrust immunity. To be considered for immunity at all, the entity or transaction in question must be mandated by legislative enactment, and anticompetitive means must be used to achieve a specific government purpose.

Group solicitation of favorable government action. Can a business procure legislative or executive action favorable to its activity under the assertion of political activity rights? The Supreme Court held that joint efforts by businessmen organized in a trade association to procure favorable anticompetitive legislation was not a Sherman Act violation. The Court rationalized that the Sherman Act did not invade the area of legitimate political activity. To do so would encroach upon the right of group petition, a freedom appended to the Bill of Rights.

More recent case law, however, shows some erosion of this doctrine, and exceptions to the rule have applied to the following:

- Attempts to use illegal means to influence government officials to use their positions to impose trade restraints.
- Efforts to influence the sale of products to public officials acting under competitive bidding statutes.
- Instances in which false information was submitted to government officials.
- Efforts to make use of government powers conferred upon a private agency for illegal ends.
- Efforts to extend the doctrine to cover judicial and administrative adjudicative proceedings.

The learned professions. The basis for exemption came from a reluctant conclusion that the learned professions are neither a "trade" nor "commerce." Most state statutes have declared that professions are not trades. And these are compatible with common-law decisions holding that clergymen, educators, and others, because of their status and noncommercial purposes, cannot commit actionable restraint of trade.

Many kinds of nonprofit organizations are statutorily exempt from antitrust laws:

Agricultural cooperatives. By congressional action, agricultural cooperatives are not to be considered illegal combinations or conspiracies in restraint of trade. The purpose of the exemption is to permit individual farmers to compete effectively in concentrated markets where they buy and sell by organizing into cooperative associations that may be nonprofit in nature.

Several court cases point to the unchecked growth of these cooperatives, even to the extent of a near monopoly.

Labor unions. Unions are a safe harbor. An early judicial decision held that a valid union objective could only violate the antitrust laws if the means used to accomplish it were beyond the scope of the union's exemption. Expanding this thesis, recent holdings have banned these acts as illegal restraints of competition:

- Engaging in violence or fraud in order to attain a direct commercial restraint.
- Engaging in activity not considered a labor dispute.

- Combining or conspiring with a nonlabor group to effect a direct commercial restraint.

The law is still in a transitional state in establishing standards to guide labor's conduct, but the courts generally allow the introduction of a bargaining agreement and negotiations as circumstantial evidence of an antitrust violation.

Nonprofit institutions. The Non-Profit Institutions Act was enacted in 1938 specifically to exempt certain nonprofit organizations from the price discrimination provisions of the Robinson-Patman Act, which prohibits price discrimination between purchasers in interstate commerce when competition would be lessened thereby.

A 1967 decision interpreted the Non-Profit Institutions Act to mean that:

- Antitrust exemption is not limited to the nonprofit party (the purchaser) alone, but also to the seller, since every sale consummated requires both a buyer and a seller.
- The purpose of the exemption "was undoubtedly to permit institutions which are not in business for a profit to operate as inexpensively as possible."
- Even if the public were shown to have substantially used the organization's facilities, the exemption would still be applicable because the organization's purchases were made by a nonprofit institution for its own use. This was sufficient to comply with the Robinson-Patman Act, which does not apply to purchases of supplies for their own use by schools, colleges, universities, public libraries, churches, hospitals, and charitable institutions not operated for profit.

It appears that where the nonprofit character of an organization is compatibly linked to the purchase of equipment that has some direct relation to the organization's nonprofit purpose, a broad exemption will be applied to such an organization under the Non-Profit Institutions Act.

The exemption given nonprofit organizations applies to their traditional noncommercial purposes as a defense to antitrust charges based on the "rule of reason." It is obvious that the weight given to noncommercial purposes will change when the nature of the organization changes from truly "charitable" to rarely "nonprofit." As nonprofit organizations become involved with profitmaking business entities, particularly when these profitmaking concerns are subject to antitrust charges, the weight given to nonprofit status will lessen.

10 ▪ 7
A FINAL OBSERVATION

Such, then, is the lot of the nonprofit organization—aggressive, but restrained and regulated at every level of government; charitable, but so diverse as to elude any pattern; tax exempt, but only sometimes, and even then forever subject to the mercies and exigencies of a leviathan tax code; governmental, in assuming obligations of society at large, but always without autonomy; and public, but always under the scrutiny of the protective consumerist whose self-proclaimed call it is to survey its every step. The nonprofit organization's role is an incredibly complex and challenging one, and that of its decisionmakers shall inevitably become even more so.

Index